INQUIRING MINDS

WANT TO LEARN

Posing Good Questions to
Promote Student Inquiry

ERIK M. FRANCIS

Solution Tree | Press
a division of
Solution Tree

555 North Morton Street
Bloomington, IN 47404
800.733.6786 (toll free) / 812.336.7700
FAX: 812.336.7790

email: info@SolutionTree.com
SolutionTree.com

Visit **go.SolutionTree.com/instruction** to download the free reproducibles in this book.

Printed in the United States of America

Library of Congress Cataloging-in-Publication Data

Names: Francis, Erik M., author.

Title: Inquiring minds want to learn : posing good questions to promote
  student inquiry / Erik M. Francis.

Description: Bloomington, IN : Solution Tree Press, 2024. | Includes
  bibliographical references and index.

Identifiers: LCCN 2023046071 (print) | LCCN 2023046072 (ebook) | ISBN
  9781954631731 (paperback) | ISBN 9781954631748 (ebook)

Subjects: LCSH: Inquiry-based learning. | Questioning. | Critical
  thinking--Study and teaching. | Learning, Psychology of. | Cognitive
  learning.

Classification: LCC LB1027.23 .F698 2024 (print) | LCC LB1027.23 (ebook)
  | DDC 371.3--dc23/eng/20231106

LC record available at https://lccn.loc.gov/2023046071

LC ebook record available at https://lccn.loc.gov/2023046072

Solution Tree
Jeffrey C. Jones, CEO
Edmund M. Ackerman, President

Solution Tree Press
President and Publisher: Douglas M. Rife
Associate Publishers: Todd Brakke and Kendra Slayton
Editorial Director: Laurel Hecker
Art Director: Rian Anderson
Copy Chief: Jessi Finn
Senior Production Editor: Christine Hood
Cover and Text Designer: Kelsey Hoover
Acquisitions Editors: Carol Collins and Hilary Goff
Content Development Specialist: Amy Rubenstein
Associate Editors: Sarah Ludwig and Elijah Oates
Editorial Assistant: Anne Marie Watkins

ACKNOWLEDGMENTS

My first acknowledgment goes to my family for supporting me in my endeavors and enduring my inquiring mind—my wife, Susie, and my daughters, Madison and Avery. Thanks for tolerating my endless (and sometimes repeated) questions and my excitement in discussing a fresh idea or something new I learned. Thanks for tolerating my domination of the family room TV watching informational or instructional videos on how to play the guitar like Eddie Van Halen or a song from an '80s hard rock band, breaking news about upcoming films from Marvel Studios, interviews with legendary professional wrestlers, or clips and documentaries about random and obscure events or topics.

Many people over the years have shaped my educational philosophy and practice toward teaching and learning through inquiry and questioning. There are many at Solution Tree—specifically Douglas Rife, Claudia Wheatley, Sarah Payne-Mills, Todd Brakke, Amy Rubenstein, and Christine Hood—who challenged, guided, and supported me in writing this book.

However, it was my father, Frederick L. Francis, who inspired me to learn, lead, and live with an inquiring mind. My father always asked questions, and he questioned everything. His favorite question was, "What do you mean?" And he didn't accept succinct answers. He also was not satisfied with acquiring simple knowledge or having surface understanding. He wanted explanations, justifications, and verifications for responses, results, or reasoning. That's what he would accept. He sought to expand others' knowledge and extend their thinking—and he did it through inquiry and questioning.

My father was also highly inquisitive. He enjoyed learning and sought to learn as much as he could about something. He strove to delve deeper and go further with everything he did professionally and personally. He saw every scenario or situation as a problem that could be solved. He attended to every challenging or complex task as a project worth completing. Most importantly, he learned from his experiences—both the successes and setbacks. It allowed him to speak with authority and conviction. It also enabled him to present himself as someone with education and experience—or expertise—gained through inquiry and questioning.

My father was not a stellar student in school. He liked to learn, but he didn't like being taught or told. He learned by asking questions. That often got him into trouble and garnered him a reputation as an agitator. However, he didn't question out of defiance or disrespect. He questioned because he was curious to understand how or why. He also questioned responses or reasoning he believed were too short, simple, or senseless. Today, he would have probably been identified as a gifted and talented student. He had an innate ability to comprehend ideas and information quickly and insightfully. He could communicate his knowledge, thinking, and feelings in a unique way that not only piqued but also persuaded others. He graduated high school, but he struggled academically and emotionally throughout his K–12 career because he was not taught the way he learned—through inquiry and questioning.

My father's inquiring mind helped him endure some of the most tragic and traumatic experiences in his life. When he lost his legs as a result of a horrific car accident in 1965 at the age of 19, he questioned what his life would be like in a world that was neither accessible nor accommodating for people with disabilities. He questioned whether people would not see anything but his amputated legs and his wheelchair. When my brother experienced permanent brain damage because of an accident at birth, my father questioned what kind of life his son would have. These questions arose from his fear. However, he transformed those questions into the fuel he needed. He changed his critical questions of *how can* to creative questions that prompted him to contemplate *how could*. He flipped his *what if* questions to consider the positives of possibilities instead of concentrating on the negatives. Most importantly, he tapped into that challenging and curious demeanor he demonstrated in school to ask *what else* and *why not*. He became determined and driven not only to take charge of both his and my brother's lives but also to change society and its systems' thoughts and treatment of individuals with disabilities—and he did this through inquiry and questioning.

My father became an activist during the Civil Rights Movement in the 1970s, who championed the rights of individuals with disabilities to make certain they received every opportunity available to them. Fred Pelka (2012) described my father as a "gifted leader in the [disabled] community. . . . He was very, very well-spoken. I mean, this guy can talk. He can speak in such a way that [is] mesmerizing" (p. 191). My father questioned the social and systemic perspectives, policies, practices, and procedures that prevented and prohibited individuals with disabilities from fully pursuing their lives. He inquired how he could implement the tactics used by antiwar protestors and other civil rights groups to bring and deepen awareness to the issues and plight plaguing the disabled community. He organized peaceful protests and engaged in numerous negotiations that brought awareness, systemic action, and social change—and he accomplished this through inquiry and questioning.

My father spent his professional career working as an advocate for individuals with disabilities. He became a valued advisor to federal and state agency commissioners on ideas and issues related to the acknowledgment and advancement of people with disabilities. His approach was to ask questions first before answering or advising. As an executive director in the Office of Vocational and Educational Services for Individuals with Disabilities in the New York State Department of Education, he established numerous policies and programs that advanced the lives of individuals with disabilities.

He convinced corporations, industries, and organizations to recognize individuals with disabilities as loyal, effective, and efficient employees in the workforce and realize the advantages of hiring them. He formed a comprehensive network of Independent Living Centers throughout the state of New York. He served as one of the architects and framers of the Americans with Disabilities Act of 1990, the federal civil rights law that prohibits discrimination to individuals based on disability. Throughout his twenty-five-year career, my father both challenged and changed society and its systems' perspectives and treatment of individuals with disabilities—and he did it through inquiry and questioning.

When I see people with disabilities living their lives to their fullest potential professionally and personally, I smile because I know my dad was responsible for helping them enjoy these experiences. He was one of the primary and prominent people responsible for making society and its systems accepting, accommodating, and appreciative of individuals with disabilities—and he did it through inquiry and questioning.

Thank you for taking the time to read this acknowledgment to my father. I wanted to share my father's accomplishments and how he learned, led, and lived successfully with an inquiring mind. I hope that you will recognize how teaching and learning with an inquiring mind makes the experience scholastically rigorous, socially and emotionally supportive, and student responsive. Also, I hope this book inspires you, your staff, and your students to learn, lead, and live with an inquiring mind by asking questions, delving deeper, going further, and sharing it with others.

Solution Tree Press would like to thank the following reviewers:

Tonya Alexander
English Teacher (NBCT)
Owego Free Academy
Owego, New York

Doug Crowley
Assistant Principal
DeForest Area High School
DeForest, Wisconsin

John D. Ewald
Education Consultant
Frederick, Maryland

Kelly Hilliard
GATE Mathematics Instructor
Darrell Swope Middle School
Reno, Nevada

Steven Weber
Assistant Superintendent
Fayetteville Public Schools
Fayetteville, Arkansas

Visit **go.SolutionTree.com/instruction** to download the free reproducibles in this book.

TABLE OF CONTENTS

Reproducibles are in italics.

Chapter 4

How Can Students Be "Hooked" Into Inquiry Using Good Questions? 91

Chapter 5

How Could Good Questions Personalize Inquiry and Promote Expertise? 115

Chapter 6

How Can Good Questions and Inquiry Address and Assess Understanding? 135

ABOUT THE AUTHOR

 **Erik M. Francis** is an international author, educator, and presenter with more than twenty-five years of experience in education as a classroom teacher, site administrator, education program specialist at a state education agency, and staff development trainer. He is consistently ranked as one of the World Top 30 Education Professionals by the international research organization Global Gurus.

Erik provides professional development, guidance, and support on how to plan and provide teaching and learning experiences that are standards based, socially and emotionally supportive, and student responsive. His areas of expertise include inquiry and questioning, teaching and learning for depth of knowledge (DOK), tiered instruction, authentic learning, differentiated instruction, personalized learning, standards-based grading and learning, and talent development.

Erik received a master's degree in education leadership from Northern Arizona University and a master's degree in television/radio/film production and management from the S. I. Newhouse School of Public Communications at Syracuse University. He holds a bachelor's degree in communication and rhetoric and English from the University at Albany.

To learn more about Erik M. Francis's work, visit Maverik Education (https:// maverikeducation.com), or follow him @Maverikedu12 on X (formerly Twitter).

To book Erik M. Francis for professional development, contact pd@SolutionTree.com.

THE QUANDARY WITH INQUIRY AND QUESTIONING IN EDUCATION

Asking questions is what brains were born to do, at least when we were young children.

—Alison Gopnik

Reflect and Respond

Are inquiry and questioning an innate or a learned skill? Why do you think children ask so many questions when they are young but stop once they enroll in school? What is the purpose of inquiry and questioning in education? What are the problems with inquiry and questioning in school? What shifts should education make as a profession and a system to engage in and encourage inquiry and questioning?

NQUIRY AND QUESTIONING are two popular, practical, and powerful practices and processes for teaching and learning. However, despite the extensive research and resources available, why do educators and students struggle to ask good questions that make teaching and learning more inquisitive rather than instructional and evaluative? Much of this is due to how educators view and use inquiry and questioning.

The Human Nature of Inquiry and Questioning

Human beings are naturally curious. Compiled research shows how our innate curiosity "facilities learning, propels discoveries, and enriches life" (Hsee & Ruan, 2016, p. 659). We want to know the answer. However, knowing is part of the battle. We also have an inherent desire to develop understanding, deepen acumen and awareness, and demonstrate personal expertise. We do this formally and informally through inquiry and questioning. *Inquiry* is how we learn. *Questioning* is what we do to learn. Both foster and fuel our innate curiosity to learn about ourselves, our world, our place, our possibilities, our potential, and our purpose.

Inquiry and questioning are how adults and children interact with each other. According to child psychologist Paul Harris (2012), children between the ages of two and five will ask approximately 40,000 questions during that age span. A research study commissioned by the online United Kingdom retailer Littlewoods found that children will ask almost 300 questions a day to the trusted adult in their life, such as their parent or guardian (Telegraph Staff and Agencies, 2013).

The complexity of young children's questions can range from factual questions that ask *who, what, where,* or *when,* to analytical and evaluative questions that seek explanations for *how* or *why,* to hypothetical questions that consider *what if, what could happen,* or *what would happen.* In fact, some children's questions may be so complicated that adults can't answer with a rote response or from memory. Even if we could answer the question, a child's inquiring mind will prompt, stimulate, or motivate them to continue asking *why* or *what if* until they either get an answer that satisfies them or sense the person to whom they are asking the questions is becoming bothered. Children also continue to ask questions because they want to make sure they are being heard and their questions are understood (Telegraph Staff and Agencies, 2013).

Children continue to interact with adults through questioning when they enroll in school. However, the nature and number of questions children ask reduces in both complexity and frequency as they progress in their age and education (Berger, 2014; Bronson & Merryman, 2010; Engel, 2013; Harris, 2012). Why the drop in numbers? There are a multitude of reasons, ranging from neurological to pedagogical to personal to social. However, a strong reason why children stop questioning as they grow older is because the purpose of questioning and who poses the questions changes when they enroll in school.

The Quandary With Questions in Education

In many classrooms, it's the teacher who asks the questions. Compiled research indicates the frequency of questions teachers ask is comparable to the vast number of questions toddlers and preschoolers ask the trusted adults in their life (Cotton, 1988; Floyd, 1960; Gall, 1970; Hattie, 2009, 2012, 2023; Levin, 1981; Marzano & Simms, 2014; Stevens, 1912; Timmins, 1998). However, while the frequency of teacher questioning is high, the complexity and demand—or cognitive rigor—of the questions teachers ask students is low. According to John Hattie (2009), "The majority of questions are about 'the facts, just give me the facts,' and the students all know that the teacher knows the answer" (p. 156). Asking questions that require students to recall information or how to do something to answer correctly is not necessarily "bad" or "wrong." These questions serve a purpose in teaching and learning. However, only asking closed-ended or factual questions limits both the complexity and quality of the teaching and learning students could experience.

Questioning in school is more instructional and evaluative than inquisitive and exploratory. It follows what Courtney Cazden (2001) describes as the traditional classroom discourse sequence of IRE/F: teacher initiation, student response, and teacher evaluation/feedback. The teacher initiates the instruction by asking a question. The purpose of the question is to check for and confirm student learning. Students must provide an answer that's not only accurate but also acceptable and appropriate according to specific criteria set by the teacher, the textbook, or the test. This emphasis and expectation to answer correctly transform questioning for students from an enriching and enjoyable experience to an activity that causes aggravation or anxiety, especially if students don't know how to respond.

Questioning in school is bound by rules. The teacher may ask, "Are there any questions?" or "Does anyone have any questions?" However, this is not an invitation for students to ask any question they might have. The questions must be about what's being taught. If the student asks a question that goes off-topic, the teacher will redirect, remind, or even reprimand them to stay on the subject or remain on task. This dissuades students from asking questions.

Students may ask questions to check or confirm they comprehend the subject correctly. However, more often, students will either state, "I don't get it," or remain silent rather than ask a question. That silence, however, can be misleading. Just because students keep quiet doesn't mean they don't have questions about what's being taught. William Berger and Elise Foster (2020) identify five reasons why students may not ask questions in school:

1. Fear (What if I ask the wrong question or a foolish question?)

2. Apathy (Why bother asking a question?)

3. Ignorance (What is the question I should ask?)

4. Time (Is there enough time to ask or address my question?)

5. Culture (Is this the right place or opportunity to ask or address my question?)

If students don't ask any questions, the teacher either presumes they can continue their instruction or administers an assignment or assessment with items that address the learning objective or target. These items are called "questions" and sometimes, they are phrased as interrogative statements that end with a question mark. However, these items are activities and tasks students must complete correctly or successfully. Consider multiple-choice questions. Students demonstrate their knowledge and thinking—or learning—by recognizing the correct response from three or four distractors. Sometimes, these "questions" are tricky rather than complex, providing students an option such as "all of the above" or asking them to choose an answer or answers. Again, the expectation is for students to answer accurately, acceptably, or appropriately based on certain criteria.

The other quandary with questions in education is how we classify and critique them. The complexity and quality of questions are typically judged based on five criteria (Francis, 2016, 2022):

1. The amount or level of difficulty students experience

2. The type and level of thinking students must demonstrate

3. The kind and depth of knowledge students must develop

4. The context or degree to which students must understand and use their knowledge, thinking, or learning

5. The extent of the response students must provide

For example, questions that ask students to recall and restate information or reproduce procedures to answer correctly are called *basic*, *lower level*, *low quality*, or even *bad*. The push for rigorous teaching and learning experiences has placed pressure on both educators and students to phrase and pose questions that prompt and promote deeper levels of thinking and depth of knowledge (DOK; Francis, 2016, 2022). These thought-provoking questions go by many names: essential questions (Sizer, 1992; Wiggins & McTighe, 2005, 2013), beautiful questions (Berger, 2014), right questions (Berger, 2014; Rothstein & Santana, 2011), and good questions (Francis, 2016). Regardless of what they are called, these questions are regarded highly as the ideal queries both educators and students should be asking and addressing.

Interestingly, these rigorous questions are like the ones preschool children ask—complex inquiries that require answers to be explained, justified, or extended. These are also the kinds of questions children stop asking once they become students because the purpose of questioning to learn shifts from addressing to answering.

For questioning to activate and advance student learning, both educators and students must shift how they view and use questions—and that's what this book will establish and explain with examples. Complicating the quandary with questioning, however, are the issues with inquiry in education—specifically, what exactly does inquiry involve, and who should be posing the questions?

The Issues With Inquiry in Education

Inquiry and questioning are considered synonymous in education. The presumption is that educators and students are engaging in and experiencing inquiry if they are both asking and addressing questions. However, while questioning is a core component of inquiry, it is just one of many actions or behaviors both educators and students engage in to deliver their instruction and deepen their learning, respectively. Also, asking and addressing questions does not necessarily mean the teaching and learning experience are inquiry based. The phrasing and purpose of the questions determine if the expectations and experience for teaching and learning are instructional or inquiry based.

The issue with inquiry-based teaching and learning, however, is that it is often presented or portrayed as a one-size-fits-all practice, process, or program. As Laura Buck, Stacey Lowery Bretz, and Marcy Towns (2008) point out, research and resources "use unique definitions and criteria for inquiry, with little overlap between them" (p. 52). For example, some practitioners present inquiry as an academic practice with prescriptive procedures or specific stages and steps that must be followed. Others portray inquiry as more behavioral or social-emotional, focusing on both the personal sensations and skills students develop and demonstrate toward learning as they engage in the experience. A few inquiry practitioners, such as Kath Murdoch (2015) and Kimberly Mitchell (2019), emphasize how inquiry should be both a pedagogical and personal experience. This balanced perspective of inquiry makes inquiry-based teaching and learning academically rigorous, socially and emotionally supportive, and student centered. It's also the core idea and philosophy of this book—that inquiry is a teaching and learning experience that's both academic and affective for educators and students.

Inquiry also differs depending on the subject area. For example, much of the research and resources available discuss scientific inquiry, which involves following the steps of the scientific method. Mathematical inquiry engages students in problem solving by using evidence and proofs to justify or refute results and solutions or conducting investigations into how they can use mathematical concepts, operations, and procedures in different contexts. In English language arts and the humanities, inquiry involves students conducting literary or style analyses of one or more texts addressing the same topic, written by the same author, within the same genre, or in different forms (for example, literary fiction versus nonfiction). Inquiry in the social sciences engages students to develop and deepen their learning so they can make informed decisions or take informed action.

A key issue with inquiry in education is that it's considered and treated as an additional activity educators and students must do on top of teaching and learning the standards and curriculum. In their research on the challenges to inquiry teaching in the science classroom, Cassie Quigley, Jeff Marshall, Cynthia Deaton, Michelle Cook, and Michael Padilla (2011) point out how educators view teaching content and inquiry as mutually exclusive, not aspects of the same goal. Compounding this issue is that educators feel that they must resort to more traditional methods of instruction because of the plethora of standards educators must address and the pressure for students and schools to perform successfully on high-stakes, standardized tests (Quigley et al., 2011). If inquiry is implemented and utilized in the classroom, it's presented more as a question-and-answer session with the teacher asking questions to assess student learning, not to activate or advance it.

The abundance of ideas and information about inquiry can be both conflicting and confusing. However, what educators and students need to recognize is there is no one way to engage in or experience inquiry. Its focus and form depend on answers to the following questions.

- Who is asking and addressing the questions—the teacher, the students, or both?

- What is the intent and intensity of the instruction expected and demanded?
- What are the goals and expectations for learning?
- What are the students' strengths or interests?
- Do the students find the subject or skill important or irrelevant to learn?

Educators and students must consider these questions when they engage in and experience inquiry-based teaching and learning experiences.

Instructional Shifts When Using Inquiry and Questioning

Inquiry and *questioning* are not synonymous. Inquiry is the teaching and learning experience. Questioning is what teachers and students do to engage in the inquiry. However, to engage in inquiry experiences through questioning, the relationship between both must be symbiotic. The questions posed prompt inquiry, and inquiry is promoted by the questions asked and addressed. That's what it means to teach and learn with an inquiring mind.

Inquiry requires both educators and students to shift how they view and use questions as:

- A method of instruction
- A means and measure for learning
- A manner to comprehend, communicate, and connect with others

Teaching and learning with an inquiring mind mean asking and addressing good questions. Good questions also can serve as assessments for student learning. However, their primary purpose is to:

- Initiate the inquiry of a subject
- Inspire further questions about what's being taught and learned
- Identify and introduce the instructional focus
- Inform the intent and purpose for learning
- Prompt inquiry
- Promote further questioning and deep discussions

- Persuade students to think about, talk about, and transfer learning
- Produce answers, arguments, or artifacts that reflect or represent learning

However, asking and addressing questions is neither easy nor simple. Phrasing and posing a good question can be just as complex and difficult as the process of answering. It involves critical, creative, and reflective thinking from both students and educators. It necessitates patience and persistence. Most importantly, it requires shifting how teachers and students view and use questions for teaching and learning.

What's in This Book

Most books on inquiry and questioning either discuss the benefits of these strategies or provide examples of engaging learning activities or assignments. However, few books delve into how to phrase and pose good questions that prompt inquiry or provoke questioning. There are even fewer books on inquiry and questioning that discuss how these strategies could address, assess, or augment standards-based learning. This book explores and discusses the following.

- How to phrase and pose good questions that not only define the instructional focus and purpose but also differ in their cognitive complexity and demand
- How to plan and provide inquiry-based teaching and learning experiences that are standards based, socially and emotionally supportive, and student centered

This book also examines the connection between inquiry, questioning, and authentic literacy, which Mike Schmoker (2018) describes as "purposeful reading, writing, and discussion as the primary modes of learning both content and thinking skills" (p. 29). Good questions ask students not only to comprehend but also to consider and convey their learning at different levels of thinking and DOK. Inquiry encourages students to inquire and investigate the ideas and information they need to succeed in a subject. Authentic literacy engages students to read texts closely, write clearly, and discuss comprehensively when responding to good questions. All three of these activities demand that students recognize, reflect, and realize how they can use their knowledge, skills, and feelings—or learning—to strengthen and support their responses, results, or reasoning.

Chapter 1 establishes and explains what an inquiring mind is and what it wants. It explores how a person with an inquiring mind exhibits the learning dispositions and virtues of a strong intellectual character and how those intellectual characteristic traits spur a spirit of inquiry. It examines and explains how an inquiring mind views and uses questions to teach and learn. The chapter concludes with an introduction of the Inquiring Minds Framework, the plan and process for inquiry and questioning that is the focus of this book.

Chapters 2 and 3 explore the academic and social-emotional practices and principles of inquiry and questioning. Chapter 2 examines the different forms of inquiry educators and students can engage in and experience. It also specifies which forms of inquiry are teacher led, student driven, or a combination of both. Chapter 3 discusses how good questions promote cognitive rigor and prompt inquiry. Both chapters answer which forms of inquiry and which good questions will guide students down a particular pathway of the Inquiring Minds Framework.

Chapters 4–8 explore how educators and students can phrase and pose good questions that prompt inquiry and propel teaching and learning down the different pathways of the Inquiring Minds Framework. Chapter 4 details how educators could engage students—or "hook 'em"—into inquiry with questioning. (Note that chapters 5–8 are in a different order than they appear in the Inquiring Minds Framework. Instead, they are presented in a way that describes how to develop good questions from simple to more complex.) Chapter 5 discusses how educators could rephrase learning objectives and targets into good questions that personalize inquiry and promote the development and demonstration of student expertise.

Chapter 6 explains, with examples, how academic standards can be rephrased into topical essential questions that will both set the instructional focus and serve as assessments for understanding. Chapter 7 examines how to use students' questions to assess and build their foundational knowledge and the functional understanding they need to achieve proficiency and succeed in a specific subject. Chapter 8 explains how inquiry and questioning could deepen both teaching and learning. This chapter also explores how teachers and students could use technology, such as search engines, generative artificial intelligence (AI), and deep machine learning, to come up with the good questions that promote inquiry.

The book concludes with directions and suggestions for what educators should not do when teaching and learning through inquiry and by questioning.

Each chapter starts with a quote and a series of questions for you to reflect on and respond to before you start reading. These quotes and questions are meant to activate and advance your inquiring mind before you read the ideas and information in the chapter. The quote is the stimulus—or what Dan Rothstein and Luz Santana (2011) call the *QFocus*—that initiates the inquiry of the ideas and information presented in the chapter. The questions serve as prompts for reflection. They also elicit and encourage questions and responses that further clarification, consideration, and conversation. Both the quote and the questions are meant to pique—or "hook"—curiosity about the chapter content. They also model how to teach and learn with an inquiring mind—by posing a question or sharing a stimulus that identifies and introduces the instructional focus, informs the purpose for learning, initiates the inquiry, and inspires further questions.

Each chapter concludes with an activity that encourages you to think critically, creatively, and reflectively about how you and your students can engage in and experience inquiry and questioning both within and beyond the classroom. These end-of-chapter activities will help you not only plan and provide teaching and learning experiences that prompt inquiry and promote cognitive rigor, they also will help you phrase and pose good questions to ensure the inquiry-based teaching and learning experiences are standards based, socially and emotionally supportive, and student centered.

Who This Book Is For

This book is for educators who want to instill a spirit of inquiry in their classroom that encourages students to take control of their learning and transforms them into lifelong learners. It is also for those who seek to stimulate the inquiring minds they had as young children and prior to attending school.

If you're a K–12 classroom teacher or instructional specialist, you will learn how to phrase and pose good questions to assess and build background knowledge, set the instructional focus, serve as assessments, and personalize inquiry-based teaching and learning. You will learn how you could use prompts and stimuli to engage students in inquiry and elicit questions from them. You also will learn how inquiry and questioning not only increase student academic achievement but also augment personal connections and engagement with the content and their classmates.

If you're an instructional coach or leader, you will understand what good inquiry and questioning should look like and how both teachers and students should experience it. You also will explore how to guide and support educators to compose and pose good questions to plan and provide inquiry-based teaching and learning experiences that differ in their cognitive complexity and demand.

If you're a curriculum or assessment developer, you will learn how to phrase and pose good questions that are standards based, socially and emotionally supportive, and student centered. You will learn how to design curricular activities and assessment items that require students to comprehend and convey their learning at different levels of thinking and DOK.

Most importantly, after reading this book, you will understand how teaching and learning with an inquiring mind provides you and your students with essential content knowledge, cognitive skills, and characteristic dispositions that benefit everyone in learning and life.

Chapter 1

WHAT IS AN INQUIRING MIND?

*There's always something to occupy the
inquiring mind.*

—Margaret Atwood

Reflect and Respond

What does it mean to have an inquiring mind? What does the expression, "Inquiring minds want to know," infer or suggest? What do you think an inquiring mind wants? How could teaching and learning with an inquiring mind fortify your and your students' intellectual character? How could teaching and learning with an inquiring mind foster a spirit of inquiry in your instructional delivery and how students develop and demonstrate their learning?

"INQUIRING MINDS WANT to know" is a common colloquialism used by someone who wants more information than what's presented or provided. It describes someone who has a curious mind and a strong desire to learn as deeply or as extensively as possible about something. However, for a person (for example, a teacher or student) with an inquiring mind, knowing is part of the battle—or rather, the journey into inquiry.

This chapter establishes and explains what an inquiring mind wants. It also examines how both educators and students with an inquiring mind approach teaching and learning.

What Does It Mean to Have an Inquiring Mind?

An inquiring mind possesses a passionate propensity to learn. A person with an inquiring mind enjoys discovering or uncovering new ideas or information. They find immense satisfaction in establishing, examining, or exploring and explaining subjects, skills, and situations. Their joy of learning is not limited to attaining answers but includes the explanation, justification or verification, and connection with those answers.

An inquiring mind also possesses a strong intellectual character, which Jason Baehr (2017) describes as "the character traits or personal qualities of a good thinker or learner" (p. 17). That's exactly who a person with an inquiring mind is—a good thinker and learner who enjoys engaging in intellectual activities and pursuits, such as inquiry. The concept of intellectual character contends that learning is about attitude as well as ability. It advocates for teaching and learning to focus on fortifying and fostering students' characteristic temperaments and tendencies to learn as well as their content knowledge and cognitive skills.

Table 1.1 lists the intellectual characteristics of an inquiring mind. This list is derived from the Intellectual Virtues Academy in Long Beach, California, founded by Jason Baehr (2013). Baehr came up with the slogans for each of the intellectual character traits. The list presents the thinking dispositions and virtues of intellectual character according to Jason Baehr (2017, 2021) and Philip Dow (2013). Table 1.1 groups the thinking dispositions and intellectual virtues under three overarching cognitive categories or dimensions identified by Ron Ritchhart (2002): creative thinking, reflective thinking, and critical thinking. An inquiring mind embodies and exhibits these character traits and virtues at deep, yet varied levels.

A person with an inquiring mind possesses a solid attitude about learning. The purpose and process of learning are both personal and pleasurable. They find learning through inquiry and questioning to be a joyful and fulfilling experience. They also feel personal satisfaction from asking, addressing, and answering their questions. A person with an inquiring mind is someone who yearns not only to learn but to show and share the depth and extent of their learning. They enjoy being the learner and the teacher, and they engage in inquiry and questioning to do both.

Table 1.1: Intellectual Characteristics of an Inquiring Mind

Thinking Dimension	Thinking Dispositions or Intellectual Virtues	Description	Slogan
Creative Thinking Looking out, up, around, about, or beyond	Curiosity	· Asks questions and wonders about things · Recognizes and realizes what's interesting or puzzling about the everyday, the familiar, the mundane, and the ordinary as well as the unexpected · Is motivated to learn	Ask questions!
	Open Mindedness and Fair Mindedness	· Thinks in a creative or original way · Considers all viewpoints and is willing to change or switch their perspective · Demonstrates flexibility and willingness to consider, learn, or try new things · Listens fairly and honestly to competing perspectives or dissenting opinions	Think outside the box!
Reflective Thinking Looking within (metacognitive)	Autonomy	· Recognizes and realizes their abilities and strengths · Is capable of active, self-directed thinking · Thinks and reasons for themselves · Forms their own judgments and draws their own conclusions · Is not easily influenced by or reliant on others · Is disciplined, focused, and independent	Think for yourself!
	Humility	· Is aware of and attentive to limitations or weaknesses · Owns and takes responsibility for mistakes · Monitors, regulates, evaluates, and directs their thinking actively and responsively · Keeps attitude, confidence, or ego in check	Admit and accept what you do and don't know!

continued →

Thinking Dimension	Thinking Dispositions or Intellectual Virtues	Description	Slogan
	Courage	• Manages and regulates anxiety or fear • Prevents anxiety or fear from impeding intellectual activities, growth, or pursuits • Takes risks with learning • Approaches learning with a growth mindset • Recognizes the lesson learned and opportunity to learn through errors or failure	Stay strong and take risks!
Reflective Thinking Looking within (metacognitive)	Tenacity	• Embraces intellectual challenges and struggles • Keeps "eyes on the prize" • Is determined to not give up or quit • Works through the difficulty and emerges smarter or stronger from the experience • Reflects and readjusts or refocuses approaches, efforts, or thoughts when unable to achieve or succeed • Demonstrates grit and resilience • Possesses passion and perseverance to achieve long-term goals	Embrace struggle!
	Honesty	• Conveys knowledge, thinking, or feelings with integrity • Values truth over the need to be "right" • Seeks to help others recognize, understand, or be aware of the truth • Cites and credits the ideas and work of others when used	Find, seek, and tell the truth!

Critical Thinking Looking at, through, for, or in between	Attentiveness	• Engages actively in learning moments • Notices or responds to details or particulars • Is aware of or sensitive to context • Commits to learning • Possesses sensory clarity and the power to concentrate	Look and listen!
	Carefulness	• Strives to be accurate, complete, or get things "just right" • Is quick to notice and avoid intellectual pitfalls and mistakes • Is skeptical of responses or results • Seeks further explanations, examples, or evidence • Follows others' reasoning and examines it carefully • Distinguishes or connects disparate ideas or information • Does not jump to conclusions • Is cautious not to use information taken out of context, to distort the truth by describing it with loaded language, or to mislead with manipulated data or statistics	Think with care!
Critical Thinking Looking at, through, for, or in between	Thoroughness	• Probes for or provides examples and evidence to support responses, results, or reasoning—be it their own or others • Probes for understanding • Looks "below the surface" • Is dissatisfied or unsatisfied with mere appearances and easy, obvious, simple, or superficial answers • Conveys learning correctly, clearly, and comprehensibly	Go deep!

Source: Baehr, 2013, 2017, 2021; Dow, 2013; Intellectual Virtues Academy, 2023; Ritchhart, 2002.

The behaviors and emotions a person with an inquiring mind experience as they learn are categorized in the Affective Domain of the Taxonomy of Educational Objectives developed by David Krathwohl, Benjamin Bloom, and Bertrand Masia (1964). Affective learning focuses on how learners feel as they study a subject, skill, or situation. It emphasizes and evaluates the attitudes, beliefs, emotions, and motivations individuals have about learning.

Table 1.2 lists the affective behaviors and emotions a person with an inquiring mind exhibits and expresses as they learn through inquiry and questioning.

Table 1.2: Affective Actions and Attitudes of an Inquiring Mind

Behaviors and Emotions	Actions and Attitudes of an Inquiring Mind
Receiving Awareness Willing to receive Controlled or selective attention	• Is open to learning • Possesses limited to little awareness and familiarity • Accepts and acknowledges differences or distinguishing details • Is attentive to factors, features, and feelings • Looks and listens to learn
Responding Acquiescence in responding Willingness to respond Satisfaction in response	• Participates in learning • Agrees to follow procedures, meet expectations, or observe rules • Takes initiative and responsibility to learn • Is eager to demonstrate and communicate learning • Finds joy and satisfaction in learning and teaching
Valuing Acceptance of a value Preference for a value Commitment	• Appreciates learning • Makes meaning • Recognizes and respects beliefs, opinions, perspectives, or thoughts—be it others' or their own • Realizes the importance and relevance of facts and feelings • Commits to a cause, claim, conclusion, or conviction
Organizing Conceptualization of a value Organization of a value system	• Prioritizes learning • Conceptualizes ideas and information through abstraction or generalization • Categorizes, considers, and critiques knowledge, thinking, and feelings based on importance, relevance, and significance • Establishes a hierarchal value system based on personal education, experience, and emotions

Characterizing Generalizing Internalizing	• Personalizes learning • Reevaluates ideas or ideals or revises judgments based on new discoveries or evidence • Answers questions, addresses problems, accomplishes tasks, or analyzes texts and topics objectively • Distinguishes facts from feelings but considers and respects both • Integrates education, experiences, and emotions into a personal perspective or philosophy about learning and life

Source: Adapted from Krathwohl, Bloom, & Bertrand Masia, 1964.

These affective attitudes are based on the principles of internalization, which Barbara Seels and Zita Glasgow (1990) describe as "the process whereby a person's affect toward an object passes from a general awareness level to a point where the affect is 'internalized' and consistently guides or controls the person's behavior" (p. 28). Adopting an affective attitude also makes learning a social-emotional experience for a person with an inquiring mind (see chapter 4, page 91).

The intellectual and affective traits of a person with an inquiring mind are instilled with the spirit of inquiry that fuels their ambition to learn. For example, the spirit of inquiry is an evidence-based philosophy and practice that's promoted in the education and professional field of nursing. The National League for Nursing (2014) describes a *spirit of inquiry* as "a persistent sense of curiosity that informs both learning and practice" (p. 1). People possessing a spirit of inquiry do the following.

- Pose questions even when the answer seems accurate, easy, obvious, or simple
- Challenge traditional or existing perspectives and practices
- Seek creative approaches to problem solving
- Demonstrate a strong sense of wonder
- Prompt or stimulate innovative, inventive, or insightful thinking
- Extend opportunities and possibilities for discovering novel solutions in both predictable and unpredictable situations (The National League for Nursing, 2014)

These are the actions and attitudes of a person with an inquiring mind. They ask questions because they are curious, interested, and skeptical. They challenge the status quo by questioning what's common or customary. They are willing to research, experiment with, or investigate new and novel ideas or ways to do something. They take and transform what they learn into personal expertise. These spirited acts and intellectual traits are what make a person with an inquiring mind a good thinker and a lifelong learner, who learns, leads, and lives based on these four tenets:

1. Ask questions.
2. Delve deeper.
3. Go further.
4. Share with others.

What Does an Inquiring Mind Want?

A person with an inquiring mind wants to know the answer. However, they know answers are a means to an end. In fact, every answer leads to another question to be addressed. It does not matter whether the question is easy or hard, simple or complex, or closed or open-ended. An inquiring mind will continue to ask *how*, *why*, *what if*, or *what else*. Those questions develop and deepen their knowledge, understanding, awareness, and expertise. They are posed to continue conversations about the subject, skill, or situation.

A person with an inquiring mind also wants to know the truth. They demonstrate a high level of existential intelligence, which Howard Gardner (2022) describes as "the cognitive capacity to raise and ponder 'big questions'—queries about love, about evil, about life and death—indeed, about the nature and quality of existence." They ponder and pose profound questions about global ideas, issues, themes, or topics. They enjoy examining and exploring these empirical questions either by themselves or with others. What makes these "big questions" both philosophical and personal is that they weigh heavily on an inquiring person's mind.

However, a person with an inquiring mind doesn't want to know "just the facts" or how to "just do it," although both are important and interesting to them. They want to understand the meaning and reasoning behind responses or results. They want to be aware of different contexts and ways something could be understood or used. They also want to take what they have learned and develop it into personal expertise that allows them to speak accurately and with authority.

A person with an inquiring mind won't accept or rely on what they are taught or told by an authority figure or a single source. They want to discover, determine, and decide the answer or truth by and for themselves. They want to think critically and creatively about how they could understand and use what they have learned to come up with or create new ideas, knowledge, or ways to perceive subjects or perform skills.

A person with an inquiring mind recognizes that answers are not final, and the truth is not finite. Their spirit of inquiry spurs them to raise questions about the accuracy of answers or the authenticity of the truth. Their intellectual character supports them in seeking the examples and evidence they need to draw conclusions or drive their decisions about the answer or the truth. For a person with an inquiring mind, the search for the answer and the truth is just as satisfying as securing both.

What Motivates an Inquiring Mind?

A person with an inquiring mind is motivated to take the time and extend the effort to learn. They are willing to conduct in-depth research and investigations so they can acquire and uncover information about a subject, skill, or situation. They want to experiment with, examine, and evaluate hypotheses, ideas, methods, strategies, and theories, and doing so fosters their critical, creative, and reflective thinking skills. It also fortifies and furthers their expertise in the subject being studied.

An inquiring mind's motivation is both extrinsic and intrinsic. They can be prompted by a question that either is posed to them or pops into their head. They can be stimulated by something they see, sense, or speculate that starts them wondering and wanting to delve deeper or go further. The prompt doesn't have to be perplexing or profound, and the stimulus doesn't have to be sensational or striking. However, both should be interesting enough to incite an inquiring mind to want to learn as much or as deeply about what the prompt is asking or the stimulus is sharing. How the prompt is presented or the stimulus is shown is what inspires the inquiring mind to want to learn.

For example, a person with an inquiring mind could be asked an easy question, shown a familiar image, or played a well-known audio or video text. The answer, idea, or truth may be concrete, obvious, or simple. However, a person with an inquiring mind will pose their own questions. They ponder the intent or purpose of the prompt or stimulus. They contemplate why this particular prompt or stimulus is being posed or shared. They speculate on the importance, relevance, or significance of the prompt or stimulus for the topic as well as for themselves. If the prompt or stimulus is not certain or communicated clearly, a person with an inquiring mind draws their own conclusions and makes their own decisions about what's interesting or fascinating about it, and that inspires them to create and ask their own questions.

This is what makes a person with an inquiring mind unique. They can "see" what's interesting or fascinating in a prompt or stimulus. They think critically about the intent of the prompt or the idea of the stimulus. They reflect on whether the prompt could be addressed using multiple methods or the stimulus could have multiple meanings. They also think creatively about how they could come up with their own connections or connotations about the prompt or stimulus.

A person with an inquiring mind is also enthused to share what they have discovered and learned. This aspiration to share is not to convey, "Look what I know, understand, or can do." They want to inform what's interesting or fascinating about the subject or skill they have learned. They want to introduce new ideas and information. They want to inspire and invite others to join them on their journey into inquiry. That's what makes a person with an inquiring mind not only a good learner but also a good teacher.

How Does a Learner With an Inquiring Mind Learn?

A learner with an inquiring mind learns through inquiry and questioning. They ask and address questions to do the following.

- Acquire foundational knowledge and functional understanding.
- Apply conceptual and procedural understanding.
- Analyze concepts, content, conditions, and connections to deepen awareness.
- Augment their knowledge, understanding, and awareness into personal expertise.
- Assess the depth and extent of someone's acumen, aptitude, or attitude.

The purpose of the questions they pose is to do one of the following.

- Attain the answer.
- Explain the answer.
- Justify or verify an answer.
- Explore or extend an answer.

For a learner with an inquiring mind, questioning is not just about answering. In fact, for a learner with an inquiring mind, *the question is the answer*. The subject of the question identifies the content knowledge covered. The question stem indicates what should be considered about the subject. The rest of the words and phrases in the question inform not only the core idea to be comprehended but also the depth and extent of the response to be conveyed. This is how a learner with an inquiring mind perceives—or "sees"—questions.

Table 1.3 (page 24) shows how a learner with an inquiring mind sees questions. They recognize the content the question covers. Then, they flip the question by rephrasing the interrogative statement into a declarative one that states the basic facts, core idea, or enduring understanding about the subject. The question stem indicates and stimulates the type and level of thinking to be demonstrated. It also informs whether the answer needs to be attained, explained, justified, or extended.

Regarding and rephrasing questions this way may feel or seem awkward. However, this table provides a lens into how a learner with an inquiring mind perceives questions. It could also help both educators and students to fathom what exactly a question asks and how deeply it must be addressed.

How Does a Teacher With an Inquiring Mind Teach?

A teacher with an inquiring mind also teaches through inquiry and questioning. The purpose of the questions, however, is not just to check for or confirm student learning. They ask questions to do the following.

- Initiate the inquiry into a subject, skill, or situation.
- Inspire further questions and conversations about what's being taught and learned.
- Identify and introduce the instructional focus.
- Inform the intent and purpose for learning.

An educator with an inquiring mind draws on their intellectual character to think critically, reflectively, and creatively about how they could plan and provide instruction through inquiry and questioning. Table 1.4 (page 26) features the overarching questions that educators with an inquiring mind might consider when developing and delivering inquiry-based instruction. These questions prompt a person with an inquiring mind to check and consider their intellect and attitude toward teaching and learning.

Table 1.3: "Flipping the Question" to Fathom the Answer

What Is the Question?	What Is the Content?	What Must Be Comprehended?	What Must Be Considered?	What Must Be Conveyed?
How can multidigit numbers be multiplied using a standard algorithm?	Multiplication of multidigit numbers with a standard algorithm	Multidigit numbers can be multiplied using a standard algorithm.	How?	Explain the answer.
What are the spelling-sound correspondences for common consonant digraphs?	Spelling-sound correspondences for common consonant digraphs	There are spelling-sound correspondences for common consonant digraphs.	What?	Attain the answer.
Why is the molecular-level structure important in the functioning of designed materials?	Molecular-level structure in the functioning of designed materials	The molecular-level structure is important in the functioning of designed materials.	Why?	Justify or verify the answer.
What were the causes and consequences of the stock market crash of 1929?	The stock market crash of 1929	The stock market crash of 1929 had many causes and consequences.	What were the causes? What were the consequences?	Justify or verify the answer.
What are the specific roles played by the following citizens in a democracy? · Voters · Jurors · Taxpayers · Members of the armed forces · Petitioners · Protesters · Officeholders	The roles of the following citizens in a democracy: · Voters · Jurors · Taxpayers · Members of the armed forces · Petitioners · Protesters · Officeholders	The following citizens in a democracy play specific roles. · Voters · Jurors · Taxpayers · Members of the armed forces · Petitioners · Protesters · Officeholders	What roles?	Explain the answer.

Why do people in one country trade goods and services with people in other countries?	Trading goods and services between countries	People in one country trade goods and services with people in other countries.	Why?	Explain the answer.
How could human activities affect the cultural and environmental characteristics of places or regions?	Human activities in places and regions	Human activities could affect the cultural and environmental characteristics of places or regions.	How?	Justify or verify the answer.
What are the ways art is used to represent, establish, reinforce, and reflect group identity?	Art and group identity	Art is used in ways to represent, establish, reinforce, and reflect group identity.	What are the ways?	Explain the answer.
What is the structure and elements of music?	Structure and elements of music	Music has specific structure and elements.	What?	Attain the answer.
What are the connections between fitness and overall physical and mental health?	Fitness, physical health, and mental health	There are connections between fitness and overall physical and mental health.	What are the connections?	Justify or verify the answer.

Table 1.4: Planning and Providing Instruction With an Inquiring Mind

Critical Learning	• What are the subjects and skills stipulated by the standards and covered by the curriculum? (Attentiveness) • How closely do the information and items offered by the curricular texts or programs address and assess the subjects and skills stipulated in the standards? (Carefulness) • What additional materials or methods could be utilized to support the standards, supplement the curriculum, and strengthen the teaching and learning experience? (Thoroughness)
Reflective Learning	• How do I determine whether the subject, skill, or situation is essential to learn, important to understand, or "nice to know"? (Autonomy) • What is my level of learning about the subject, skill, or situation? (Humility) • How capable or confident do I believe I am to teach the subject, skill, or situation to my students? (Courage) • What exactly do I need to learn so my instruction is effective and engaging and student learning is educational and encouraging? (Tenacity) • Do I believe my students have the ability or interest to learn the subject or skill at the level expected and the depth demanded? (Honesty)
Creative Learning	• Why is the subject or skill essential to address and assess, important to teach and learn, or interesting to know and understand? (Curiosity) • What else should be clarified, confirmed, or considered when teaching and learning the text, topic, or technique? (Fair-Mindedness/Open-Mindedness)
Affective Learning	• How could my students learn the subject, skill, or situation? (Receiving) • How could my students participate in the learning? (Responding) • How could my students appreciate what they are learning? (Valuing) • How could my students prioritize what they are learning? (Organizing) • How could my students personalize what they are learning? (Characterizing)

An educator with an inquiring mind also develops and delivers their instruction with a spirit of inquiry, as in the following examples.

- A mathematics teacher might question the different ways the mathematics could be performed. They also might reflect on how they could show and share these different ways to students without confusing or overwhelming them.

- A reading and literacy teacher might question the different central ideas or themes of a text. They also might reflect on how they could encourage students to choose or come up with a central idea and theme of a text and support their choice or claim with textual evidence.

- A science teacher might question how science impacts science fiction or whether science fiction influences science. They also might reflect on how they could encourage students to examine or explore and explain the impact and influence both have on each other.

- A history teacher might question how the textbook presents or portrays a historical yet controversial idea, individual, incident, or issue. They also might reflect on how they could present the idea, individual, incident, or issue in an accurate, honest, and unbiased manner.

- An art or music teacher might question how students could appreciate art and music as a genre and a craft. They also might reflect on how they can encourage students not only to create their own art and music but also critique the works of others.

- A physical education teacher might question how they could help students develop healthy lifestyles. They also might reflect on how they could teach the sport to students as well as how and why the sport could be played in different contexts or ways.

- A foreign language teacher might question how they could educate students on the target language but also expose them to cultures that speak different forms of the language. They also might reflect on how they could have students explore the interrelationship between communication and culture.

- A career and technical education teacher might ask questions about the vocational and specialized skills students need to succeed in a career or profession. They also might reflect on how they could simulate real-world and work experiences that would encourage students to draw on and use both their academic and vocational knowledge and skills.

For a person with an inquiring mind, teaching and learning is a continuous practice and process of asking and addressing questions. Their approach and attitude toward learning and life follows this quote by WWE Hall of Fame professional wrestler "Rowdy" Roddy Piper (1984): "Just when you think you have the answers, I change the questions." That's exactly what a teacher with an inquiring mind will do—change their question to continue the conversation or cause further contemplation.

The philosophy and practice of teaching and learning with an inquiring mind promotes the following ideas.

- Intelligence is affective (socioemotional) as well as academic (knowledge) and analytical (cognitive).

- Instruction should equip students with the content knowledge, cognitive skills, and characteristic dispositions they need to become good thinkers and lifelong learners.

- Effective learning is marked and measured by achievement (Did they learn?), aptitude (Can they learn?), and attitude (Do they want to learn?).

- Educators teach, and students learn through inquiry and questioning.

Teaching and learning with an inquiring mind follow the traditional structure of classroom discourse known by the acronym IRE/F (Cazden, 2001; Hattie, 2012, 2023). However, the pattern of teacher-student discourse occurs as follows:

- The teacher *initiates the inquiry* by presenting a prompt or sharing a stimulus.

- The students *reflect* on the prompt or stimulus before *responding*.

- The teacher *elicits* and *encourages further inquiries and explanations* from the students.

Figure 1.1 distinguishes traditional (teacher-directed) delivery and discourse of IRE/F with the pattern that prompts and promotes inquiry.

Teacher Directed	Inquiry Driven
1. The teacher initiates instruction by posting an objective, presenting the information, providing an assignment, or posing a question that must be answered correctly. 2. The student responds to instruction within an expected or set amount of time. 3. The teacher evaluates and provides feedback on the student's response.	1. The teacher initiates the inquiry by presenting a prompt or sharing a stimulus that identifies and introduces the instructional focus and informs the purpose for learning. 2. The student reflects on the prompt or stimulus before responding. 3. The teacher elicits and encourages further inquiries and explanations from the students.

FIGURE 1.1: Teacher-directed versus inquiry-driven steps of IRE/F.

Notice how the traditional structure is more instructional, while the inquiry-driven pattern is more interactive. Inquiry also transforms teaching and learning into an exchange and experience that Hattie (2012) describes as "dominated more by dialogue than by monologue about learning" (p. 150). The goal is for educators to talk less and use questions to trigger rather than test learning. The expectation is for students to comprehend, consider, and convey what they are learning.

What Is the Inquiring Minds Framework for Teaching and Learning?

I created the Inquiring Minds Framework as a plan and process for developing and delivering inquiry-based teaching and learning experiences driven by good questions. It establishes a balance between academic and social-emotional learning by offering students opportunities to develop, demonstrate, and deepen their intellectual character. It also instills a spirit of inquiry by engaging and encouraging students to ask and address questions about what they are learning.

Figure 1.2 (page 30) is a visual representation of this redefined IRE/F progression of classroom discourse that promotes inquiry and questioning.

The Inquiring Minds Framework is not a taxonomy. It's a nominative framework that describes four different pathways to engage in and experience inquiry. The pathway to inquiry and its progression depends on the following.

- The demand for the academic standard being addressed and assessed
- The strengths, needs, and interests of students
- The intent and purpose of the teaching and learning experience

Teaching and learning with an inquiring mind don't have to start on the foundational pathway to inquiry. The focus and form of the inquiry flow both down and across the different pathways. That's why figure 1.2 (page 30) has dashed lines connecting each of the boxes along each pathway. The only requirement is that the journey down or across each pathway starts with presenting a prompt or sharing a stimulus that will engage students—or hook 'em—into experiencing inquiry.

The Inquiring Minds Framework ensures the inquiry students engage in and experience is standards based, socially and emotionally supportive, and student responsive. Each pathway addresses and assesses specific aspects of academic standards and has a particular instructional focus and purpose for learning the subject, skill,

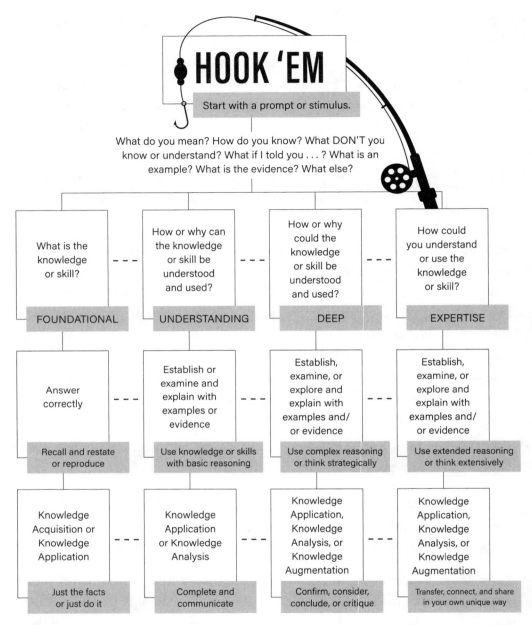

FIGURE 1.2: The Inquiring Minds Framework for teaching and learning.

Visit **go.SolutionTree.com/instruction** *for a free reproducible version of this figure.*

and stipulations stated in the standards. These pathways also encourage students to comprehend and communicate their learning at different levels of thinking and DOK. (For more information on DOK levels, see table 3.1, page 74.) For example:

- **Foundational:** The *Foundational Pathway to Inquiry* stimulates students to ask and answer their own questions so they can develop and demonstrate the foundational knowledge and functional understanding they need to succeed in a specific subject. Inquiry and questioning along this pathway require students to understand and use their learning at either DOK 1 or DOK 2, depending on the questions they ask.

- **Understanding:** The *Inquiry Pathway to Understanding* is standards based, prompting students to establish or examine and explain how and why the knowledge and skills can or could be understood and used to answer questions, address problems, accomplish tasks, or analyze the ideas and information presented in texts or about topics. Inquiry and questioning along this pathway require students to understand and use their learning at either DOK 2 or DOK 3, depending on the questions derived from the standard.

- **Deep:** The *Deep Pathway to Inquiry* takes students beyond the standards and curriculum, engaging them to establish, examine, or explore and explain how and why the knowledge and skills can and could be understood and used in different contexts and deeper ways. Inquiry and questioning along this pathway will be either DOK 2, DOK 3, or DOK 4, depending on the depth and extent students are engaged to delve into the subject or skills being studied.

- **Expertise:** The *Inquiry Pathway to Expertise* motivates students to consider and convey how they can understand and use what they have learned in-depth, insightfully, innovatively, inventively, or in their own unique way. Inquiry and questioning along this pathway will be either DOK 2, DOK 3, or DOK 4, depending on the depth and extent students are engaged to express, examine, or extend what they are learning.

Though teaching and learning with an inquiring mind is standards based, it's unrealistic and even unreasonable to address every standard in a certain content area at a given grade level through inquiry and questioning. The Inquiring Minds Framework, however, provides educators with a process to prioritize which standards students must address to demonstrate understanding and pick those they could investigate to deepen awareness. It ensures that educators and students will engage in and experience inquiry and questioning with a guaranteed and viable curriculum that will enhance teacher instruction and encourage student learning. Most importantly, the Inquiring Minds Framework ensures that the inquiry students engage in and experience addresses, assesses, and augments their individual strengths, interests, and needs in learning.

This framework serves as the focus and foundation of this book. However, before exploring how to plan and provide inquiry-based teaching and learning experiences driven by good questions, we examine how good questions prompt students to engage in and experience inquiry at different and deeper levels of cognitive rigor.

Summary

A person with an inquiring mind possesses a strong intellectual character and spirit of inquiry. They want to know the answer or the truth. However, they want to discover or uncover both for themselves. A learner with an inquiring mind asks questions to assert or attain, explain, justify, or extend the answer. A teacher with an inquiring mind asks questions to initiate the inquiry into a subject, skill, or situation; inspire further questions and conversations; identify and introduce the instructional focus; and inform the intent and purpose for learning.

Teaching and learning with an inquiring mind involve initiating the instruction with a prompt or stimulus that students reflect on before responding. The teacher elicits and encourages further questions and responses from students. The Inquiring Minds Framework provides a plan and process for developing and delivering inquiry-based teaching and learning experiences driven by good questions that differ in their cognitive rigor.

Application: Do You Have an Inquiring Mind to Learn?

Either individually or with your team, complete the Survey for the Intellectual Characteristics of an Inquiring Mind and the Profile of Your Inquiring Mind reproducibles on pages 34–37. Use this survey to gauge the depth and extent of your thinking dispositions and intellectual characteristics, and how they distinguish your inquiring mind. Use this Likert scale to rate each statement.

5 = I am like this all the time.

4 = I am often like this.

3 = I am sometimes like this.

2 = I can be like this.

1 = I am not this way at all.

Note: You can also conduct this self-assessment with students.

1. Copy the Survey for the Intellectual Characteristics of an Inquiring Mind and the Profile of Your Inquiring Mind reproducibles on pages 34–37.

2. Read the statements that describe the thinking dispositions and intellectual virtues of an inquiring mind.

3. Write a score after every statement that you associate with or that sounds like you.

4. Use the bar graph to chart your response to each statement. (For example, if you rated statement number one a 5, color your bar to the column marked 5.)

5. Share and compare results with your colleagues.

Survey for the Intellectual Characteristics of an Inquiring Mind

Intellectual Characteristics of an Inquiring Mind	Score
1. I enjoy asking questions to deepen my understanding.	
2. I often find myself seeking new knowledge and information.	
3. I approach challenges with curiosity and a desire to explore different perspectives.	
4. I actively engage in research to expand my understanding of various subjects.	
5. I regularly seek out opportunities for learning and personal growth.	
6. I am open-minded and willing to consider different ideas and opinions.	
7. I enjoy exploring complex problems and finding innovative solutions.	
8. I have a natural inclination to investigate and analyze situations thoroughly.	
9. I am comfortable with uncertainty and see it as an opportunity for discovery.	
10. I enjoy exploring different fields and disciplines to broaden my knowledge.	
11. I actively seek out feedback and input from others to gain different insights.	
12. I often find myself reflecting on my own assumptions and beliefs.	
13. I have a natural curiosity about the world and a desire to understand how things work.	
14. I am constantly looking for ways to expand my intellectual horizons.	
15. I am comfortable challenging conventional wisdom and exploring alternative viewpoints.	
16. I have a knack for spotting patterns and making connections between different ideas.	

page 1 of 3

Intellectual Characteristics of an Inquiring Mind	Score
17. I enjoy exploring the underlying principles and theories behind various concepts.	
18. I actively seek out diverse sources of information to gain a comprehensive understanding.	
19. I am persistent in finding answers to questions that intrigue me.	
20. I am comfortable with ambiguity and am willing to explore multiple possibilities.	
21. I enjoy engaging in intellectual discussions and debates.	
22. I have a natural inclination to dig deeper and get to the root cause of issues.	
23. I am eager to explore new technologies and their potential applications.	
24. I enjoy experimenting and testing new ideas to see how they work in practice.	
25. I actively seek out challenging tasks that require critical thinking and problem solving.	
26. I am constantly seeking to improve my analytical skills.	
27. I am not afraid to challenge authority or established norms if I believe there is a better way.	
28. I have a strong desire to unravel complex concepts and make them more understandable.	
29. I enjoy exploring philosophical questions and contemplating the meaning of life.	
30. I am constantly seeking out new perspectives to broaden my worldview	
31. I have a natural curiosity about different cultures and customs.	
32. I am comfortable with intellectual uncertainty and am always seeking to learn more.	
33. I enjoy exploring different methodologies and approaches to problem solving.	

Intellectual Characteristics of an Inquiring Mind	Score
34. I am skilled at asking probing questions to get to the heart of the matter.	
35. I actively seek out feedback to gain a better understanding of my blind spots.	
36. I am driven by a desire to acquire knowledge for its own sake.	
37. I enjoy exploring the connections between seemingly unrelated concepts.	
38. I actively seek out opportunities for self-reflection and introspection.	
39. I am constantly seeking out new challenges to keep my mind engaged.	
40. I enjoy reading and researching topics outside of my immediate area of expertise.	
41. I am comfortable with uncertainty and am willing to take risks in pursuit of knowledge.	
42. I enjoy examining different assumptions and questioning established beliefs.	
43. I am curious about the natural world and how it functions.	
44. I actively seek out new experiences to broaden my understanding of the world.	
45. I enjoy engaging in debates and discussions to explore different viewpoints.	
46. I have a knack for identifying gaps in knowledge and seeking to fill them.	
47. I am comfortable with complexity and enjoy unraveling intricate concepts.	
48. I actively seek out mentors and experts to learn from their experiences.	
49. I enjoy exploring the history and evolution of various ideas and concepts.	
50. I am driven by a constant thirst for knowledge and understanding.	

Profile of Your Inquiring Mind

	1	2	3	4	5
1					
2					
3					
4					
5					
6					
7					
8					
9					
10					
11					
12					
13					
14					
15					
16					
17					
18					
19					
20					
21					
22					
23					
24					
25					
26					
27					
28					
29					
30					
31					
32					
33					
34					
35					
36					
37					
38					
39					
40					
41					
42					
43					
44					
45					
46					
47					
48					
49					
50					

Chapter 2

WHAT FORMS OF INQUIRY CAN STUDENTS ENGAGE IN AND EXPERIENCE?

*Inquiry is more important than answers,
for it is the questions we ask and the way
in which we ask them that defines us.*

—John Paul Caponigro

Reflect and Respond

What exactly does inquiry involve? Is inquiry about answering questions or asking and addressing them? Who could and should be asking and addressing the questions when students engage in and experience inquiry? How could inquiry shift from a teacher-led experience to a student-driven experience? How could educators participate in inquiry with students?

NQUIRY IS BOTH an instructional practice and learning process that emphasizes and encourages seeking and sharing knowledge and understanding through asking questions, investigating, and exploring. Teachers and students with inquiring minds ask and address questions through a variety of means to satisfy their natural curiosity and thirst for learning. This chapter explores what it means to engage in inquiry as well as the different forms of inquiry students can experience.

What Is Inquiry?

Inquiry is both a teaching and a learning experience. It is an intentional yet involved approach to teaching and learning that prompts or stimulates both educators and students to develop and demonstrate deeper insights, perspectives, and understanding of a subject.

Teaching and learning through inquiry involve the following.

- Asking questions to acquire, activate, advance, or assess learning
- Reading and researching texts and sources in detail, in-depth, and insightfully
- Establishing, examining, or exploring and explaining ideas and information
- Defending, disproving, or drawing conclusions
- Engaging in deep dialogues, discussions, and debates

Through inquiry, students develop and demonstrate the following essential learning and life skills that will benefit them both in and beyond school.

- **Critical thinking:** The ability to analyze information, evaluate evidence, consider multiple ideas or perspectives, and make informed decisions or judgments.
- **Problem solving:** The ability to identify and analyze problems, gather information, develop hypotheses or solutions, and conduct analyses or experiments.
- **Creative thinking:** The ability to develop original ideas, design unique products, or demonstrate innovative or inventive ways of thinking.
- **Collaboration:** The ability to work well with others to answer a question, address a problem, or accomplish a task correctly or successfully.
- **Communication:** The ability to express and share ideas and information clearly, comprehensibly, and creatively with others.
- **Academic and authentic literacy:** The ability to read, write, and discuss ideas and information purposefully within a specific academic area or in a real-world context.

Inquiry is both an academic and social-emotional experience. Not only does it strengthen students' content knowledge and conceptual understanding of a specific subject. It also supports students in developing critical learning and life skills that will benefit them academically and personally both within and beyond school. Most importantly, inquiry is both a method and a means for students and educators to address and approach teaching and learning with an inquiring mind.

What Are the Different Forms of Inquiry?

There is no one way to engage in and experience inquiry. It can take different forms, depending on the following.

- What is the intent and purpose of the inquiry?
- Who is asking and addressing the questions?

According to Heather Banchi and Randy Bell (2008), the frequent forms of inquiry experienced in K–12 education include the following.

- Confirmation or controlled inquiry
- Structured inquiry
- Guided inquiry
- Open or free inquiry

These are the four core methods of inquiry identified by Joseph Schwab (1962) and formalized by Marshall Herron (1971). Each of these experiences is initiated by the teacher. However, the responsibility and roles of the students shift from following directions to working individually and independently to engage in and experience the inquiry. Since the early 2000s, other forms of inquiry have been introduced and implemented in education.

- Coupled inquiry (Dunkhase, 2000; Martin-Hansen, 2002)
- Authentic inquiry (Bell, Smetana, & Binns, 2005)
- Synergistic inquiry (Kuntzleman, 2019)

Table 2.1 (page 42) presents the different forms of inquiry that educators and students can engage in and experience. Note that each form of inquiry differs in its intent and purpose. However, these forms share some common characteristics.

Table 2.1: Different Forms and Common Characteristics of Inquiry

Characteristics of Inquiry	Forms of Inquiry						
	Confirmation	Structured	Guided	Open or Free	Coupled	Authentic	Synergistic
Subject Studied	Teacher led	Teacher led	Teacher led	Teacher led	Teacher led	Student driven	Collaboration
Prompt/Stimulus	Teacher led	Teacher led	Teacher led	Teacher led	Teacher led	Student driven	Collaboration
Information Items Resources Tools	Teacher led	Teacher led	Teacher led	Teacher led or student driven	Teacher led or student driven	Student driven	Collaboration
Expectations	Teacher led	Teacher led	Teacher led	Teacher led or student driven	Teacher led or student driven	Student driven	Student driven
Questions	Teacher led	Teacher led	Teacher led or student driven	Student driven	Teacher led or student driven	Student driven	Collaboration
Analysis/Evaluation	Teacher led	Teacher led	Student driven	Student driven	Student driven	Student driven	Collaboration
Answers	Teacher led	Student driven	Student driven	Student driven	Student driven	Student driven	Collaboration
Examples/Evidence	Teacher led	Student driven	Student driven	Student driven	Student driven	Student driven	Student driven
Conclusions	Teacher led	Student driven	Student driven	Student driven	Student driven	Student driven	Collaboration
Response Results Reasoning	Teacher led	Student driven	Student driven	Student driven	Student driven	Student driven	Collaboration

The descriptors within this matrix describe who decides and dictates the depth and direction of the inquiry and designate the roles of responsibilities of an inquiry experience.

All these forms of inquiry can be applied to a teaching and learning experience at any grade level and in any subject area. They also can be scaffolded so students learn the following.

- How to engage in and experience inquiry by addressing and asking questions
- How to learn about a subject through inquiry and questioning

The rigor of an inquiry-based teaching and learning experience can vary and depends on the following.

- The demand of the tasks that students must complete
- The complexity of the mental processing students must perform
- The extent of the response students required by the questions posed
- The time, thought, and temperament needed to engage in the inquiry

What Distinguishes Controlled Inquiry From Confirmation Inquiry?

Controlled and confirmation inquiry are the simplest forms of inquiry students can engage in and experience. What makes both simple is that every step of inquiry is set and specified by teachers from start to finish. This makes both forms of inquiry more instructional than inquisitive or individualized.

The goal of controlled and confirmation inquiry is for students to learn how to check and confirm responses, results, or reasoning. The focus and purpose of controlled and confirmation inquiry is for students to learn how to use the following.

- Subject-specific concepts or procedures for answering a question, addressing a problem, accomplishing a task, or analyzing a text or topic
- Active learning skills, stages, and steps of research, experimentation, evaluation, investigation, debate, and design

Responses, results, or reasoning are predetermined. The expectation is students will learn how to verify or validate the accuracy, appropriateness, or authenticity of answers and arguments through inquiry and questioning.

Both forms of inquiry are teacher led. The teacher selects the subject that students will investigate. They present the prompt and share the stimulus students must address and analyze. They also decide on the depth and direction of the inquiry students will engage in. The teacher or the curricular text provides the questions asked and addressed. The answers students attain, the conclusions students draw, and the details students understand and use to support responses, results, or reasoning are all prescriptive and provided to them. However, what distinguishes both forms of inquiry is their intention of the instruction and the expectation of student performance.

Controlled Inquiry

With *controlled inquiry*, students learn to inquire about and investigate how they can understand or use a concept, strategy, or technique to answer a question, solve a problem, or accomplish a task. For example, the expectation could be for students to inquire and investigate the following.

- How to apply an algorithm, formula, method, operation, or procedure to solve an algebraic, word, or real-world problem
- How to summarize key details and ideas or cite evidence from a text using different reading methods or strategies (for example, SQ3R, KWL charts, annotation, Cornell notes)
- How to follow the writing process to plan and produce a particular type of text
- How to use the scientific method to conduct experiments and test hypotheses or ideas
- How to apply civic virtues or principles in different scenarios, settings, or situations
- How to use maps or graphs to identify locations or explain spatial patterns
- How to use materials and tools to create works of art
- How to use notation or recording technology to perform or produce music
- How to conjugate verbs or form sentence types in a target language
- How to play a sport or execute specific plays

Confirmation Inquiry

Confirmation inquiry is more complex. The goal is for students to verify or validate responses, results, or reasoning. The answer and conclusion are predetermined. The practices and procedures students must understand and then use are also prescriptive. However, the purpose of confirmation inquiry is for students to learn how to reinforce or refute an answer or argument with examples or evidence. This type of inquiry allows students to develop their inquiry and questioning skills. Confirmation inquiry experiences could engage students to do the following.

- Work with mathematical properties of operations, prescriptive algorithms and formulas, or proofs to explain or justify responses, results, or reasoning

- Explain how the key details and ideas or craft and structure of a text strengthen and support the central idea or the author's main point of view or purpose

- Conduct experiments or construct arguments supported by evidence to defend or disprove a scientific hypothesis or theory

- Use a chronological sequence of historical events to compare developments that happened at the same time or analyze connections among events and developments in broader historical contexts

- Explain why an object, artifact, or work of art is valued over others based on given criteria

- Identify and explain how cultural and historical context inform and influence a specific performance

The form of inquiry that students engage in and experience depends on the intent of the instruction and the purpose of the learning. If you want students to learn subject-specific concepts and procedures and how they can use them to answer a question, address a problem, accomplish a task, or analyze a text or topic, then engage them in controlled inquiry. If you want students to learn how and why to use specific concepts and procedures to explain or justify a response, result, or reason, then engage them in confirmation inquiry.

What Does Structured Inquiry Involve?

Structured inquiry is primarily teacher led. However, unlike controlled or confirmation inquiry, the answer or conclusion is not provided. The goal is for students to think critically about how they can explain or justify responses, results, or reasoning using the data and details they acquire through analysis and evaluation as examples and evidence. Table 2.2 explains how structured inquiry strengthens and supports the thinking dispositions and intellectual virtues of critical thinking.

Table 2.2: How Structured Inquiry Strengthens Students' Intellectual Character

Thinking Dispositions and Intellectual Virtues	What Students Learn Through Structured Inquiry
Attentiveness Look and listen!	Students learn to pay close attention to data and details that can provide further information and insight. They also learn how these data can serve as examples or evidence to strengthen and support responses, results, or reasoning.
Carefulness Think with care!	Students learn to check and confirm the accuracy, acceptability, appropriateness, or authenticity of claims, conclusions, conjectures, or critiques. They also learn to approach learning with a sense of caution and skepticism.
Thoroughness Go deep!	Students learn not to accept or stop with simple or superficial answers. They also learn to specify and explain, delve deeper, or go further by asking *how, why, what if, or what else*.

With structured inquiry, the complexity—or rigor—of the experience depends on the following.

- Expectations established by the teacher
- Cognitive complexity and demand of the questions posed by the teacher
- Depth of the analysis and evaluation the students must conduct
- Extent of the response the students must provide

Structured inquiry experiences might be described as "easy" or "hard" based on the following.

- Time and effort for students to engage in the inquiry
- Capability and confidence of students to complete the inquiry successfully
- Conditions and criteria of the inquiry

An easy structured inquiry experience can be completed quickly. A hard structured inquiry experience involves more time and effort. The complexity of a structured inquiry experience is designated by the following.

- The type of thinking students must demonstrate
- The kind of knowledge students must acquire and apply
- The level of DOK students must understand and use

Easy structured inquiry experiences require students to obtain the correct answer. Hard structured inquiry experiences demand that students explain, justify, or extend their responses, results, or reasoning with examples or evidence.

What Does Guided Inquiry Enable and Encourage?

Guided inquiry enables and encourages students to learn how to engage in and experience inquiry independently. The goal of guided inquiry is to support students in strengthening their inquiry, critical thinking, and problem-solving skills while building their content knowledge and understanding. To accomplish these goals, the teacher must lessen their control and loosen the structure of the inquiry experience. The teacher's responsibility and role in inquiry shift from being the instructor who asks questions and gauges student understanding to being the facilitator who guides student learning by questioning. This enables and encourages students to develop and demonstrate their inquiry and questioning skills.

With guided inquiry, the teacher establishes the framework and focus for the inquiry. They begin the inquiry by posing the prompt or sharing the stimulus students must address. They provide the background information, resources, and tools students must understand and set the expectations for inquiry. By asking questions the students must address throughout the inquiry, teachers guide and support their students. Students are encouraged to ask and address their own questions as part of their analysis and evaluation of the subject to make the guided inquiry experience more interactive and iterative than informative and instructional.

Table 2.3 (page 48) features the kinds of questions educators and students can pose to facilitate and foster the guided inquiry experience. These are the criteria for how good questions strengthen and support student learning through inquiry. (This topic is discussed further in chapter 3, page 65.)

Table 2.3: Kinds of Questions That Facilitate and Foster Guided Inquiry

Facilitating Questions	How Questions Facilitate and Foster Guided Inquiry
Open-Ended	Stimulates different levels of thinking
Clarifying	Engages and encourages students to express and share their learning
Probing	Checks for and confirms knowledge, understanding, and awareness
Deep	Expands students' knowledge and extends their thinking
Hypothetical	Piques students' curiosity, imagination, interest, and wonder
Reflective	Prompts students to reflect and review before responding
Leading	Phrases the instructional focus and purpose for learning as an interrogative statement

Guided inquiry engages and encourages students to analyze and evaluate how they can understand and use the data, details, and procedures to strengthen their answers and support their conclusions. The teacher poses facilitating questions to guide and support students through the inquiry experience.

How Does Open or Free Inquiry Engage Students in Active Learning Experiences?

Open and free inquiry are essentially the same. They engage students in a deep or extensive experience that requires them to do the following.

- Read texts closely or research credible sources to retrieve data and details.
- Elaborate on, experiment with, or evaluate concepts, ideas, or procedures.
- Inquire about and investigate the impact and influence of events, individuals, or issues.
- Debate claims and conclusions or design plans, techniques, processes, or products.

These are the practical skills students will perform both within and beyond school. They also comprise a learning process I call REID to Learn.

- R = Read, research, retrieve, report
- E = Examine, experiment, explain, evaluate
- I = Inquire, investigate, inspect, imagine
- D = Debate, dialogue, discuss, design

Figure 2.1 summarizes the goals and expectations of the practical skills students perform through open or free inquiry. The delivery and intensity of the inquiry depend on the complexity of the questions posed and how they are used to engage students in the inquiry experience.

REID to Learn	Goals and Expectations of Open or Free Inquiry
Read Research Retrieve Report	Acquire the knowledge by reading texts closely or researching credible sources to retrieve data and details.
Examine Experiment Explain Evaluate	Apply the knowledge by elaborating on, experimenting with, examining, and evaluating how and why concepts, ideas, and procedures can be used to answer questions, address problems, or accomplish tasks.
Inquire Investigate Inspect Imagine	Analyze the knowledge to inquire about, investigate, inspect, or imagine the impact or influence of ideas, events, individuals, or issues.
Debate Dialogue Discuss Design	Augment knowledge or skills by debating claims or conclusions, discussing approaches or ideas, or designing plans, techniques, processes, or procedures that are innovative, insightful, or inventive.

FIGURE 2.1: REID to Learn with open or free inquiry.

The good questions that prompt students to engage in open or free inquiry could include the following.

- *Universal essential questions* that examine or explore broad or grand ideas, issues, themes, or topics
- *Driving essential questions* that personalize learning and promote the development and demonstration of expertise

- *Hypothetical questions* that pique students' curiosity to consider alternatives, options, possibilities, or potential

- *Argumentative questions* that require students to defend, justify, or refute actions, alternatives, answers, or arguments—be it their own or those made by others (Francis, 2016)

Each question establishes not only the depth of the inquiry that students engage in, but also the direction the experience takes. For example, universal essential questions make the open or free inquiry experience thought-provoking, prompting students to think reflectively by reporting, elaborating, and debating. Driving essential questions personalize the open or free inquiry by stimulating students to read or research, experiment, investigate, and design. Hypothetical questions prompt students to draw on their imagination to make a prediction or presumption. Argumentative questions demand students seek evidence to support their choices and claims and strengthen their conclusions.

Open or free inquiry engages students in the following active learning experiences, which I call PIPES:

- **P**roject-based learning
- **I**nvestigative learning
- **P**roblem-based learning
- **E**xpeditionary learning
- **S**ervice learning

Figure 2.2 summarizes how each of these active learning experiences engages students to participate in open or free inquiry. Each of these active learning experiences requires students to take the lead in their learning. They challenge students to expand on or extend the information, resources, or tools the teacher provides. Students pose their own questions, plan their own procedures or designs, conduct their own analyses and evaluations, and come up with their own answers or conclusions based on their efforts or the evidence they gather.

Open or free inquiry serves multiple purposes. It engages students to utilize the content, conceptual, and critical learning skills they developed through confirmation and controlled, structured, and guided inquiry experiences. It provides students the opportunity to engage in inquiry experiences independently and responsibly with limited guidance or support from the teacher. It allows students to use the practical skills they need to succeed, survive, and thrive academically,

Active Learning Experience	How to Engage in Open or Free Inquiry
Project-Based Learning	Students are presented with a topical or driving essential question that prompts and guides them through the process of planning, developing, and implementing a plan or process or creating a product for a specific purpose. Projects can be possible (one that can be completed or produced successfully) or impossible (one that cannot be completed or produced successfully due to lack of knowledge, resources, or capability).
Investigative Learning	Students are presented with a prompt or stimulus that engages them to conduct in-depth research, examinations, or explorations into an idea, event, individual, or issue. Students must gather and evaluate sources for their credibility and use the information they acquire as evidence to attain answers and defend, disprove, or draw conclusions—be it their own or those made by others.
Problem-Based Learning	Students are presented with a driving essential question or problem that prompts or stimulates them to address, handle, resolve, settle, or solve a circumstance, issue, or situation. The problem can be tame (formulaic with one solution), complex (multiple perspectives, multiple potential processes, multiple possible solutions), or wicked (no concrete, final, or mutually agreed-on solution; Rittel & Webber, 1973).
Expeditionary Learning	Students are posed a prompt or presented with a stimulus that sends them on a journey to learn through inquiry that extends across the curriculum or beyond the classroom physically or virtually. The purpose of expeditionary learning is for students to inquire and investigate how they could understand and use the knowledge and skills they learn in school in a real-world context.
Service Learning	Students are engaged or encouraged to inquire and investigate how they could address, explain, or respond to a circumstance, issue, or problem within the community— be it school, local, statewide, regional, national, global, socioeconomic, or cultural.

FIGURE 2.2: Active learning experiences that engage students in open or free inquiry.

professionally, and personally. It engages students to engage in inquiry actively through experiences that strengthen thinking and support talent development.

Most importantly, the expectation of open or free inquiry shapes students' intellectual character and spurs their inquiring minds to address and approach learning with a strong sense of curiosity, imagination, interest, and wonder.

Figure 2.3 explains how open or free inquiry deepens students' intellectual character by prompting or stimulating them to think creatively.

Thinking Dispositions and Intellectual Virtues	What Students Learn Through Open or Free Inquiry
Curiosity Ask questions!	Students learn how to motivate themselves intrinsically ("I want to learn this!") and extrinsically ("This makes me want to learn this!"). They learn to consider "what if" or "what else" even after they attain answers or draw conclusions.
Open-Mindedness Fair-Mindedness Think outside the box!	Students learn to consider all alternatives, options, and possibilities—even after they attain answers or make decisions. They learn to consider and comment on opposite perspectives, opinions, or thoughts when defending, disproving, or drawing conclusions.

FIGURE 2.3: How open or free inquiry strengthens students' intellectual character.

How Does Coupled Inquiry Combine Guided and Open or Free Inquiry?

Coupled inquiry combines the practices and processes of guided and open or free inquiry. The teacher initiates the inquiry by selecting the subject to be studied and providing the prompt or sharing the stimulus students must address and analyze. They also provide the background information, resources, or tools, and pose questions to engage students in the inquiry. However, students must acquire the information, resources, and tools they need to answer the question correctly or defend, disprove, or draw their conclusions successfully. Students must ask questions about the subject studied. They craft the procedures or design, conduct the analysis or evaluation, and come up with their own answers or conclusions. This is how the coupled inquiry shifts from a teacher-led to a student-driven experience.

What distinguishes coupled inquiry is that it is standards based. The prompt students must address is derived from the learning intention, objective, or target of a grade-level or content-area academic standard. The stimulus students analyze could be an audio, print, or visual text that elaborates on or extends the following.

- The type and level of cognition the standard challenges students to demonstrate
- The content knowledge the standard expects students to develop

- The context the standard demands students to understand and use in their learning

For example, in mathematics, a coupled inquiry experience engages students to inquire and investigate how and why they could understand or use the mathematical concept, operation, or procedure addressed in a specific standard to solve numerical or word problems. Figure 2.4 shows the Inquiry Grid—a resource educators and students can use as a planning tool for engaging in and experiencing inquiry. (You can find more information on designing Inquiry Grids in chapters 4 and 7, pages 91 and 159.)

Subject	Perform Operations With Multidigit Whole Numbers
Standard (Goal and Expectations)	Fluently multiply multidigit numbers using a standard algorithm. (MATH.NYS.5.NBT.1)
Prompt (Instruction and Evaluation)	How can multidigit whole numbers be multiplied fluently using a standard algorithm? (DOK 2) How could you multiply multidigit whole numbers fluently using a standard algorithm? (DOK 3)
Stimulus (QFocus)	542 × 398 801 × 246 245 × 938 126 × 408 824 × 953 975 × 624 293 × 845 579 × 264 763 × 154 629 × 475 367 × 541 249 × 567 315 × 476 851 × 245 571 × 643 158 × 452 468 × 210 515 × 842 864 × 102 458 × 215

Source for standard: New York State Department of Education, 2019.

FIGURE 2.4: Coupled Inquiry Grid for multiplying multidigit whole numbers.

The prompt in figure 2.4 features two essential questions derived from the academic standard being addressed and assessed. The first is a topical essential question that prompts students to establish and explain how multidigit numbers can be multiplied fluently using a standard algorithm. It's DOK 2 because it asks students to apply knowledge, concepts, and skills. The other is a driving essential question that prompts students to think strategically about how they could multiply multidigit numbers fluently using a standard algorithm. It's DOK 3 because it asks students to examine and explain with evidence. The mathematics problems students must solve serve as the stimulus to address the standard. They also serve as examples and evidence students need to support their responses to the questions.

With coupled inquiry in literacy and language arts, the text of literary fiction or nonfiction students read and review serves as the stimulus of the inquiry. In figure 2.5, the poem "I Like to See It Lap the Miles" (a.k.a. "The Railway Train") by Emily Dickinson (1891) serves as the stimulus.

The prompt consists of good questions that address the standard and ask specifics about the text being read and reviewed. These questions initiate the inquiry, provide the purpose or reason for reading, and serve as assessments.

Subject	Figurative Language: Poetry—Emily Dickinson
Standard (Goal and Expectations)	Describe how the author's use of figurative language such as metaphor and personification achieves specific purposes. (TEKS.ELA.6.9I)
Prompt (Instruction and Evaluation)	• How does an author's use of figurative language achieve specific purposes? (DOK 3) • How does Emily Dickinson use figurative language to depict the train as a giant, powerful, living, horse-like creature? (DOK 2) • How does Emily Dickinson's use of figurative language support the poem's central idea or theme of the advancement, power, and wonder of technology? (DOK 3)
Stimulus (QFocus)	"I Like to See It Lap the Miles" (a.k.a. "The Railway Train") by Emily Dickinson I like to see it lap the miles, And lick the valleys up. And stop to feed itself at tanks; And then—prodigious, step Around a pile of mountains, And, supercilious, peer In shanties by the sides of roads And then a quarry pare To fit its sides, and crawl between, Complaining all the while In horrid, hooting stanza; Then chase itself down hill And neigh like Boanerges; Then, punctual as a star, Stop—docile and omnipotent— At its own stable door.

Source for standard: Texas Education Agency, 2019.

FIGURE 2.5: Coupled inquiry for figurative language in poetry by Emily Dickinson.

This method of coupled inquiry can be implemented in science and social studies courses that utilize data-based or document-based questioning (DBQ). Art and music courses could engage students in similar coupled inquiry experiences by prompting students with questions that not only address the standard but also ask specifics about a work of art or a musical piece.

Educators can engage students in coupled inquiry by utilizing the gradual release of responsibility (GRR) instructional framework developed by P. David Pearson and Margaret Gallagher (1983) and extended by Doug Fisher and Nancy Frey (2021). Figure 2.6 shows the stages and steps to integrate coupled inquiry into the GRR model.

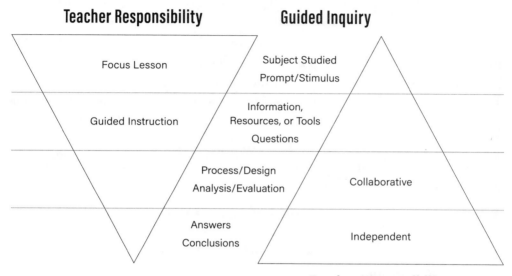

Teacher Responsibility   Guided Inquiry

Focus Lesson — Subject Studied / Prompt/Stimulus

Guided Instruction — Information, Resources, or Tools / Questions

Process/Design Analysis/Evaluation — Collaborative

Answers Conclusions — Independent

Teacher Responsibility

Source: Adapted from Fisher & Frey, 2021. Used with permission.

FIGURE 2.6: Using the GRR model with coupled inquiry.

Selecting the subject studied and the prompt or stimulus to be addressed or analyzed is what educators do—or "I do." Gathering information, resources, or tools and formulating questions is what "we do" with students. Students then work through the coupled inquiry experiences independently and responsibly. Next, give students the opportunity to conduct their analyses and evaluations, informing them, "You do it together." Then encourage them to come up with their answers and defend, disprove, or draw conclusions based on their questions, analyses, and evaluations—"You do it alone."

The Inquiring Minds Framework that serves as the focus and foundation of this book is based on coupled inquiry. The prompt or stimulus presented or shared serves to engage students—or hook 'em—into the inquiry experience. It also establishes the pathway to inquiry students will take. Once the intent and purpose of inquiry is set, you can facilitate the experience as students venture down a particular pathway. I will explore this practice and process in greater detail in subsequent chapters of this book.

How Can Inquiry Be Authentic?

Authentic inquiry is completely student driven. These inquiry experiences prompt and promote learner or student agency, which Diane Larsen-Freeman, Paul Driver, Xuesong (Andy) Gao, and Sarah Mercer (2021) describe as "the feeling of ownership and sense of control that learners have over their learning" (p. 6). Every aspect of the inquiry is decided and driven by students. They select the subject or situation they want to study; ask the questions they want to address; gather the information, resources, and tools they need to succeed; and conduct the analysis and evaluation. They also attain their own answers, draw their own conclusions, and explain or justify responses, results, or reasoning—be it their own, those made by others, or those they discovered or uncovered. Examples of authentic inquiry experiences are capstone projects, dissertations, term papers, independent studies, or passion projects that prompt students to inquire and investigate a subject of their choice beyond the classroom.

With authentic inquiry, the teacher offers students the opportunity to choose what they want to learn. They could ask them about their hobbies or interests and encourage them to examine or explore what they enjoy or excites them. They also could prompt students to consider and convey, "What do you want to know, understand, or learn about [subject]?" They should stress to students that this is their inquiry to engage in and experience. Once the student selects the subject or situation they want to study, the teacher steps back and lets the student learn through inquiry and questioning.

The teacher has little to no role or responsibility in an authentic inquiry experience. However, that does not mean they just step back and let students engage in inquiry freely or unsupervised. Authentic inquiry can be a difficult experience for students—especially if they lack familiarity or interest in inquiring and investigating a subject, skill, or situation. The teacher needs to be available, ready, and willing to guide and support students through the experience—especially if they struggle or get stuck. The inquiry also might need to shift or tier to a form that requires the teacher to take a more advisory or instructional role.

Authentic inquiry is both academic and affective. Not only does the experience enable students to deepen their awareness of the subject, skill, or situation; it also encourages them to reflect on and take responsibility for their learning. Figure 2.7 shows how authentic inquiry supports the attributes of reflective thinking and strengthens students' intellectual character.

Thinking Dispositions and Intellectual Virtues	What Students Learn About Themselves Through Authentic Inquiry
Autonomy Think for yourself!	Students learn they can work independently and responsibly. They also learn how to become self-disciplined and self-reliant.
Humility Admit and accept what you don't know!	Students learn what their limitations and weaknesses are and how to accept them. They also learn it's appropriate to ask for assistance when necessary or needed.
Courage Stay strong and take risks!	Students learn how to manage their fears and frustrations. They learn every obstacle or setback is a lesson learned. They take and transfer those lessons to other learning experiences.
Tenacity Embrace struggle and don't give up!	Students learn how to persevere and progress despite adversity or drawbacks. They learn how to stay focused on the goal and figure out how to achieve it.
Honesty Find, seek, and tell the truth!	Students learn to check and confirm the accuracy and sincerity of claims and conclusions—both their own and those made by others. They learn to give credit where credit is due and acknowledge their influences or sources of information.

FIGURE 2.7: How authentic inquiry is a social-emotional experience.

Authentic inquiry encourages students to develop a solid attitude toward learning through inquiry and questioning. Figure 2.8 shows how authentic inquiry prompts and promotes personal actions and attitudes about learning that are both positive and productive. The intellectual virtues of reflective thinking and attitudinal attributes of affective learning make authentic inquiry a social-emotional experience through which students learn how to respond to and regulate their emotions.

Affective Actions and Attitudes	What Students Learn Through Authentic Inquiry
Receiving I am willing to learn.	Students are open and attentive to learning about ideas, incidents, individuals, or issues in greater detail or depth.
Responding I want to share what I learn.	Students are willing to learn and share the depth and extent of their learning.
Valuing I appreciate what I learn.	Students realize the importance, relevance, and significance of what they are learning.

FIGURE 2.8: How authentic inquiry prompts and promotes affective learning.

continued →

Affective Actions and Attitudes	What Students Learn Through Authentic Inquiry
Organizing I prioritize what I learn.	Students prioritize what's essential to learn, important to understand, and "nice to know."
Characterizing I act and feel based on what I learn.	Students personalize their learning to establish their perspective and philosophy about learning and life.

Teachers should invite students to share their learning with the class. However, the teacher should never allow students to abandon the authentic inquiry if they encounter obstacles, face setbacks, or become frustrated. The teacher should inform the students that these complications and the feelings they arouse are a part of the experience. These are the important and valuable life lessons students learn through inquiry and questioning—how to persevere when encountering obstacles or opposition. These life lessons also strengthen and support the development of students' intellectual character—specifically, the thinking dispositions and intellectual virtues that reflect reflective thinking.

What Does Synergistic Inquiry Involve?

Synergistic inquiry is a collaborative experience developed by Tom Kuntzleman (2019) that has teachers and students "work together to pose questions and attempt to answer them." Everyone in the class—including the teacher—engages in synergistic inquiry as stakeholders with a common goal. The class functions more as an organization, team, or unit, with the teacher and students working collaboratively to achieve a goal, accomplish a task, or address a problem. This makes synergistic inquiry not only educational but authentic and vocational. The experience mirrors how disciplinary experts and professionals in postsecondary institutions and the workforce collaborate to achieve goals, accomplish tasks, address problems, or answer questions through inquiry and questioning.

Synergistic inquiry also fosters learner agency—specifically, *co-agency*, which Charles Leadbeater (2017) defines as "individuals cooperating to achieve shared goals" (p. 5). What distinguishes co-agency is that "teachers and students [become] co-creators in the teaching-and-learning process" (Organisation for Economic Co-operation and Development, 2019, p. 2). What distinguishes synergistic inquiry from the other forms is the role and responsibility of the teacher as a collaborator and participant in inquiry with the students.

Synergistic inquiry starts with the teacher initiating the inquiry. They may suggest the subject or situation the class will address and analyze. They might suggest an idea or issue to inquire and investigate. However, the goal is to have the class decide the focus, define the purpose, and determine the depth and direction of the inquiry. Once the intent of the inquiry is stipulated, the teacher takes on multiple roles. They act as the facilitator who oversees the experience and steps in only when necessary or needed. They act as the advisor with expertise who students can rely on and come to when they need guidance and support. The teacher also acts as a collaborator with whom students can brainstorm or troubleshoot. The teacher could take on responsibilities that only contribute to the inquiry, or they could assist students in their work. For example, they could establish contact or connections with resources students might not be able to access.

Synergistic inquiry not only synthesizes the characteristics of all forms of inquiry; it also combines different elements of authentic learning experiences. For example, synergistic inquiry could engage the class—or team—to research and investigate (investigative learning) an issue or situation (problem-based learning) in the local community (service learning) and determine whether the problem can be addressed, handled, resolved, settled, or solved—or abandoned. This experience could involve going beyond the classroom physically or virtually (expeditionary learning). It could involve developing or designing a plan, process, or product (project-based learning) to address the problem in the community. However, what makes this inquiry synergistic is that everyone in the class—including the teacher—is involved in the experience. Synergistic inquiry would be effective in classes or clubs, such as student government, newspaper, and yearbook, in which the teacher serves as an advisor rather than an instructor.

Which Paths of the Inquiring Minds Framework Engage Students in Specific Forms of Inquiry?

All forms of inquiry start with posing a prompt or sharing a stimulus that engages students—or "hooks 'em"—into the experience. However, the different pathways of inquiry that students take engage them in a particular form, as demonstrated in the following examples.

- The *Foundational Pathway to Inquiry* engages students in a controlled, confirmation, structured, or coupled inquiry experience driven by questions the teacher poses and prescriptive expectations they establish for the inquiry. The teacher could also engage students in coupled inquiry that's standards based and combines the stages and steps of guided and open or free inquiry.

- The *Inquiry Pathway to Understanding* engages students in structured, guided, or coupled inquiry. This structured inquiry experience is more instructional and requires students to come up with their own answers, conclusions, responses, results, or reasoning. The coupled inquiry experience is standards based and utilizes the GRR to involve students in establishing, examining, and explaining how and why they use subject-specific skills. Students explain why disciplinary practices and processes are used to answer questions, address problems, accomplish tasks, or analyze the ideas and information presented in texts or topics.

- The *Deep Pathway to Inquiry* engages students in guided, open or free inquiry, or coupled inquiry experiences. This pathway requires students to delve deeper into subjects or go beyond the goals and expectations set by the grade level's learning intention or the content area academic standards being addressed and assessed. This is the pathway that asks students to develop, demonstrate, and deepen their learning using the REID to Learn practices (see figure 2.1, page 49) and through active learning experiences such as project-based, investigative, and problem-based learning.

- The *Inquiry Pathway to Expertise* engages students in guided, open or free, coupled, authentic, or synergistic inquiry experiences that are mostly or entirely student driven. Educators serve as an advisor, facilitator, or participant in these experiences rather than an instructor or teacher.

The pathway to inquiry taken depends on the demand of the standard and the strengths of the students. Engaging students in a specific form of inquiry depends on who's asking and addressing the questions that help develop the skills and demonstrate the knowledge they need to succeed.

Summary

There's no one way to engage in or experience inquiry. The form of inquiry students engage in depends on the intent and purpose of the inquiry as well as who is asking and addressing the questions. Each form of inquiry has a specific instructional focus and purpose for learning. The goal is to shift the inquiry from a teacher-led and subject-specific experience to a student-driven one that requires students to inquire and investigate a subject independently and responsibly. Students will take the initiative to inquire and explain answers. They are expected to investigate and then defend, disprove, and draw conclusions.

Application: Which Form of Inquiry Should Students Experience?

Either individually or with your team, choose the form of inquiry students will engage in and experience. Use the Form of Inquiry Planner reproducible (page 63) to clarify both your roles and responsibilities and those of your students in the inquiry experience. You can use this tool to plan the form of inquiry students will engage in and experience. You can copy and distribute the reproducible to students to complete if it is a student-centered or student-driven inquiry.

1. Copy the Form of Inquiry Planner reproducible on page 63.

2. Choose the form of inquiry participants will engage in and experience.

3. Decide whether and which characteristics and aspects of inquiry will be teacher led and subject specific, student driven, or both.

4. State the subject for inquiry and investigation.

5. Present the prompt that will set the instructional focus and serve as an assessment.

6. Select the stimulus that elaborates on or extends the subject studied and the prompt posed.

7. Identify or itemize the information, items, resources, or tools needed to engage in the inquiry experience.

8. Formulate the questions that will determine and drive the depth and direction of the inquiry.

9.   Set the procedures to follow or determine the design to develop.

10.   Establish the scope and stipulations for analysis and evaluation.

11.   State the answer that must be attained through the inquiry.

12.   Gather the examples or evidence to be used to defend, disprove, or draw conclusions.

13.   Defend, disprove, or draw conclusions from the answer attained and supporting examples or evidence.

14.   Share responses, results, or reasoning.

Form of Inquiry Planner

Form of Inquiry		
Characteristics of Inquiry	Who's responsible?	State what the inquiry will focus on and feature.
Subject Studied		
Prompt		
Stimulus		
Information, Items, Resources, and Tools Needed		
Procedures or Design		
Expectations		
Questions		
Analysis and Evaluation		
Answer		
Conclusion		
Responses, Results, or Reasoning		

Chapter 3

HOW DO GOOD QUESTIONS PROMOTE COGNITIVE RIGOR AND PROMPT INQUIRY?

Good questions outrank easy answers.

—Paul Samuelson

Reflect and Respond

What does a good question do? What determines the rigor of a good question? Is it the type and level of thinking it stimulates or the DOK it requires? What distinguishes a good question from a "bad" one? How could a "bad" question become a good one that promotes cognitive rigor and prompts inquiry? How could educators and students teach and learn through inquiry by asking and addressing good questions?

AS MENTIONED PREVIOUSLY, inquiry is the teaching and learning experience. The form of the inquiry depends on the complexity of the questions posed, who is asking the questions, and how deeply they must be addressed or answered. This chapter explores what good questions do and what constitutes a "bad" question. It also examines what determines the cognitive rigor of good questions and how teachers can prompt students to engage in different forms of inquiry.

65

What Does a Good Question Do?

When educators consider or critique what makes a question "good," they generally presume it depends on the type of thinking it expects students to demonstrate or the extent of response it requires students to provide. However, a good question:

- Stimulates different levels of thinking
- Checks for and confirms knowledge, understanding, and awareness
- Expands students' knowledge or extends students' thinking
- Piques curiosity, interest, imagination, and wonder
- Engages and encourages students to express and share their expertise
- Prompts students to reflect before responding
- Phrases the instructional focus and purpose as an interrogative statement (Francis, 2016, 2022)

With good questions, it's not about the thinking students must perform or the response students must provide. It's how and why the question is phrased and posed that make it "good." As Jay McTighe and Grant Wiggins (2013) explain, "Intent trumps form. Why you ask a question (in terms of the desired result of asking it) matters more than how you phrase it" (p. 7). Therefore, any question could be a good one depending on how it's asked and addressed.

For example, suppose you are teaching a unit or lesson on addition. You initiate the inquiry by asking, "What is 2 + 2?" This is a simple question because it does not require deep thought or much effort to attain the answer. However, it meets the criteria of what a good question does. It stimulates students' thinking. Specifically, it asks them to recall how to use addition to answer correctly, which designates the level of DOK required by this question DOK 1. This question could also be used to check for and confirm knowledge, understanding, and awareness. It could also pique students' curiosity—especially older students learning more complex mathematics. They might wonder why the teacher is posing such a seemingly easy and simple question. That prompts them to reflect before responding.

After students provide an answer, follow up with a clarifying question such as, "What do you mean?" Now students must apply knowledge, concepts, and skills to establish and explain how they attained their answer, making the level of inquiry students engage in DOK 2. The question serves not only to check for and confirm students' knowledge, understanding, and awareness. It also encourages students to express and share their expertise in their own unique way. The question could expand students' knowledge and extend their thinking by prompting them to consider, choose, and convey how they can use a specific addition strategy that works best with the assigned problem (for example, using an open number line, objects, or drawings; skip counting; clapping; mental images; fingers; and so on).

You could also deepen the inquiry by asking students, "Could two plus two equal five?" Most likely, students will respond *no*. You could ask them to explain why to check for and confirm their knowledge and understanding. However, you could also ask them, "What could you do to make two plus two equal five?" You could also ask, "What if you used addition, decimals, or rounding?" These questions stimulate students' thinking. However, they also pique their curiosity and interest. They also deepen the demand of the inquiry to DOK 3 because students must think strategically to examine and explain with evidence why the action and answer are valid or viable. Addressing these questions also expands students' knowledge and extends their thinking about how these mathematical concepts and operations could be used in different contexts.

Notice how deeply and extensively these questions prompt students to communicate and demonstrate their learning—and it all starts with asking a simple question that requires students to recall how to answer correctly. They also encourage students to develop the thinking dispositions and intellectual virtues that define and deepen their intellectual character. They also foster a spirit of inquiry by engaging students to ask, reflect on, and respond to questions; challenge common or traditional perspectives and practices; seek and use evidence to explain or justify reasoning or results; and discover innovative or inventive methods or ways to do or use something. That's what makes them "good."

How Do Good Questions Prompt Inquiry?

Good questions prompt inquiry by encouraging educators and students to do the following.

- Acquire and assess foundational knowledge and functional understanding.
- Comprehend and demonstrate conceptual and procedural understanding.
- Deepen understanding, aptitude, and awareness.
- Extend or enrich personal expertise.

Figure 3.1 identifies which good questions will engage students to venture along or down the pathways of the Inquiring Minds Framework. Any good questions could hook 'em into inquiry and questioning, including a factual question that only demands students to answer correctly. After students respond with an answer (which could be correct or incorrect), the teacher would pose a supporting question such as, "What do you mean?" or "What else?" These elaborative questions not only drive the direction of the inquiry but also guide students along and among the different pathways of the Inquiring Minds Framework.

Keep in mind that it's not the kind of good question posed that will promote cognitive rigor and prompt inquiry. It's how that good question is posed. Any good question will hook 'em into inquiry. To quote the classic Eric Clapton song, "It's in the way that you use it" (with Robertson, 1986). Specifically, it's in the way that question is asked and addressed that determines the delivery and intensity of the inquiry.

What Determines the Cognitive Rigor of a Good Question?

The cognitive demand of a good question depends on the following.

- The type of thinking students must demonstrate
- The kind of knowledge students must develop
- The depth and extent to which students must understand and use their learning (Francis, 2016, 2022; Hess, Carlock, Jones, & Walkup, 2009; Hess, Jones, Carlock, & Walkup, 2009)

These are the measures of cognitive rigor, a concept developed by Karin Hess (with Carlock, Jones, & Walkup, 2009a, 2009b). The type and level of thinking prompted by good questions are classified by cognitive taxonomies such as Bloom's Taxonomy of Educational Objectives revised by Lorin Anderson and David Krathwohl (2001) and the Levels of Questioning developed by Art Costa (with Bena Kallick, 2000). Both frameworks feature and list verbs that indicate the cognitive actions good questions prompt students to perform. However, they do not feature question stems that prompt or stimulate a specific type or level of thinking. To help teachers and test makers classify and create questions that prompt or stimulate students to demonstrate a specific type and level of thinking, I revised and extended Bloom's taxonomies and Costa's levels to feature the question stems that address and assess the type and level of thinking categorized within them.

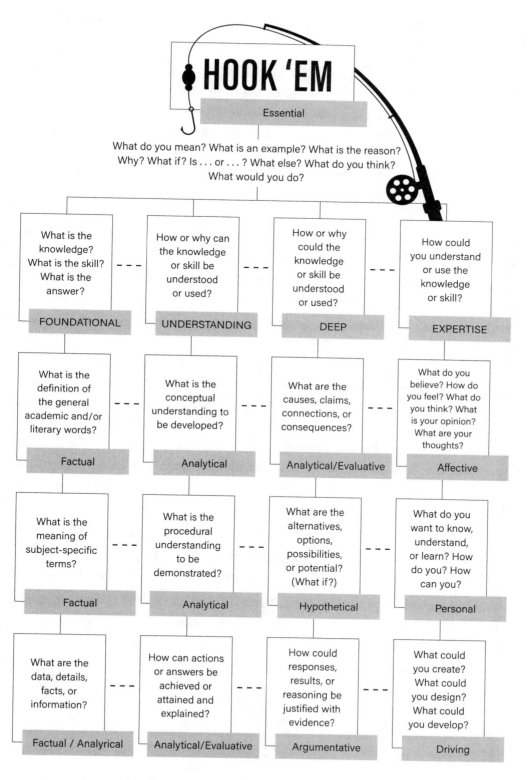

FIGURE 3.1: Planning and providing pathways to inquiry with good questions.

*Visit **go.SolutionTree.com/instruction** for a free reproducible version of this figure.*

Figure 3.2 is Bloom's Questioning Inverted Pyramid. It's represented as an inverted pyramid to signify how the type and level of thinking students demonstrate deepen as they engage in and experience inquiry.

The question stems featured at each level prompt students to demonstrate a specific type of thinking at a particular level of Bloom's taxonomy. I changed the base level of the pyramid from *Remember* to *Recognize* to show how the thinking demonstrated with inquiry is active and observable. It also reintroduces *Synthesize* as a level within the taxonomy between the levels *Evaluate* and *Create*. This is the level where the instructional focus and purpose for learning shifts from subject specific to student centered. The question stems prompting students to synthesize connect the cognitive domain of Bloom's Revised Taxonomy to the affective domain, which categorizes the complexity of emotions students experience as they learn. (Chapter 5, page 115, further explores teaching and learning through inquiry and questioning with the affective domain.)

Costa's Levels of Questioning is often portrayed as a house because it's based on the central idea of "The Three-Story Intellect" by Oliver Wendell Holmes (1872/1884). In this passage, Holmes compares levels of thinking to a three-story house with skylights. Each floor or story of the house represents a specific cognitive process and purpose for thinking. The complexity and intent of the cognition deepen with each subsequent level. The skylights symbolize how cognitive skills developed and demonstrated by moving through the intellect house transform into thinking dispositions. However, Costa's framework lists the cognitive action—or Bloom's—verbs that indicate the type of thinking students develop and demonstrate at each level of learning.

Figure 3.3 (page 72) shows the Three-Story Inquiry House of Question Stems. This house graphic features the question stems that prompt students to demonstrate the cognitive actions identified by the verbs listed in Costa's levels.

Similar to Bloom's Questioning Inverted Pyramid, the Three-Story Inquiry House of Question Stems extends Costa's framework by featuring the question stems that will prompt or stimulate students to engage in and experience inquiry at different levels of cognitive complexity. The "roof" represent how these cognitive processes and skills foster intellectual character and fortify a spirit of inquiry toward learning and life.

Creating good questions with these frameworks starts with unpacking and deconstructing the statements of objectives of academic standards and learning targets.

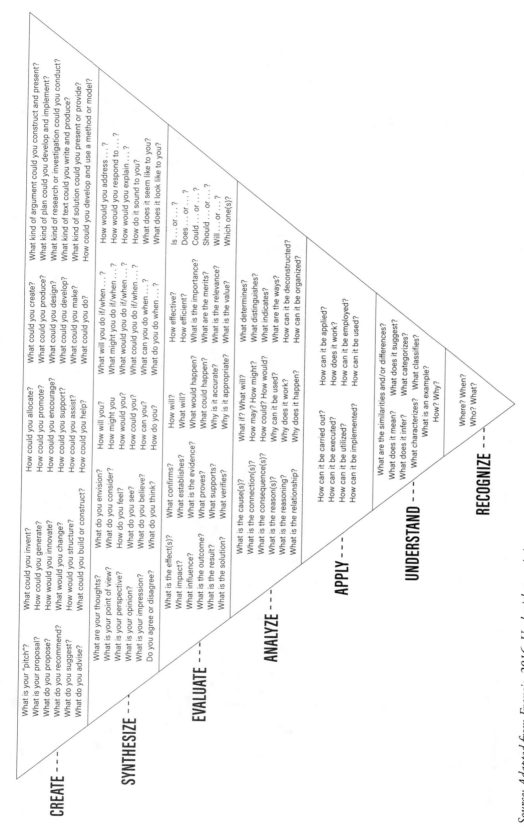

Source: Adapted from Francis, 2016. Used with permission.

FIGURE 3.2: Bloom's questioning inverted pyramid.

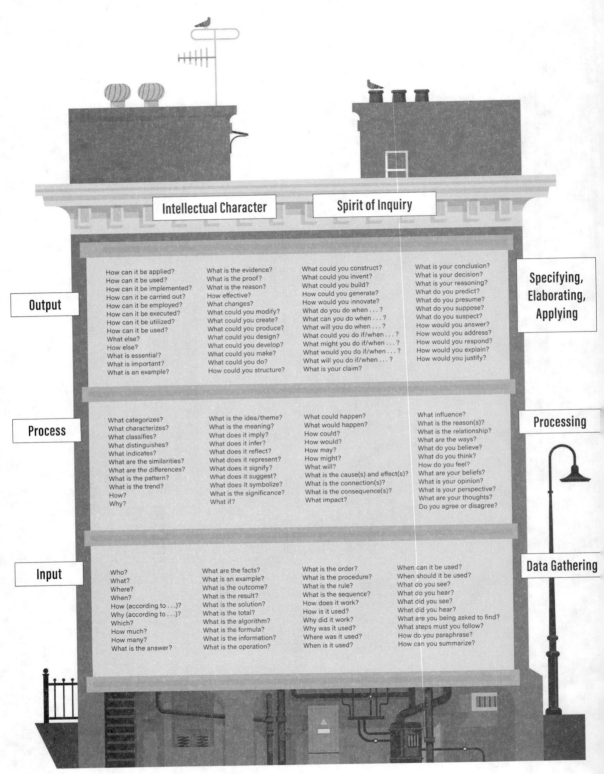

Intellectual Character   Spirit of Inquiry

Output

| | | | Specifying, Elaborating, Applying |

How can it be applied?
How can it be used?
How can it be implemented?
How can it be carried out?
How can it be executed?
How can it be employed?
How can it be utilized?
How can it be used?
What else?
How else?
What is essential?
What is important?
What is an example?

What is the evidence?
What is the proof?
What is the reason?
How effective?
What changes?
What could you modify?
What could you create?
What could you produce?
What could you design?
What could you develop?
What could you make?
What could you do?
How could you structure?

What could you construct?
What could you invent?
What could you build?
How could you generate?
How would you innovate?
What do you do when . . . ?
What can you do when . . . ?
What will you do when . . . ?
What could you do if/when . . . ?
What might you do if/when . . . ?
What would you do if/when . . . ?
What will you do if/when . . . ?
What is your claim?

What is your conclusion?
What is your decision?
What is your reasoning?
What do you predict?
What do you presume?
What do you suppose?
What do you suspect?
How would you answer?
How would you address?
How would you respond?
How would you explain?
How would you justify?

Process   **Processing**

What categorizes?
What characterizes?
What classifies?
What distinguishes?
What indicates?
What are the similarities?
What are the differences?
What is the pattern?
What is the trend?
How?
Why?

What is the idea/theme?
What is the meaning?
What does it imply?
What does it infer?
What does it reflect?
What does it represent?
What does it signify?
What does it suggest?
What does it symbolize?
What is the significance?
What if?

What could happen?
What would happen?
How could?
How would?
How may?
How might?
What will?
What is the cause(s) and effect(s)?
What is the connection(s)?
What is the consequence(s)?
What impact?

What influence?
What is the reason(s)?
What is the relationship?
What are the ways?
What do you believe?
What do you think?
How do you feel?
What are your beliefs?
What is your opinion?
What is your perspective?
What are your thoughts?
Do you agree or disagree?

Input   **Data Gathering**

Who?
What?
Where?
When?
How (according to . . .)?
Why (according to . . .)?
Which?
How much?
How many?
What is the answer?

What are the facts?
What is an example?
What is the outcome?
What is the result?
What is the solution?
What is the total?
What is the algorithm?
What is the formula?
What is the information?
What is the operation?

What is the order?
What is the procedure?
What is the rule?
What is the sequence?
How does it work?
How is it used?
Why did it work?
Why was it used?
Where was it used?
When is it used?

When can it be used?
When should it be used?
What do you see?
What do you hear?
What did you see?
What did you hear?
What are you being asked to find?
What steps must you follow?
How do you paraphrase?
How can you summarize?

Source: Adapted from Costa, 2000. Used with permission.

FIGURE 3.3: Three-story inquiry house of question stems.

Once the cognitive action verb has been identified and isolated, confirm where it is categorized in Bloom's Revised Taxonomy or Costa's Levels of Questioning. Then, cross-reference and choose a correlating question stem from Bloom's Questioning Inverted Pyramid or the Three-Story Inquiry House of Question Stems that will prompt or stimulate students to demonstrate a specific type or level of thinking (see chapter 4, page 91).

What Determines the Depth of Knowledge Level Required by a Good Question?

Depth of Knowledge (DOK) is just one way to determine the rigor of a good question. When developing good questions, you also need to clarify and confirm the following.

- The extent of the response students must provide
- The demand of the mental processing students must perform
- The complexity of the activity or task students must complete (Francis, 2022)

These are the criteria that designate the level of DOK required by a good question. DOK is an academic concept and framework that was first developed by Norman Webb (1997, 1999) as a criterion for alignment studies of academic standards, curricular activities, and assessment items. The concept and its framework—the DOK levels—have evolved into a measure of cognitive rigor (Hess, 2006, 2013, 2018) and a method and model for teaching and learning (Francis, 2022).

Table 3.1 (page 74) is the DOK Matrix for Good Questions. The phrases in the matrix are the DOK descriptors that designate and distinguish what a good question requires students to understand and how to use it in their learning. Teachers and students can use this matrix to determine and decide the cognitive demand of the inquiry and the questions asked and addressed.

Like the DOK level of a learning objective depends on what comes after the verb, the words and phrases that follow the question stem designate the level of DOK required by a good question. Consider the following good questions that address a Next Generation Science Standard (NGSS, 2013) on Earth's systems.

Table 3.1: DOK Matrix for Good Questions

DOK Level	DOK Response	DOK Skill	DOK Task	DOK Goal and Expectations
DOK 1 Recall and Reproduce	Answer correctly	Recall information Recall how to	Just the facts Just do it	Attain the answer. (Answer it.)
DOK 2 Apply Knowledge and Skills or Use Basic Reasoning	Establish and explain answers with examples	• Apply knowledge, concepts, and skills • Use information and basic reasoning	• Show and share or summarize • Comprehend and communicate • Specify and explain • Give examples or nonexamples • Express and share your opinion or outlook	Explain the answer. (Explain it.)
DOK 3 Strategic Thinking or Complex Reasoning	Examine and explain with evidence	• Think strategically • Use complex reasoning supported by evidence	• Delve deeper • Inquire and investigate • Think critically • Problem solve • Think creatively • Defend or disprove • Consider, confirm, conclude, or critique	Justify or verify an answer. (Check, conclude, confirm, consider, or critique it.)
DOK 4 Extended Thinking and Reasoning	Explore and explain with examples and evidence	• Use extended reasoning supported by examples and evidence • Think extensively	• Go deep within a subject area • Go through multiple texts or topics • Go across the curriculum • Go beyond the classroom	Explore or extend an answer. (Go do something with it. Go for it.)

1. What are Earth's four major systems?

2. What are the geosphere, biosphere, hydrosphere, and atmosphere?

3. What are the ways Earth's major systems interact with each other?

4. What impact do human activities have on Earth's major systems?

5. What if one of Earth's major systems was disrupted or removed?

6. What kind of scientific model could you develop and use to describe ways Earth's major systems interact?

7. What kind of scientific model could you use to address or respond to a real-world scenario or situation involving the interactions of Earth's major systems? (NGSS-5-ESS2–1; NGSS Lead States, 2013)

Each of these questions asks *what*. However, the words and phrases that follow the question stem inform the depth and extent to which students must respond. For example, consider the following.

- The first two questions are factual questions that ask students to attain and assert *what*. These questions are DOK 1 because they require students to recall information to answer correctly.

- The third question is an analytical question that asks students to use information and basic reasoning to explain, with examples, what the ways of interaction are. That makes it DOK 2.

- The fourth is an evaluative question that asks students to confirm what impact. The fifth is a hypothetical question that prompts students to consider *what if*. Both questions are DOK 3 because they ask students to think strategically or use complex reasoning to examine and explain with evidence.

- The sixth and seventh questions are driving questions that ask students how they could develop and use a scientific model. The sixth question is DOK 3 because it engages students to think strategically about how they could develop and use a model to describe ways Earth's four major systems interact. The seventh is DOK 4 because it asks students to think extensively about how they could address, explain, or respond to a real-world scenario or situation involving Earth's four major systems. The model the student develops serves as the example and evidence students will use to support their solution or suggestion.

How Can the Cognitive Rigor of a Good Question Be Marked and Measured?

The cognitive rigor of a good question is marked and measured by the following.

- *The level of thinking the question stem prompts or stimulates students to perform*
- *The depth and extent of the question requires students to respond* (Francis, 2022)

Figure 3.4 is a modified version of the Hess Cognitive Rigor Matrix (CRM) that marks and measures the cognitive rigor of good questions. It features the cognitive levels listed in Bloom's Questioning Inverted Pyramid. It also includes the extent of the response students must provide at each DOK level, as well as where the good questions on Earth's major systems would be placed and printed in the Hess CRM for Good Questions.

To confirm the cognitive rigor of a good question, check where the question stem is categorized in the Bloom's Questioning Inverted Pyramid to determine in which row to place the good question in the Hess CRM. Then, clarify what exactly and how deeply the question requires students to respond to determine in which DOK column to place the question. Then, code the cognitive rigor of the question with the name of the framework, the number of the row, and the column in which it should be placed (for example, Bloom's 4/DOK 3).

How Can Good Questions Be Difficult to Answer?

Good questions can be difficult to answer. These questions are described as easy or hard—or difficult—based one or more of the following factors.

- The amount of time and effort it takes a student to answer the question correctly
- The capability or confidence of the student to answer the question successfully
- The number of questions students must answer correctly or successfully
- The percentage or proportion of students who answer a question accurately (Francis 2022)

DOK Levels / Bloom's Revised Taxonomy	DOK 1	DOK 2	DOK 3	DOK 4
	Answer correctly.	Establish and explain answers with examples.	Examine and explain with evidence.	Explore and explain with evidence.
Recognize	What are Earth's four major systems? (Bloom's 1/DOK 1) What is the geosphere, biosphere, hydrosphere, and atmosphere? (Bloom's 1/DOK 1)			
Understand		What are the ways that Earth's major systems interact with each other? (Bloom's 2/DOK 2)		
Apply				
Analyze			What if one of Earth's major systems was disrupted or removed? (Bloom's 4/DOK 3)	
Evaluate			What impact do human activities have on Earth's major systems? (Bloom's 5/DOK 3)	
Synthesize				
Create			What kind of scientific model could you develop and use to describe ways Earth's major systems interact? (Bloom's 7/DOK 3)	What kind of scientific model could you develop and use to address, explain, or respond to a real-world scenario or situation involving the interactions of Earth's major systems? (Bloom's 7/DOK 4)

Source: Adapted from Francis, 2022; Hess, 2006, 2018. Used with permission.

FIGURE 3.4: Hess cognitive rigor matrix for good questions.

Difficulty is subjective and continues to change. One student may find answering a good question to be easy, while another may find it hard. However, answering questions may become easier for students as they become more familiar with particular subjects or skills. You could make questions easier or harder by simply changing the conditions of the inquiry (for example, you might assign fewer or more questions for students to answer, or you might shorten or extend the amount of time you give students to answer).

The difficulty of a good question can be calculated statistically using the formula $P = c/n$. This is the formula psychometricians and test makers use to analyze the difficulty of assessment items. Determining the difficulty—or P-value—involves dividing the number of students who answer the question correctly (the value of c) by the total number of students who were asked the question (or the value of n).

For example, if you asked thirty students the same question and eighteen answered correctly, you would divide eighteen (the value of c) by thirty (the value of n) to attain a P-value of 0.6 (the value of D). You can express the P-value as a decimal or a percent if you multiply the quotient by 100, so $P = c/n \times 100$. Once you determine the value, check the item difficulty index to determine its level of difficulty.

Figure 3.5 features an example of an item difficulty index that includes the range of P-values for difficulty as a decimal and a percentage.

Keep in mind, however, that the P-value is used primarily to determine the difficulty of questions that typically appear on assignments or assessments. Those questions can be activities, tasks, or other items students must complete correctly or accomplish accurately. Examples of assignment and assessment questions are multiple choice, short answer, fill-in-the-blank, numeric responses, survey, true/false, or matching.

Difficult good questions can serve as items on an assignment or assessment. However, their primary purpose is to activate and advance student learning, not assess it. The P-value could be used to determine the difficulty of good questions. However, the other three factors—amount of time and effort, individual capability or confidence, and number of questions—are stronger determinants of the level the difficulty for the question asked and the inquiry students engage in and experience.

P-Value		Item Difficulty	
Decimal Range	Percent Range	Determination	Characteristics and Conclusions
0.0–0.3	< 30 percent	Extremely difficult	The question may be too difficult for students to answer due to conditional factors or personal reasons.
0.31–0.50	31 percent to 50 percent	Very difficult	The question challenges even the top-performing students. However, students can answer the questions under certain conditions or favorable factors.
0.51–0.70	51 percent to 70 percent	Moderately difficult	The question is tough but answerable. These questions are called "easy" or "hard" based on the proportion of student success and students' personal perceptions.
0.71–0.90	71 percent to 90 percent	Moderately easy	Students can answer questions correctly and independently with little to no intervention or support. Some students may require extra time and support to demonstrate proficiency or perform successfully.
0.91–1.0	91 percent to 100 percent	Very easy	Students can answer questions correctly and easily with little or no time, effort, or support required.

FIGURE 3.5: Item difficulty index for good questions.

How Could Good Questions Be Demanding to Address?

Good questions could be demanding to address. These questions are deemed simple or complex depending on the depth and extent to which students must comprehend and convey their learning.

Simple questions only require students to recall, understand, or apply what they are learning to attain or explain answers correctly. For example, the questions, "What is the solution to the mathematics problem?" or "What is the main idea of the text?" are simple because there are only two ways students can answer—correctly or incorrectly. Students might devote a significant amount of time or effort to answer these questions. However, time and effort determine difficulty, not demand.

Complex questions engage students to explain, justify, or expand on their responses with examples or evidence. These questions also prompt authentic literacy, which utilizes "purposeful reading, writing, and discussion as the primary modes of learning both content and thinking skills" (Schmoker, 2018, p. 29).

A complex question might ask students to explain, "How can the mathematics be used to solve the problem?" or "What is the central idea or theme of the text?" A more complex question could be, "Why is the solution to the problem accurate?" or "How do the details in the text strengthen and support the central idea or theme?" Not only do these questions require students to talk more extensively about the subject or skill, but they also require students to transfer their learning in different contexts.

The simplicity and complexity of a demanding question do not change. They remain constant regardless of the level of learning students develop and possess. This makes demanding questions equitable in that all students are engaged and encouraged to address the question at its level of complexity. Cognitively demanding questions should not be relegated or reserved for students in classes designed as advanced or honors. All students, regardless of their ability or age, should be posed cognitively demanding questions and given the opportunity to address them.

The rigor of demanding questions also depends on the response students must provide. You can simplify the process to address and answer the question, especially with the use of technology (think calculators and artificial intelligence). However, the depth and extent of the response remains the same. That's why, with demanding questions, the rigor is in the response.

Figure 3.6 features how students are expected to address and respond to good questions. It clarifies a student's responses as either irrefutable (correct or incorrect) or disputable (right or wrong).

Student Goal	Student Expectation	Student Response
Answer	Acquire or attain the answer.	Correct or incorrect/irrefutable
Explain	Establish and explain the answer with examples.	Correct or incorrect/irrefutable
Justify or verify	Examine and explain actions, answers, arguments, or assumptions with evidence.	Right or wrong/disputable
Explore or extend	Innovate, invent, or investigate (over an extended period of time).	Right or wrong/disputable

FIGURE 3.6: Rigor in the response for demanding questions.

Should Good Questions Be Difficult or Demanding?

Good questions that prompt inquiry and promote cognitive rigor could and should be difficult or demanding. In fact, they can be both. Difficult good questions challenge students intellectually and emotionally, teaching them how to be reflective and resilient throughout the inquiry they engage in and experience. Demanding good questions engages students to consider how they could understand and use their learning in different contexts and deeper ways. Both strengthen and support students' thinking dispositions and intellectual virtues.

However, there is no one-to-one correspondence between the level of difficulty and demand for a good question. For example, a question may be difficult yet simple to answer if the student struggles to attain or explain a single response. Conversely, a complex question may be easy to address if the student possesses the knowledge, skills, or disposition they need to succeed. You might make the process to answer a complex question easier or simplified by reducing the number of steps students must perform. However, the level of thinking expected and DOK required by the question remains constant. That's why it's important to determine the intent of the inquiry and the purpose of the question. Do you want students to work harder to answer the question, or do you want students to think and talk about how they could address the question?

What Makes a Question "Bad"?

The designation of questions as "good" insinuates that they can also be "bad." However, "good" characterizes a question that prompts students to comprehend, consider, and convey what they are learning. "Bad" is a critique of a question that's based more on perspective than purpose.

For example, many educators believe factual questions are bad because they neither expect nor demand students comprehend and convey their learning at deeper levels. That's the fallacy of factual questions—that they are basic because they only require students to recall and restate who, what, where, or when. However, factual questions are good questions. Not only are they useful to check and confirm knowledge, understanding, and awareness, but they also stimulate students to think—just not at the higher levels of academic frameworks and learning taxonomies. They encourage students to express and share their expertise by citing, paraphrasing, or summarizing. These questions prompt students to reflect before responding. Plus, factual questions serve a specific purpose in the progression of student learning. These are the good questions that will help students build foundational knowledge and functional understanding about a subject. That's why questions that ask students to share "just the facts" or how to "just do it" should not be considered or critiqued as bad. Asking and addressing factual questions also provides students with the examples and evidence they need to strengthen and support their explanation, justification, or extension of answers.

Dichotomous or Polar Questions

Bad questions limit or restrict responses. For example, dichotomous or polar questions can be bad because they only require a single, succinct response such as *yes* or *no*, *true* or *false*, and *agree* or *disagree*. These questions are "cognition and conversation killers" because that's what they do. Once a student chooses or gives a response, all talking and thinking about the subject or skill ceases. However, there is a way to turn dichotomous or polar questions into good questions. One is to provide alternatives, options, or possibilities they can choose, consider, or champion. For example, asking, "Should the death penalty be abolished?" only allows a *yes* or *no* response. However, asking, "Should the death penalty be abolished, legal, or invoked depending on the situation?" not only provides choices but also prompts reflection before responding, which is a criterion for what a good question does.

Leading or Loaded (Trick) Questions

Leading or loaded (trick) questions are bad because they do not prompt critical thinking. These questions are directive and deceptive. For example, "Why is *Maus* by Art Spiegelman an inappropriate book to teach in school?" is a leading question. It's not analytical or argumentative. It presupposes that the book is inappropriate. It also pressures someone to respond with acceptable or appropriate reasons. Loaded or trick questions that prompt students to consider "Which one(s)?" or choose "All of the above" engage students to think critically about how to respond. However, loaded or trick questions cause confusion and doubt. Even if students choose at least one of the correct answers, they still get marked down or off because they did not choose *all* the correct answers. Good questions teach students, not trick them.

While both leading and loaded (trick) questions are meant to stimulate student thinking and prompt students to reflect before responding, they unfortunately do so in an unfair and unpleasant way. They instill doubt instead of initiating deep thought. Students wonder whether the question is tricking them instead of teaching or testing them. That's why I don't consider either of these to be good questions. They cause students to develop and demonstrate suspicious minds, not inquiring ones.

Are Questions in Textbooks and on Tests Good or Bad?

The questions in curricular texts and on tests are neither good nor bad. In fact, they are not questions at all. Even though they may be phrased as interrogative statements, they are typically activities, items, and tasks that students must complete correctly or successfully. They are meant to assess and affirm the depth and extent of student learning, not activate learning or drive instruction.

Consider multiple-choice questions. They are used to check for and confirm knowledge, understanding, and awareness, which is a criterion of a good question. However, they serve more as evaluative items than inquiries that prompt learning. However, multiple-choice items could become good questions if used as a stimulus that incites inquiry and inspires questioning. Consider the following, for example.

- Present a multiple-choice item and prompt students to reflect and respond with the answer they think is correct and explain why.

If students answer incorrectly, provide them with the correct answer and engage them to examine and explain why their choice was incorrect.

- Show a multiple-choice item, tell students what the correct answer is, and challenge them to examine and explain why the answer is correct.

- Share a multiple-choice item from an assessment the students completed. Inform students what the correct answer is and engage them to examine and explain why the other choices are incorrect.

- Find a multiple-choice item from an assessment that either all or many students answered incorrectly with the same incorrect response. Engage students to examine and explain why their classmates chose the same incorrect response. Encourage students to communicate to their classmates what they should consider or be careful of when presented with similar items.

These inquiry-based teaching and learning experiences are DOK 4. Instead of answering the multiple-choice items correctly, students are engaged to explain with evidence why the choices provided are correct or incorrect. Multiple-choice questions are transformed into a tool for teaching, not a task for testing.

The good questions in curricular texts are featured in the margins of teacher editions. These are the good questions the text offers to introduce the instructional focus and inform the purpose for learning. Educators can use these questions as prompts that will initiate the inquiry and inspire students—or hook 'em—to ask their own questions (see chapter 4, page 91).

Are Questions That Can Be Googled Good or Bad?

In my seminars, trainings, and workshops, I start my presentation by asking, "What is a good question?" Someone always responds, "One that can't be googled." This is a common opinion shared by many educators. Their reasoning is that googling neither expects nor demands students to comprehend, consider, or convey their learning at higher levels of thinking. It makes teaching and learning too automated and reduces the rigor students engage in and experience.

Students also don't have to consider or create a response to a "googleable" question. They can just google it and report what their search returns. Many educators share similar criticisms about other technologies such as artificial intelligence (AI) or machine learning—that both have made the time and thought it takes to answer questions too easy and effortless. This is a traditional mindset of teaching and learning through inquiry and questioning—that the experience should be time-consuming as well as thought-provoking. Students should be expected to demonstrate their thinking at the higher levels of cognitive frameworks such as Bloom's Revised Taxonomy.

The debate over googling is not limited to education. A *Newsweek* article by reporter Jack Beresford (2021) documented an online debate over whether googling is an essential skill set for employment. The debate was sparked over an X (formerly Twitter) post by a software developer who stated, "Got a [curriculum vitae] today and the guy literally listed one of his skills as 'Googling.' We're interviewing him" (as cited in Beresford, 2021). This post incited a virtual debate among professionals not only on X but also on other social media platforms such as LinkedIn. Some defended the validity of googling as a valuable skill. Others dismissed the ability to google as basic or inconsequential. The comments and conclusions were a divisive split—much like when educators discuss whether to ask questions that students can google for answers.

Googling has become an everyday yet essential skill for learning and life. What do we do if we don't know, don't have, or can't recall the ideas, information, or instructions we need? We google it. Google and other search engines such as Bing and Yahoo are encyclopedic libraries one can access with the stroke of a keyboard or through a vocal command (if you use voice assistant technology, such as Google Assistant, Amazon Alexa, or Apple's Siri). These technologies not only provide the answers we need or seek with little to no time, effort, or restrictions; they also save and store the answers to their digital memory so you can retrieve the information when you need it again. This frees up your brain capacity and power to think deeper about the subjects and skills you study and learn. However, it requires your inquiring mind to distinguish and decide which answers are essential to learn, important to understand, or "nice to know."

However, using Google and googling are two separate skills. Using Google is a functional skill. It involves knowing how to enter the information in the search bar to conduct the search, scrolling through the results returned, clicking on the link to access a page, and bookmarking the page to access it again. From a DOK perspective, using Google is DOK 1 because it retrieves, restates, and recalls information. Googling, however, requires advanced thinking or even expertise. It involves utilizing complex cognitive abilities and skills such as research, investigation, critical thinking, analysis and interpretation, synthesizing, and—most importantly—questioning.

To get the most accurate, acceptable, appropriate, or authentic answer, you must be able to ask the good question in the Google toolbar in a format or way that will return the responses or results you need or seek. However, what Google—or any technology for that matter—cannot tell you is whether the source providing the information is credible. That demands further inquiry and questioning—or googling. It also makes googling more DOK 3 or DOK 4 because you must check and critique the credibility of the responses and sources Google retrieves.

What Is Bad About Addressing and Answering Questions With Technology?

What makes "googleable" questions bad? These types of questions are only bad if questioning stops and inquiry ends after students attain an answer. Additionally, questions addressed with technology through Google and other search engines may return answers that are inaccurate, incomplete, inconsistent, or even incorrect.

For example, if you ask Google, "What is Depth of Knowledge?", you'll receive up to a million sites and sources—depending on the day—that explain, feature, or reference the topic, the phrase, or one of the words within it. If you enter, "What is DOK?" Google will return sites that reference the academic framework or refer to a stool softener. Asking Google either question will also return images of the DOK wheel, which is an inaccurate depiction of Depth of Knowledge (Francis, 2022; Hess, 2018). The problem with the majority of sites all search engines retrieve and return from this search is that most of them provide information that's incomplete, inconsistent, and possibly incorrect.

Search engines and voice assistants have made it easier to retrieve answers. Advances in generative AI and deep machine learning have made asking and addressing questions more immediate, informal, and interactive. These technologies return numerous bits and bytes of information, disinformation, and misinformation students need to consider, critique, and cut through. Professors of library and information science Annette Lamb and Larry Johnson (2010) emphasize:

> [Educators] should help young people learn how Google tools available for accessing, organizing, and sharing information can facilitate learning. Rather than teaching these tools in isolation, use a subject area activity such as exploring a mathematical theorem, examining an endangered species, or addressing a social problem. (p. 83)

Most importantly, students must learn that the inquiry does not end, and questioning doesn't stop once they receive their responses from Google or other forms of technology. They need to check the accuracy of the answers presented and the authenticity of the sources provided. That's what googling through inquiry and questioning demands and involves.

What Is Beneficial About Addressing and Answering Questions With Technology?

Technology has transformed how educators and students engage in and experience inquiry. It has also redefined the rigor of inquiry and questioning by focusing more on the depth and extent the experience requires students to reflect, research, and respond versus the amount of time or level of thought it takes to answer the question correctly or complete the task successfully. Students must learn how to verify the accuracy and authenticity of the answers from e-resources and tech tools.

The answers attained from technology should serve as the starting point for deeper inquiry and further questioning. Technology platforms require students to think critically, reflectively, and creatively about the ideas and information attained through online searches. They should drive students to want to delve deeper or go further into the subject, skill, or situation. Remember that an inquiring mind wants to learn the answer but also the *truth*. To quote the tagline of the television series *The X-Files*, "The truth is out there" (cited in Hurwitz & Knowles, 2008). Technology enables and encourages students to discover the truth and determine its validity through inquiry and questioning.

Advances in technology make inquiry and questioning easier and effortless—and that's okay! Inquiring and questioning should be challenging on an intellectual level but not an emotional one. The goal and expectations of teaching and learning through inquiry and questioning are to advance or further learning, not to frustrate or aggravate. Educators need to accept that technology has transformed inquiry and questioning. Educators should neither discourage nor disparage technology's role or use in teaching and learning. Instead, they should acknowledge and appreciate how advantageous and assistive technology can be to teach and learn through inquiry and questioning (see chapter 8, page 183).

Summary

A good question promotes cognitive rigor and prompts inquiry by engaging and encouraging students to comprehend, consider, and convey their learning at different levels of thinking and DOK. The cognitive rigor of a good question is marked and measured by the level of thinking the question stem prompts or stimulates students to perform and the depth and extent to which the question requires students to respond.

To confirm the cognitive rigor of a good question, first check where the question stem is categorized in the Bloom's Questioning Inverted Pyramid. Then, clarify the extent of the DOK response that the question requires students to provide. The Hess CRM for Good Questions is a tool you can use to mark and measure the cognitive rigor of good questions.

"Bad" questions limit or restrict student responses. They also can be directive and deceptive. The questions featured in curricular texts and on tests are neither good nor bad because they are items students must complete correctly or successfully, not inquiries that activate or advance learning. Questions that can be googled or addressed and answered with technology are not "bad" because they teach students how to develop and demonstrate essential skills such as researching and investigating.

Application: How Good Are Your Questions?

Either individually or with your team, use the Hess Cognitive Rigor Matrix for Good Questions and Inquiry reproducible to categorize and code the cognitive rigor of your questions or the ones provided in your curricular texts.

1. Copy the Hess Cognitive Rigor Matrix for Good Questions and Inquiry reproducible.

2. Identify the question stem that introduces the good question in the Bloom's Questioning Inverted Pyramid (see figure 3.2, page 71). Place the question in the corresponding row of the reproducible.

3. Determine the DOK response that the good question requires students to provide. Place the question in the designated DOK level column of the reproducible.

4. Code the cognitive rigor of the good question with the name of the framework and the number of the row and column in which it's placed (for example, Bloom's 4/DOK 3).

5. Consider how you could raise the cognitive rigor of the question by increasing the level of thinking the good question requires students to demonstrate, or deepening the level of DOK that the good question requires students to understand and use.

Hess Cognitive Rigor Matrix for Good Questions and Inquiry

DOK Levels/ Bloom's Revised Taxonomy	DOK 1	DOK 2	DOK 3	DOK 4
	Answer correctly.	Establish and explain answers with examples.	Examine and explain actions, answers, arguments, or assumptions with evidence.	Explore and explain with examples and evidence.
Recognize				
Understand				
Apply				
Analyze				
Evaluate				
Synthesize				
Create				

Source: Adapted from Francis, 2022; Hess, 2006, 2018. Used with permission.

Chapter 4

HOW CAN STUDENTS BE "HOOKED" INTO INQUIRY USING GOOD QUESTIONS?

The feeling of being interested can act as a kind of neurological signal, directing us to fruitful areas of inquiry.

—B. F. Skinner

? Reflect and Respond

When do educators and students typically ask questions in a teaching and learning experience? How could the teacher use questioning to engage students—or hook 'em—into an inquiry experience? How could educators present prompts or share stimuli to pique students' curiosity and interest to want to learn?

PREVIOUS CHAPTERS ESTABLISHED what inquiry involves, identified the different forms of inquiry students could engage in and experience, and examined how good questions promote cognitive rigor and prompt inquiry. This chapter explores how we, as educators, can phrase and pose good questions that will engage students—or "hook 'em"—into teaching and learning experiences that promote cognitive rigor and prompt inquiry.

What Does It Mean to "Hook 'Em" Into Inquiry?

Teaching and learning with an inquiring mind start with educators. To make sure students are fully engaged in the inquiry process, teachers should:

- Present prompts that set the instructional focus, serve as the assessments, and start students' thinking
- Share a stimulus that elaborates on or extends the subject and serves as the source of the questions students ask and address about the subject

This is what Doug Lemov (2010) calls "The Hook"—"a short introductory moment that captures what's interesting and engaging about the material and puts it out front" (p. 75). The prompt or stimulus is presented or shared at the beginning of a teaching and learning experience to set the tone of the inquiry students will experience. Robin Hunter (2004) calls this part of the teaching learning experience "prime learning time" (p. 39) when educators do the following.

- Give students something to think about, recall, or practice if there is wait time before class can start
- Use an anticipatory set that focuses students on the content to be learned, assesses what students already know or have learned, and introduces new learning
- Clear students' inquiring minds of irrelevant things so they can focus on the present lesson
- Inform students what the objective (intended learning) is and why it is important (unless you wish them to discover it or be surprised)

Figure 4.1 shows how the Inquiring Minds Framework uses a prompt or stimulus to initiate the inquiry. The prompt or stimulus is meant to motivate students to be curious, care, and converse about the subject or skill. It sets the form and tone of the inquiry. The teacher follows up the prompt or stimulus with clarifying questions that will encourage students to consider responses, results, or reasoning—be it their own or those presented by others. The clarifying questions elicit and encourage further questions and conversations about the prompt or stimulus.

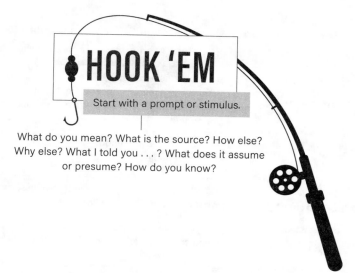

FIGURE 4.1: How to hook 'em into inquiry and questioning.

The Hook introduces the essential question of the unit, lesson, or activity by doing the following.

- Starting the inquiry
- Setting the instructional focus
- Serving as the assessment
- Stating the purpose for learning

Figure 4.2 (page 94) categorizes the different kinds of essential questions that engage students—or hook 'em—into inquiry. These good questions "set the instructional focus and expectations for students to demonstrate deeper, more authentic learning about universal themes, core ideas, and topical understandings of a lesson or unit in their own unique way" (Francis, 2016, p. 21). These questions should address or allude to the subject studied.

When choosing or coming up with The Hook, teachers should consider the following questions.

- Should the form of inquiry engage students to address a prompt that introduces the instructional focus and informs the purpose of learning?
- Should the form of inquiry engage students to analyze a stimulus that inspires them to ask questions and address the subject being studied?

Essential Questions	What Does It Prompt Students to Comprehend or Consider? (Content Area and Subject-Specific Examples)
Universal Question	What is the global issue or topic? What is the grand or greater idea or theme? What is the abstract concept, feeling, quality, or sensation (for example, love, fear, anger)? What is the existential or philosophical belief, ideology, or outlook?
Overarching Question	What are the core ideas and enduring understandings of the academic area, discipline, or subject?
Topical Question	What is the instructional focus and summative assessment of the unit or lesson? What does the grade level or content area standard ask students to address?
Driving Question	What can you create, design, develop, or do that reflects and represents your thinking and talent?

FIGURE 4.2: Good essential questions that hook 'em into inquiry.

Use these guiding questions to decide how to initiate the inquiry that students will engage in and experience. These questions can help determine if the instructional intent is to address an essential question and present a prompt to initiate the inquiry, or if the purpose of learning is to reflect and respond to a print or visual text or share a stimulus to initiate the inquiry.

How Does the Socratic Approach Hook 'Em Into Inquiry and Questioning?

Teaching and learning with an inquiring mind align with the philosophy and practices of the Socratic inquiry. The goal of Socratic inquiry is for students to attain answers or defend, disprove, or draw conclusions on their own through shared discovery and discussion. The purpose of the questions is to prompt students to consider and convey the extent and essence of their knowledge, thinking, and feelings. The expectation is that students will learn to think critically, creatively, and reflectively when studying a subject or talking about a topic. Figure 4.3 features the different types and examples of questions that support Socratic inquiry and dialogue.

Clarifying	What do you mean? Why do you say that? How does this connect or relate to the subject studied or topic taught? How could you elaborate on or explain that point clearer or further? What if I told you . . . ?
Probing	What do you know or understand? What don't you know or understand? How did you come to that conclusion? What caused you to take that action? What caused you to make that decision? Is there a reason to doubt or question the response, result, or reasoning? How could someone . . . ? Why would someone . . . ? What could possibly . . . ?
Assumptive	What if? What would happen? What could happen? What is the assumption? What is the belief? What is the presumption? What is the notion? What do you assume? What do you presume? What do you guess? What do you imagine? What do you suppose? Why do you suppose?
Implicating and Consequential	What effect does it have? What impact does it have? What influence does it have? What generalizations can be made? What are the consequences? What are the costs? What is the price for . . . ? What is the significance? What are you implying? What are you suggesting? How does this connect or tie into to your previous learning or prior experiences?
Evidentiary	What is the evidence? What is the proof? What is the reasoning? What is the justification? What is the rationalization? What is the source? How credible is the source? How could it be defended, justified, refuted, or validated? How could you defend, justify, refute, or verify?
Viewpoint and Perspective	Who else? What else? Where else? How else? Why else? What would be an alternative? What are other options? What is another way to look at it? How else could someone perceive, seem, or look at it? How else might someone perceive, seem, or look at it? Why is it the best? Why is it the most appropriate? What are the strengths and weaknesses? What are the pros and cons?
Questioning the Question	What is the intent of the question? What is the point of the question? What is the purpose of the question? What is the relevance of the question? Why is this essential? Why is this important? Why is this relevant? Why should you learn this? How does . . . apply to everyday life? How does . . . apply to or impact your life? What is a better question to ask or address? What could be a better question to ask or address? What would be a better question to ask or address?

FIGURE 4.3: Good elaborative questions that support Socratic inquiry.

The Inquiring Minds Framework is based on the Socratic method of teaching and learning. Like Socrates, start the lesson by presenting a prompt or sharing a stimulus that will engage students into the inquiry experience. However, you should neither elaborate on the prompt nor explain the stimulus. You also should not express nor share your own knowledge, thinking, or feelings about the subject or topic. Instead, ask Socratic supporting questions to elicit deeper thinking and encourage in-depth discussions from students. You can use Socratic questioning to guide students along and down the different pathways of the Inquiring Minds Framework. The pathway the Socratic inquiry takes depends on the following.

- The goal and expectations of the learning intention, objective, or target addressed
- The intent and purpose of the inquiry and questioning
- The depth and direction of the conversations between students

For example, you might initiate the inquiry—or hook 'em—with a universal question that addresses a grand idea or theme or probing question that checks for and confirms the depth and extent of students' learning. Depending on how students respond, you might follow with a clarifying, probing, or evidentiary question that asks them to explain their response or justify their reasoning. Then, ask a viewpoint or perspective question that asks for other answers, options, or solutions. Continue or conclude the conversation by asking an implicating or consequential question for students to consider the effect or impact. Have the students consider the question to provide feedback or further thoughts. Never provide an answer or present a perspective through Socratic inquiry because the role and responsibility of the teacher is to be the questioner who commences and continues the conversations through inquiry and questioning.

How Can Educators Use Socratic Questions to Hook 'Em Into Inquiry?

After students have reflected on or responded to the prompt or stimulus, the teacher poses clarifying questions to hook 'em further into the inquiry experience. Socratic questions prompt students to do the following.

- Elaborate on their responses, results, or reasoning
- Establish or examine the accuracy of their answers
- Expand their knowledge
- Extend their feelings
- Enthuse their curiosity and interest to learn

For example, suppose you asked students an easy yet simple question they could answer, such as, "What is 3 × 2?" After students respond, pose a clarifying question such as, "What do you mean?" Now students must explain their answers. This deepens the cognitive demand of the inquiry from DOK 1 to DOK 2. Clarifying questions prompt students to check and confirm the accuracy of their answers. For example, if students responded with "five" as the answer instead of "six," you could ask, "What do you mean?" This allows them to check and self-correct their responses, results, or reasoning. In doing so, students are engaging in inquiry at DOK 3 because they must justify their response.

Clarifying questions shift how you deliver instruction and disseminate important or interesting information. For example, whenever I wanted to provide my students with important or interesting information on a text or topic, instead of making declarative statements through a lecture, I would ask, "What if I told you . . . ?" and finish the question with the details or facts they needed to know or understand. This transforms the declarative statement that's informational into an interrogative one that's more conversational. Students still learn the content. However, instead of listening to and receiving the information, asking, "What if I told you . . . ?" prompts students to reflect on what they are being taught or told.

Socratic inquiry uses questions to prompt students to think deeply and talk about the ideas and information presented in a text, pertaining to a topic, or pro- moted by a theory. However, it could cause an opposite reaction or response from students. They might feel as if they are being challenged personally, not pedagogi- cally. Students might become embarrassed or exasperated if they struggle to express themselves clearly or correctly. This may increase the risk of students having what I call "the downs"—the meltdown or the shutdown—if they sense their responses or reasoning are not respected or if they are regarded as "wrong" either by you or their classmates.

You need to ensure the Socratic questioning used to engage students in inquiry is rigorous yet respectful. Avoid bombarding students with questions or badgering them for a response. The questions posed to students should be intentional yet inviting. The purpose of the questions is to prompt students to think and talk about the subject they are studying, not push them to answer. You don't want students to feel as if they are in a courtroom instead of a classroom. Engage and encourage them to learn through inquiry and questioning.

How Do Prompts Hook 'Em Into Inquiry?

When teaching and learning with an inquiring mind, the term *prompt* has a dual meaning and purpose. A prompt is the good question that initiates the inquiry. The good questions posed to or by students prompt them to reflect before responding. The prompt elicits and encourages questions and responses from students that lead to clarification, consideration, or conversation. In essence, prompt students into inquiry by posing a prompt.

Any good question could serve as a prompt. It does not need to be a profound question that requires students to demonstrate deeper levels of thinking. It should not require students to comprehend, consider, or convey their learning at deeper levels of DOK. However, the prompt should address one or more of the following.

- The type and level of cognition the inquiry expects students to demonstrate
- The content covered in the inquiry
- The conditions and criteria of the inquiry
- The central or underlying idea or intention the inquiry

The prompt could be a standards-based or subject-specific question that asks and addresses the learning intention, objective, or target to be achieved. These questions should feature the following.

- The question stem that triggers the thinking students must demonstrate
- The content knowledge students must understand or use
- The context in which students must understand and use their learning

However, the prompt does not need to address a standard explicitly or the subject directly. Teachers could ask and address questions that prompt students to delve deeper into the subject or go beyond the curriculum and classroom. These could be universal, essential questions that ask and address "grander or more global ideas, issues, themes, or topics" (Francis, 2016, p. 27). Clarifying questions prompt students to elaborate on, expand on, or extend their knowledge, thinking, or feelings. The purpose of these questions is to prompt students to continue to talk about, think, and transfer their learning.

Figure 4.4 features examples of good questions that prompt students into inquiry. The topical and driving questions are derived from the learning intention of the mathematics standard being addressed and assessed. These questions set the instructional focus and serve as the assessments for the inquiry experience.

Subject	Perform Operations With Multidigit Whole Numbers
Standard	Fluently multiply multidigit numbers using a standard algorithm. (MATH.NYS.5.NBT.1)
Prompt (Instruction and Evaluation)	How can multidigit numbers be multiplied fluently? (DOK 2) How could multidigit numbers be multiplied fluently using a standard algorithm? (DOK 3) How could you multiply multidigit numbers fluently using a standard algorithm? (DOK 3)
Socratic (Discussion)	Is there only one way to do something, or could there be multiple ways? How could this notion of "more than one way" be applied to mathematics? Has the way to do mathematics changed, or has how the ways we teach and learn mathematics changed? How many ways could you multiply multidigit numbers? Which algorithm do you prefer using and why?

Source: New York State Department of Education, 2019.

FIGURE 4.4: Using standards-based prompts to hook 'em into inquiry and questioning.

The questions featured in the row labeled *Socratic* are meant to capture students' attention and commence or continue conversations. They vary in their type and purpose. For example, the first question is a universal question that prompts students to reflect on the grand mathematical topic before responding. The second is an analytical question that prompts students to consider and be curious about the many ways multidigit numbers could be multiplied. The third is an affective question that prompts students to express and share the depth and extent of their learning in their own unique way. Any of these questions will elicit and encourage students to ask and address further questions about the subject.

The prompt spurs students—or hooks 'em—to think about the subject being studied. However, it should state the subject that students must learn. This is essential with standards-based inquiry experiences in English language arts, music, and the arts. The standards for these academic subjects are more conceptual, focusing on the components and craft of art, music, and literature than specific content (for example, theme and structure versus a specific piece or work of art, music, or literary text). The question that serves as the prompt should reference the academic standard being assessed. It should also address the specific text, topic, or technique being read and reviewed. The objectives of the standard could also be rephrased into questions that not only initiate the inquiry but also set the instructional focus and serve as the assessment for the inquiry (I will explore this concept further in chapter 5, page 115).

Figure 4.5 is an example of good questions I used when I taught *The Outsiders* by S. E. Hinton (1967). The good questions that served as the prompt address both the learning intention of the academic standard students must achieve and the text students are reading and reviewing. The Socratic questions are more personal and provocative. Their purpose is to pique curiosity, prompt thinking, and provoke discussions. However, do not share opinions, perspectives, or thoughts. Teach like Socrates—pose questions and preside over the discussions with students.

Subject	Literary Elements in *The Outsiders* by S. E. Hinton
Standard	Analyze how particular elements of a story or drama interact (for example, how the setting shapes the characters or plot). (DOK 3) (ELA-LITERACY.RL.7.3)
Prompt (Instruction and Evaluation)	How can the elements of a story interact with each other? How does the setting of *The Outsiders* by S. E. Hinton shape the characters and plot of the story? (DOK 2) How does *The Outsiders* by S. E. Hinton explore the conflicts and stereotypes that exist between different social classes through its characters and setting? (DOK 3)
Socratic (Discussion)	What does it mean to be "rich"? What does it mean to be "poor"? Is it better or more beneficial to be rich or to be poor? What are the benefits and drawbacks of being rich or poor? Could you be rich but also be poor? Could you be poor but also be rich? Which has a greater impact or influence—education or experience? How could your education or experiences impact or influence you positively or negatively? Does your address or zip code define who you are and decide who you will become, or do you determine your fate and future?

Source: Hinton, 1967.
Source for standard: NGA & CCSSO, 2010b.

FIGURE 4.5: Standards-based and subject-specific prompts for inquiry in literature.

Using a prompt to hook 'em into inquiry ensures the experience addresses or references key parts of the standard being assessed. The prompt that references and rephrases the learning intention, objective, or target is derived from a standard that sets the instructional focus and serves as the assessment for the learning. Socratic questions are more personal and provocative, prompting deeper thinking and provoking in-depth discussions to ensure the inquiry is socially and emotionally supportive. The prompt engages and encourages students to participate in conversations and ponder what is being asked and addressed.

How Can Educators Use Prompts to Hook 'Em Into Inquiry?

Hooking 'em with a prompt can be as simple and straightforward as asking a question the moment the class starts. For example, a mathematics teacher could start the class by asking, "How can multidigit numbers be multiplied using a standard algorithm?" Or an English teacher might ask, "How does *The Outsiders* by S. E. Hinton explore the conflicts and stereotypes that exist between different social classes through its characters and setting?" Students are not expected to answer—at least, not immediately or initially. These questions are meant to spark students' thinking about the subject and commence conversations with classmates.

Educators could pose a factual question with a seemingly obvious answer to hook 'em into inquiry. For example, one of my favorite topics to teach with inquiry is the U.S. Constitution. One of the academic standards students must achieve features a learning intention like this one: "Identify the issues that led to the creation of the U. S. Constitution, including the weaknesses of the Articles of Confederation" (TEKS.HIS. 5.3[A]; Texas Education Agency, 2022).

One of the weaknesses of the Articles of Confederation was that it did not establish a centralized government at the federal level. There was a president of the United States—in fact, eight men were appointed to the position under the Articles of Confederation (National Endowment for the Humanities and National Trust for the Humanities, 2018). The position was called President of the United States in Congress Assembled. However, these men lacked any power in their position—specifically, the executive power granted to the president of the United States elected under the U.S. Constitution. That was one of the weaknesses of the Articles of Confederation that the U.S. Constitution attempted to address. Who was the "real" first president of the United States? is a question that is debated amongst historians and discussed on various credible and personal websites.

It's not widely known that there were eight men appointed as Presidents of the United States in Congress Assembled (I call them POTUSICAs) prior to George Washington's election under the United States Constitution (National Endowment for the Humanities and National Trust for the Humanities, 2018). I did not want to teach this topic through a lecture or presentation. Instead, I started the class with the prompt, "Who was the first president of the United States?" All my students answered, "George Washington," feeling confident they were correct.

Then I asked, "What do you mean?"

My students were surprised yet puzzled by my clarifying question that asked them to explain the answer. Some of them stated, "George Washington was the first president of the United States." Sometimes, a student would specify that "George Washington was the first elected president." That led to me asking them, "What if I told you there was a president of the United States before George Washington? In fact, what if I told you there were eight Presidents of the United States in Congress Assembled before George Washington, who were appointed under the Articles of Confederation?" That's how I hooked 'em into inquiry. They were curious and interested to learn who these appointed presidents were and why they are not more well known. It also served as The Hook that led them across all four pathways of the Inquiring Minds Framework throughout the unit.

Figure 4.6 outlines the inquiry into the presidency under the Articles of Confederation. This is a deep inquiry experience that delves into the subject addressed and assessed by the standard—specifically, the weakness of the position of presidency in the Articles of Confederation and how it led to establishing the executive power of the presidency under the U.S. Constitution. Notice the good question that serves as The Hook. It seems like an easy or simple question to answer. However, the intent and purpose of the question is to pique students' curiosity and interest in engaging in the deep inquiry experience. Each subsequent question students address along the pathways of the Inquiring Minds Framework also hooks 'em deeper and further into inquiry.

Starting the class with a prompt is one of purest ways to engage students to experience inquiry. It also aligns with the Socratic method of teaching and learning through continuous questioning and discussion. Pose questions to prompt students into the inquiry and then preside over the discussion.

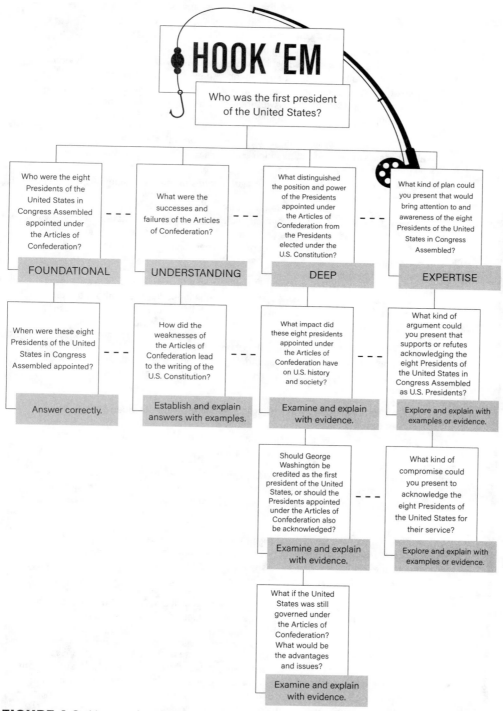

FIGURE 4.6: How to hook 'em into deep inquiry of the Articles of the Articles of Confederation.

Figure 4.7 (page 104) lists examples of stimuli that can serve as a QFocus and hook 'em into inquiry and questioning.

Stimulus	Engagement and Experience
Standard	Share with students the learning intention of the academic standard that will be addressed and assessed as part of the unit or lesson. Ask students which words, terms, and details they do not understand and express this in the form of a question. Have students share their questions with the whole class, in pairs, or in groups. Then, challenge students to answer their classmates' questions. The questions they cannot answer will set the instructional focus and purpose of the inquiry.
Sample Items	Share the sample items students must answer correctly. They need to establish and explain with examples, examine and explain with evidence, or explore and explain with examples or evidence. Ask students to pose questions about the items. Examples of sample items could be mathematics problems or scientific models.
Section, Segment, or Statement	Share a section, segment, or statement from the text or topic being read and reviewed. It could be a quote or a cited statement from a source. Ask students what questions they have about the text segment. Have students share their questions with the whole class, in pairs, or in groups. Then, challenge them to answer their classmates' questions.
Snippet	Present students with a brief clip of a multimedia text (for example, a snippet of a sound, song, or video). Ask students what questions they have about the text segment. Have them share their questions with the whole class, in pairs, or in groups. Then, challenge them to answer their classmates' questions.
Sound	Play a sound that relates to the subject or skill being studied. Ask students what questions they have about the sound. Have students share their questions with the whole class, in pairs, or in groups. Then, challenge them to answer their classmates' questions.
Speech	Present a speech to students. It could be an audio, print, or video speech. Ask students what questions they have about the sound. Have students share their questions with the whole class, in pairs, or in groups. Then, challenge them to answer their classmates' questions.
Song	Play a song for students. It could be a snippet or the whole song. Ask students what questions they have about the sound. Have students share their questions with the whole class, in pairs, or in groups. Then, challenge them to answer their classmates' questions.
Visual	Present students with a visual related to the subject or skill studied. It could be a chart, a graphic, a painting, or a photo. Ask students what questions they have about the visual. Have students share their questions with the whole class, in pairs, or in groups. Then, challenge them to answer their classmates' questions.
Video	Show students a video related to the subject or skill studied. It should not be longer than five minutes. Have students share their questions with the whole class, in pairs, or in groups. Then, challenge them to answer their classmates' questions.
Sensation	Present students with something that will activate and appeal to their senses. It could be something they see, hear, feel, smell, or taste. Ask students what questions they have about the sound, smell, taste, and so on. Have them share their questions with the whole class, in pairs, or in groups. Then, challenge them to answer their classmates' questions.
Reflection	Have students reflect on the questions that are on their inquiring minds. It could be about the subject, the skill, or something that's important or interesting to them. Keep the environment quiet or play music in the background to help activate and appeal to their senses. Then, have students choose a question they want to answer.

FIGURE 4.7: Stimuli that will hook 'em into inquiry.

As you can see, there are many ways to present stimuli to students. Stimuli can appeal to students' senses and different ways of learning. But specifically, how can teachers use stimuli to deeply engage students in inquiry and questioning?

How Can Educators Use Stimuli to Hook 'Em Into Inquiry?

Sharing a stimulus is the first step of the Question Formulation Technique (QFT), a formal instructional process for questioning developed by Dan Rothstein and Luz Santana (2011) and used by the Right Question Institute (rightquestions.org). With the QFT, the teacher hooks 'em into inquiry by sharing a stimulus—or QFocus—that serves as the source of students' questions. The purpose of the QFocus "is to get the students to ask their own questions" (Rothstein & Santana, 2011, p. 44). For example, they could share a visual of the water cycle with students, as shown in figure 4.8.

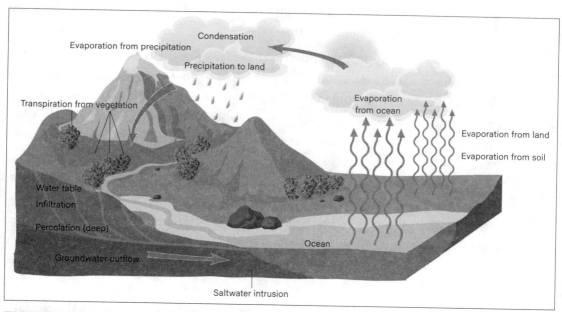

FIGURE 4.8: Using a stimulus to hook 'em into inquiry about the water cycle.

However, the teacher does not discuss this stimulus. They simply share it with students without any explanation or elaboration. After sharing the stimulus with students, the teacher sets the following procedures and protocols for posing questions.

1. Ask as many questions as you can.

2. Do not stop to discuss, judge, or answer any of the questions.

3. Write down every question exactly as it was stated.

4. Change any statements into questions. (Rothstein & Santana, 2011, p. 32)

Once the teacher shares the stimulus and sets the rules, students write down as many questions as they can about the stimulus within a given timeframe. They don't stop to consider or critique their questions—at least, not yet. They just compose and craft their questions as they come to their mind. The teacher has no influence and provides no input during this experience. They simply walk around the room and observe.

After the questions period has expired, the teacher directs students to categorize their questions as open ended or closed ended. They can also challenge students to convert their questions into more complex ones. The QFT ends with students prioritizing which questions to address and explaining their choices. Throughout the process, the teacher encourages students to reflect on the experience and share their reasoning for the questions they posed.

A stimulus can support the prompt that identifies the instructional focus and informs the purpose for learning. For example, a mathematics teacher could initiate the inquiry into multiplying multidigit whole numbers by showing the scene from *Incredibles 2* (Bird, 2018), in which Mr. Incredible becomes frustrated with helping his son Dash with his mathematics homework and proclaims, "I don't know that way! Why would they change math? Math is math!" After showing the scene, the teacher could ask students, "How many of you have felt like Mr. Incredible when it comes to mathematics?" The purpose of this question is to encourage students to reflect on and respond with their feelings and emotions. The teacher could then pose clarifying questions to encourage students to ask further questions or have deeper conversations.

After the discussion, the teacher could present the standards-based prompt: "How can multidigit whole numbers be multiplied using a standard algorithm?" They could share a stimulus, such as the one in figure 4.9, which shows all the different methods for multiplying multidigit whole numbers. Seeing all the different algorithms could confuse or overwhelm students to the point where they become disengaged or disinterested. However, the teacher could reengage students back into the inquiry by prompting them to consider, "Which method would work best for you and why?"

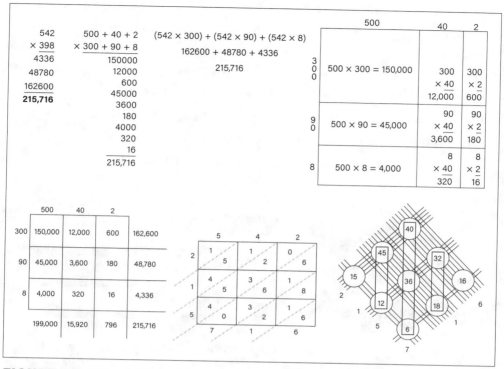

FIGURE 4.9: Stimulating students to choose a method for multiplying multidigit numbers.

Teachers wouldn't expect students to use all these methods. They only want them to choose one. The stimulus shows students all the strategies they can choose from. It also makes them curious and interested to learn about a particular algorithm.

Using a stimulus to hook 'em into inquiry will make the experience socially and emotionally supportive, student centered, and multisensory. It's meant to appeal to students' emotions, interests, and senses. It should be something that stirs a feeling inside them and be recognizable, relatable, or remarkable. It should also be something students can see, hear, feel, or even taste. Most importantly, it should stimulate students to want to discover or learn more or as much as they can about the subject they are studying.

How Does Rapid-Fire Questioning Hook 'Em Into Inquiry?

When I was a classroom teacher, and before I learned about Rothstein and Santana's (2011) QFT, I engaged my students in inquiry through what I called

Rapid-Fire Questioning. Like the QFT, the goal and expectation of Rapid-Fire Questioning to encourage students to ask and address their own questions. My purpose for engaging students in Rapid-Fire Questioning, however, was to teach them how they could tap into and trigger their inquiring minds to ask questions as well as become lifelong learners who learn through inquiry and questioning.

Figure 4.10 features an example of how my inquiring mind works. It lists some of the questions I asked when I first started watching the news about COVID-19.

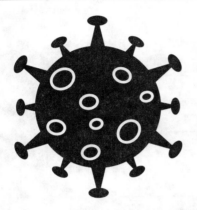

- What is a pandemic?
- What causes a pandemic?
- What's the difference between an epidemic and a pandemic?
- When have pandemics occurred throughout history?
- What caused different pandemics in history?
- How were pandemics addressed, handled, and resolved throughout history?
- How were pandemics addressed, handled, and resolved in other countries?
- How were pandemics addressed, handled, and resolved in other cultures?
- When has the United States ever experienced a pandemic?
- What should be done to reduce the burdens, issues, and problems associated with this pandemic?
- Why is the name of this virus *coronavirus*?
- Why is the disease caused by this virus called COVID-19?
- How is COVID-19 different from other viruses throughout history that have caused epidemics and pandemics?
- What distinguishes the COVID-19 pandemic from other pandemics throughout history?
- What could happen to me or my family if I get COVID-19?
- How will we know when the pandemic is over?
- What are or will be the lingering consequences of this pandemic or COVID-19?

FIGURE 4.10: Using stimuli to hook 'em into inquiry through Rapid-Fire Questioning.

News was the stimulus that hooked me into asking questions and engaging in inquiry to learn more. I decided to write down the questions as they came to my mind. Notice how the questions are listed in succession to match the rapid speed in which I asked them. That's how my inquiring mind works when I'm prompted or stimulated by something I see, hear, feel, or sense. I just "fire off" those questions as quickly as they come to mind. I don't consider, "Should I ask that?" or contemplate, "How could I make the question better?" I just ask the questions as they come to me.

To engage students—or hook 'em—into inquiry with Rapid-Fire Questioning, present a prompt or share a stimulus, and ask students, "What questions come to your inquiring mind about this?" Then let students ask questions either verbally or in writing. Encourage them to share their questions with the class, and reassure them that their questions will be respected and valued. Students might discover that others have some of the same questions; and they could check if anyone could address or answer the questions. During this process, hang back and observe but do not offer suggestions. Just let students pose their questions in response to the shared stimulus.

The difference between Rapid-Fire Questioning and the QFT is in the methodology in instruction and motivation for learning through inquiry and questioning. The QFT is a more formal instructional process for asking questions, with specific protocols and a particular purpose for questioning. Rapid-Fire Questioning, on the other hand, is more freewheeling and spontaneous.

Sometimes, I prompted students to ask a *specific type* of good question. For example, "What kind of good analytical questions could you ask about this?" or "What kind of personal questions do you want to ask about this?" I did not have them change or improve their questions after asking them. These were the questions they wanted to ask. My purpose with Rapid-Fire Questioning was to teach students how to incite their inquiring mind to experience inquiry and questioning as a part of life.

In my experience, Rapid-Fire Questioning is effective with younger students, especially those in preschool through third grade. Though students may be developing the literacy competency to respond to stimuli by reading and writing, they are fearless questioners who demonstrate an immense ability to ask questions to learn. In fact, students in preschool through third grade are more likely to ask more complex and creative questions than their peers in the upper grades—if you encourage them to do so freely. One of the goals of engaging older students in Rapid-Fire Questioning is to encourage them to become the fearless questioners they were when they were young.

Again, there's a fine line between the QFT and Rapid-Fire Questioning as a method and motivation to engage in inquiry through questioning. Deciding whether to hook 'em into inquiry using QFT or Rapid-Fire Questioning depends on the intent of the instruction and the needs of students individually and collectively as a class.

Summary

Teaching an inquiring mind starts with engaging students in inquiry. The teacher initiates inquiry by presenting a prompt or sharing a stimulus that piques students' curiosity and interest—or hooks 'em—to learn. The prompt is a question that students must address. It could be a standards-based or subject-specific question. Also, prompts could be Socratic questions that are more conversational and informal. The stimulus is the question focus—or QFocus—that serves as the source of students' questions. It could be an audio, print, or visual text students must analyze to serve as the source of their questions.

The Inquiring Minds Framework is based on the principles and practices of the Socratic method. Teachers use Socratic questioning to guide students along and down the different pathways of the Inquiring Minds Framework. The QFT and Rapid-Fire Questioning can engage students in formulating their own questions about the subject.

Application: How Can You Hook 'Em Into Inquiry and Questioning?

Either individually or with your team, plan a teaching and learning experience that uses one or more of the following to engage students in inquiry.

- A prompt that is standards based or subject specific
- An audio, print, or visual text that serves as the QFocus to stimulate questioning
- Socratic questions that commence and continue conversations with and amongst students

Follow these steps to develop and deliver a lesson plan that will engage students in inquiry and questioning.

Develop a Lesson Plan

1. Copy the Inquiry Grid reproducible on page 113.
2. Select the subject to be studied. Write this in the first row of the Inquiry Grid labeled *Subject*.

3. Identify the academic standard or standards students must achieve. Write the standard or standards in the second row of the Inquiry Grid labeled *Standard.*

4. Produce a standards-based or subject-specific prompt students must address and write it in the third row of the Inquiry Grid labeled *Prompt.* The prompt should be a good question that features one or more of the following:

   ¤ The question stem that triggers the type and level of thinking students must demonstrate

   ¤ The content knowledge students must understand or use

   ¤ The context in which students must understand and use their learning

5. Select an audio, print, or visual text to serve as the QFocus. The QFocus should support the standard, supplement the prompt, and stimulate students to ask their own questions. Write the stimulus in the row of in the Inquiry Grid labeled *Stimulus.*

6. Come up with conversational and informal questions that can be posed through Socratic inquiry and questioning. These questions should be personal and provocative enough to prompt deeper thinking and provoke in-depth talking. List these questions in the row of the Inquiry Grid labeled *Socratic.*

Deliver the Lesson

1. Start the class by presenting the prompt featuring the standards-based or subject-specific questions that set the instructional focus, serve as the assessment, or personalize the inquiry. Provide students the opportunity and time to reflect on and retrieve the data and details they need to respond to the questions.

2. Start the class by posing a question that seems simple to answer. After students respond, ask, "What do you mean?" Students must explain or justify their response. Continue asking Socratic questions that elicit deeper thinking and encourage in-depth conversations. Use questioning to guide students along and down the different pathways of the Inquiring Minds Framework. Complete the Socratic inquiry by presenting the standards-based or subject-specific

prompt that sets the instructional focus, serves as the assessment, or personalizes the inquiry.

3. Start the class by sharing an audio, print, or visual text that addresses the standard and augments the prompt. This will be the QFocus that stimulates students' thinking and serves as the source of students' questions. Use the QFT to encourage students to choose the questions they want to address about the stimulus and the subject.

4. Develop conversational Socratic questions that will capture students' attention and commence or continue conversations. These questions should be personal and provocative to prompt deeper thinking and provoke in-depth discussions. Use the Socratic method of teaching and learning through inquiry and questioning to initiate the inquiry and inspire further questions or discussions.

5. Decide what information is important or interesting for students to know and understand about a text, topic, theory, or technique. Ask, "What if I told you . . . ?" and follow the question stem with the declarative statement featuring the important detail or interesting fact you want students to know and understand. Give them the opportunity and time to reflect on and respond to the question.

6. When a student answers a question with a single or simple response, ask, "What do you mean?" to encourage them to elaborate on their answer, explain how they attained it, or ensure their response or reasoning is accurate.

7. After presenting the prompt or sharing the stimulus that hooks 'em into inquiry, use Socratic questioning to guide students along or down the pathways of the Inquiring Minds Framework.

Inquiry Grid

Subject		
Standard (QFocus)		
Prompt (Good Questions)		
Socratic (Discussion)		
Stimulus (QFocus)		

Define Academic Vocabulary	Describe Subject-Specific Terminology	Explain Data and Details

Chapter 5

HOW COULD GOOD QUESTIONS PERSONALIZE INQUIRY AND PROMOTE EXPERTISE?

The marvelous thing about a good question is that it shapes our identity as much by the asking as it does by the answering.

—David Whyte

Reflect and Respond

How do you feel when someone asks you a question? How do you think students feel when you ask them a question? When you ask the class questions to initiate inquiry and inspire discussion, do you use the pronouns *I*, *we*, or *you*? How could you pose questions that not only prompt inquiry and promote cognitive rigor but also personalize inquiry and promote expertise?

P REVIOUSLY, YOU EXPLORED how to phrase and pose good questions as a prompt that will engage students in the inquiry experience. This chapter explains how you could rephrase the learning intentions, objectives, and targets of academic standards into good questions that personalize inquiry and promote expertise simply by using a question stem that features *you* as the pronoun referent.

How Could Inquiry Be Personalized?

The goal of teaching with an inquiring mind is for students to become resourceful, responsive, and responsible for their own learning. The expectation is that students will learn how to prompt or stimulate themselves to learn individually and independently through inquiry and by inquiry.

To accomplish this, plan and provide inquiry experiences that do the following.

- Personalize the intent and purpose of the learning for students
- Promote the development of student expertise in a subject or with a skill

To personalize learning and promote expertise, engage students in the following forms of inquiry.

- *Guided inquiry* that shifts the responsibility of the inquiry from educators to students
- *Open or free inquiry* that expects students to engage in the inquiry individually and independently
- *Coupled inquiry* that tiers the experience based on the success and struggles of the students
- *Authentic inquiry* that engages students to determine and decide the depth and direction of the inquiry from start to finish
- *Synergistic inquiry* that involves both students and educators working collaboratively and interdependently throughout the experience

When deciding which form of inquiry students should engage in and experience, the teacher should consider the following questions.

- What is the purpose of the inquiry?
- How prepared are students to engage in the inquiry?

Your responses to these questions not only determine the form of inquiry students engage in and experience; they also determine what responsibility and role the teacher and students will have in the inquiry. However, before educators choose the form of inquiry, they first need to come up with good questions that personalize the learning for students and promote the development and demonstration of their expertise.

How Could You Rephrase Learning Objectives and Targets Into Good Questions?

Learning objectives and targets are not questions—good or otherwise. Learning objectives refer to the intended student learning outcomes that "indicate what we want students to learn" (Anderson & Krathwohl, 2001, p. 12). They are typically phrased as imperative statements that begin with a cognitive action verb indicating the type of thinking students must demonstrate. The noun and noun phrases in the objective identify the concepts and content students must understand and learn. The rest of the words and phrases following the initial cognitive action verb inform what exactly and how deeply students must understand and use their knowledge and thinking, or learning.

Learning targets are phrased as simple declarative statements written from students' points of view. That's why they start with an introductory first-person phrase such as *I can* or *We will*. Susan Brookhart and Connie Moss (2013) explain how learning targets "guide learning [and] describe, in language that students understand, the lesson-sized chunk of information, skills, and reasoning processes that students will come to know deeply" (p. 9). The key difference between learning objectives and targets is that the former indicates the goal for teaching and learning, and the latter informs the teacher and students of what needs to be addressed and accomplished to achieve the learning goal or expectation.

The simplest way to rephrase a learning objective or target into a good question is to use one of the following question stems.

- How do you . . . ?
- How can you . . . ?
- How could you . . . ?

That's it! That's all you need to do to compose and pose a good question. With learning objectives, place one of these question stems in front of the cognitive action verb and put a question mark at the end. With learning targets, replace the introductory first-person phrase with one of these question stems and replace the period with a question mark. Using these question stems rephrases the learning objective or target into a good question that's standards based. The pronoun *you* in the question stem makes the good question student centered, specifying that the question asks how the student personally understands or could use what they are learning.

Figure 5.1 shows how these three question stems rephrase the learning objectives and targets of academic standards into good questions that personalize inquiry. The question stem used to introduce a good question depends on the instructional focus and purpose of the teaching and learning experience. For example, consider the following.

- The question stem "How do you . . . ?" is evaluative. It checks and confirms the depth and extent of students' personal knowledge, understanding, or awareness. These questions serve as assessments.

- The question stem "How can you . . . ?" is instructional. It phrases and presents the instructional focus and purpose for learning as an interrogative statement. These questions can also be used to assess student learning.

- The question stem "How could you . . . ?" is inquisitive. It stimulates different levels of thinking; piques students' curiosity, interest, imagination, and wonder; and prompts students to reflect before responding. These questions initiate the inquiry and inspire further questioning.

Notice how these question stems not only change the phrasing of the learning objective or target but transform the tone of how instructional goals and expectations are communicated or presented. Instead of directing students to "do this" or having them state, "I can do this," the question stems prompt students to communicate "how do you . . . ?," comprehend "how can you . . . ?," or consider "how could you . . . ?" These questions encourage dialogue between the teacher and the students and discussion among the students also. Most importantly, these question stems make the complex language and sentence structure of learning objectives and targets clearer and more comprehensible to students.

Why Should You Use the Pronoun *You* in Good Question Stems?

Some teachers may want to use the pronouns *I* or *we* instead of *you* with the question stems that personalize inquiry. All three pronouns express the questions in student-friendly language that makes the goal and expectations of the inquiry understandable. They permit students to see themselves in the learning. However, there is a distinct difference in what these pronouns convey or infer.

Subject	Learning Objective	Learning Target	Assessment	Instruction	Inquiry
Mathematics	Solve with fluency one- and two-step problems involving multiplication and division, including interpreting remainders. (TEKS.MATH.4.4[H])	I can solve with fluency one- and two-step problems involving multiplication and division, including interpreting remainders.	How do you solve with fluency one- and two-step problems involving multiplication and division, including interpreting remainders?	How can you solve with fluency one- and two-step problems involving multiplication and division, including interpreting remainders?	How could you solve with fluency one- and two-step problems involving multiplication and division, including interpreting remainders?
English Language Arts	Determine the meaning of words and phrases as they are used in a text, including figurative and connotative meanings. (CCRS.ELA-.LIT.RL.5.3)	I can determine the meaning of words and phrases as they are used in a text, including figurative and connotative meanings.	How do you determine the meaning of words and phrases as they are used in a text, including figurative and connotative meanings?	How can you determine the meaning of words and phrases as they are used in a text, including figurative and connotative meanings?	How could you determine the meaning of words and phrases as they are used in a text, including figurative and connotative meanings?
Science	Analyze and interpret data on natural hazards to forecast future catastrophic events and inform the development of technologies to mitigate their effects. (NGSS-MS-LS2–2)	I can analyze and interpret data on natural hazards to forecast future catastrophic events and inform the development of technologies to mitigate their effects.	How do you analyze and interpret data on natural hazards to forecast future catastrophic events and inform the development of technologies to mitigate their effects?	How can you analyze and interpret data on natural hazards to forecast future catastrophic events and inform the development of technologies to mitigate their effects?	How could you analyze and interpret data on natural hazards to forecast future catastrophic events and inform the development of technologies to mitigate their effects?
Civics	Apply civic virtues and democratic principles in school and community settings. (C4.D2.Civ.7.6–8)	I can apply civic virtues and democratic principles in school and community settings.	How do you apply civic virtues and democratic principles in school and community settings?	How can you apply civic virtues and democratic principles in school and community settings?	How could you apply civic virtues and democratic principles in school and community settings?
Economics	Use benefits and costs to evaluate the effectiveness of government policies to improve market outcomes. (C4.D2.Eco.8.9–12)	I can use benefits and costs to evaluate the effectiveness of government policies to improve market outcomes.	How do you use benefits and costs to evaluate the effectiveness of government policies to improve market outcomes?	How can you use benefits and costs to evaluate the effectiveness of government policies to improve market outcomes?	How could you use benefits and costs to evaluate the effectiveness of government policies to improve market outcomes?

continued →

FIGURE 5.1: Rephrasing learning objectives and targets into good questions.

Subject	Learning Objective	Learning Target	Assessment	Instruction	Inquiry
Geography	Construct maps and other graphic representations of both familiar and unfamiliar places. (C4.D2.Geo1.3–5)	I can construct maps and other graphic representations of both familiar and unfamiliar places.	How do you construct maps and other graphic representations of both familiar and unfamiliar places?	How can you construct maps and other graphic representations of both familiar and unfamiliar places?	How could you construct maps and other graphic representations of both familiar and unfamiliar places?
History	Chart the secession of the southern states and explain the process and reasons for secession. (UCLA.NHS.USE.1A.5–12)	I can chart the secession of the southern states. I can explain the process and reasons for secession.	How do you chart the secession of the southern states? How do you explain the process and reasons for secession?	How can you chart the secession of the southern states? How can you explain the process and reasons for secession?	How could you chart the secession of the southern states? How could you explain the process and reasons for secession?
World Languages	Use the target language to acquire goods, services or information orally and in writing. (AERO.COMM.1.1.G6.a)	I can use the target language to acquire goods, services, or information orally and in writing.	How do you use the target language to acquire goods, services, or information orally and in writing?	How can you use the target language to acquire goods, services, or information orally and in writing?	How could you use the target language to acquire goods, services, or information orally and in writing?
Art	Combine ideas to generate an innovative idea for artmaking. (NCAS.VA.CR1.1.6a)	I can combine ideas to generate an innovative idea for artmaking.	How do you combine ideas to generate an innovative idea for artmaking?	How can you combine ideas to generate an innovative idea for artmaking?	How could you combine ideas to generate an innovative idea for artmaking?
Music	Improvise rhythmic and melodic patterns and musical ideas for a specific purpose. (NCAS.MU:Cr1.2a)	I can improvise rhythmic and melodic patterns and musical ideas for a specific purpose.	How do you improvise rhythmic and melodic patterns and musical ideas for a specific purpose?	How can you improvise rhythmic and melodic patterns and musical ideas for a specific purpose?	How could you improvise rhythmic and melodic patterns and musical ideas for a specific purpose?
Physical Education	Dribble with dominant hand using a change of speed and direction in a variety of practice tasks. (S1.M8.6)	I can dribble with my dominant hand using a change of speed and direction in a variety of practice tasks.	How do you dribble with your dominant hand using a change of speed and direction in a variety of practice tasks?	How can you dribble with your dominant hand using a change of speed and direction in a variety of practice tasks?	How could you dribble with your dominant hand using a change of speed and direction in a variety of practice tasks?

Source for standards: American Education Reaches Out, 2018; National Center for History in the Schools, 1996; National Core Arts Standards State Education Agency Directors of Arts Education, 2014; National Council for the Social Studies, 2013; NGA & CCSSO, 2010b; NGSS Lead States, 2013; SHAPE America, 2013; Texas Education Agency, 2014.

- The pronoun *I* prompts students to consider their own knowledge, thinking, and feelings about a subject or skill. It also individualizes the inquiry. However, there's no difference between posing a question that asks, "How can I . . . ?" and presenting a learning target that states, "I can . . ." or "We will. . . ." Both are examples of "teacher talk" in which the teacher directs or leads conversations about the subject, skill, or situation. In fact, asking "How can I . . . ?" makes the question a leading one because it directs students to ask themselves that question. It also gives students the opportunity to respond, "I can't."

- The pronoun *we* initiates the inquiry for the entire class and makes it inclusive. It introduces the instructional focus and informs the purpose for learning by communicating, "This is what everyone in the class will establish, examine, or explore and explain." However, while asking "How could we . . . ?" makes the inquiry a collective and shared experience, it does not individualize or personalize the learning for students. In fact, asking "How could we . . . ?" could cause students to become disinterested in the question and detached or disconnected from the inquiry—especially those who are more intrapersonal in their approach and attitude toward learning.

There's nothing necessarily wrong with asking "How could I . . . ?" or "How could we . . . ?" in a good question because it allows students to see themselves as the subject of the question. It prompts them to consider what the question is asking. These pronouns help them understand what the learning objective or target from which it is derived is expecting and requiring them to comprehend and convey. However, using *you* as the pronoun referent prompts students to reflect and respond. This is a criterion for what a good question does, and it ensures that the inquiry and questioning are more of an exchange of learning between educators and students versus a transmission of knowledge from teachers to students. Also, the worst thing students could reply or respond to a question that asks, "How could you . . . ?" is "I don't know." Do not take this as the student avoiding the question or disengaging from the inquiry. Regard it as the student informing what direction the inquiry and questioning should take.

Don't question or doubt this practice because it seems easy and simple. It *is* that easy and simple! This is how educators can shift their instructional delivery from directing to inquiring because it ensures the inquiry students engage in and experience is both standards based and student centered.

How Could Good Driving Questions Promote Expertise?

Good question stems that feature the pronoun referent *you* promote the development and demonstration of student expertise. These questions are a form of essential questions called *good driving questions* that encourage students "to think creatively and strategically about what they can create, design, develop, do, plan, or produce, based on their Depth of Knowledge" (Francis, 2016, p. 32).

Table 5.1 features question stems that could introduce good driving questions. Most of the good driving question stems ask, "How could you . . . ?" not only to personalize inquiry but also to prompt critical and creative thinking.

Table 5.1: Good Driving Question Stems

Good Driving Question Stems	
• What could you create?	• How would you motivate?
• What could you design?	• How could you persuade?
• What could you develop?	• How could you assist or help?
• What could you do?	• How could you support?
• What could you make?	• What do you propose?
• What could you produce?	• What do you recommend?
• What could you invent?	• How would you argue?
• How would you innovate?	• What do you suggest?
• How could you generate?	• What is your "pitch"?
• What would you change?	• What is your solution?
• What could you build?	• How could you develop and use a model?
• What could you construct?	• How could you develop and use a method?
• How could you use a model?	• How could you develop and use a strategy?
• How could you use a method?	• How could develop and use a technique?
• How could you use a strategy?	• How could you construct and present an argument with specific claims?
• How could you use a technique?	
• What do you advise?	• How could you write and present an expository/informative text?
• How could you advocate?	
• How could you promote?	• How could you write and produce a narrative?
• How could you encourage?	• What kind of plan could you develop and implement?
• How could you convince?	• What kind of research/experiment/investigation could you conduct?

Good driving questions strengthen and support talent development, which Francois Gagné (2009) describes as "the progressive transformation of gifts into talents" (p. 1). They prompt students to think critically or creatively about how they could draw on their innate abilities and skills to produce innovative products or present new ideas that showcase their unique expertise. Good driving questions showcase expertise to specify the product students will create or the purpose for thinking critically and creatively. For example, some good driving question stems identify what exactly students will create. Consider the following.

- How could you develop and use a model?
- How could you construct an argument or explanation?
- How could you construct maps, graphs, or other representations?

Others include the creative action students will perform. For example:

- Create
- Develop
- Design
- Innovate
- Invent

Good driving questions set the purpose and steer the process of authentic and extensive teaching and learning experiences, such as project-based and problem-based learning. According to John Larmer, John Mergendoller, and Suzie Boss (2015), a good driving question should have the following three attributes.

1. **Engaging for students:** The question should be written in a student-friendly language so students can easily comprehend what the question asks and addresses. The question stem should communicate and create a sense of personal ownership for students.

2. **Open-ended:** The question should require students to explain, justify, or extend actions or answers—be it their own or others'. A good question should require students to search for and investigate examples and evidence that strengthen and support responses and reasoning.

3. **Aligned with learning goals:** The question could address the learning intention of a specific academic standard explicitly. However, it should prompt students to develop and demonstrate the knowledge and skills featured within it. It should be mission driven and goal oriented.

There are four different ways to phrase and pose good questions that engage students in authentic learning experiences that extend their expertise.

1. Place the question stem "How could you . . . ?" before the imperative statement of the learning objective being addressed and assessed. For example, "How could you write opinion pieces on topics or texts, supporting a point of view with reasons?"

2. Replace the first-person phrase that introduces a learning target with the question stem "How could you . . . ?" For example, rephrase the learning target: "I can make a line plot to display a data set of measurements in fractions of a unit $(\frac{1}{2}, \frac{1}{4}, \frac{1}{8})$" into a good question that prompts students to think creatively: "How could you make a line plot to display a data set of measurements in fractions of a unit $(\frac{1}{2}, \frac{1}{4}, \frac{1}{8})$?"

3. Specify the creative cognitive action in the question stem followed by the determiner *that* and the imperative statement of the learning objective or target being addressed and assessed. For example, "What could you create that . . . ?" or "What could you invent that . . . ?"

4. Specify the artifact or product students must create or produce in the question stem. For example, "What kind of narrative could you write and produce . . . ?" or "How could you develop and use a model . . . ?"

How Could Good Questions Prompt Students to Express Their Emotions?

Good questions that personalize inquiry address and assess students' individual content knowledge and cognitive skills. They prompt and promote affective learning, which emphasizes and evaluates students' attitudes, interests, values, and character development as they learn. Table 5.2 lists the question stems that prompt and promote affective learning. Notice how each of these question stems feature *you* or *your* as the pronoun referent to emphasize that students should express their personal emotions or thoughts.

Good questions for expertise align with the behavioral and emotional actions and expectations categorized by the affective domain of Bloom's taxonomy developed by Krathwohl, Bloom, & Macias, 1964. These good questions address objectives

Table 5.2: Good Affective Question Stems

Good Affective Question Stems			
• What do you believe?	• What is your opinion?	• What is your goal?	• What do you do if/when . . .?
• What do you think?	• What is your perspective?	• What is your objective?	• What can you do if/when . . . ?
• How do you feel?	• What is your point of view?	• What is your intent?	• What could you do if/when . . . ?
• What do you suppose?	• What are your thoughts?	• What is your purpose?	• What would you do if/when . . . ?

"expressed as interests, attitudes, appreciation, values, and emotional sets or biases" (Krathwohl et al., 1964, p. 7). Examples of affective objectives include those that expect students to construct an argument using facts and feelings as evidence, express their personal opinions, or share their individual experiences.

Like the cognitive domain, the affective domain features and lists verbs that specify the different behavioral reactions and emotional responses exhibited and experienced at each level. However, like the cognitive domain, most of the verbs that indicate emotional reactions and responses are intrinsic, making them difficult not only to measure but also to observe.

To encourage students to express their feelings, I developed the Affective Questioning Inverted Pyramid shown in figure 5.2 (page 126). It features the question stems that will prompt students to consider and convey the behaviors and emotions they experience as they learn about a subject, skill, or situation.

The question stems from the Affective Questioning Inverted Pyramid encourage students to contemplate how they could synthesize their emotions, education, and experiences into personal expertise. That's why many of these question stems are listed in the synthesize level of Bloom's Questioning Inverted Pyramid in figure 3.2 (page 71). Synthesizing is when the instructional focus and purpose of inquiry transitions from processing to personalizing learning. Synthesizing encourages students to consider and convey their emotions about their education and experiences. In contrast, creating encourages students to consider and convey how they could employ their gifts and talents—or endowments—to express the depth and extent of their learning innovatively, inventively, or in their own unique way as expertise.

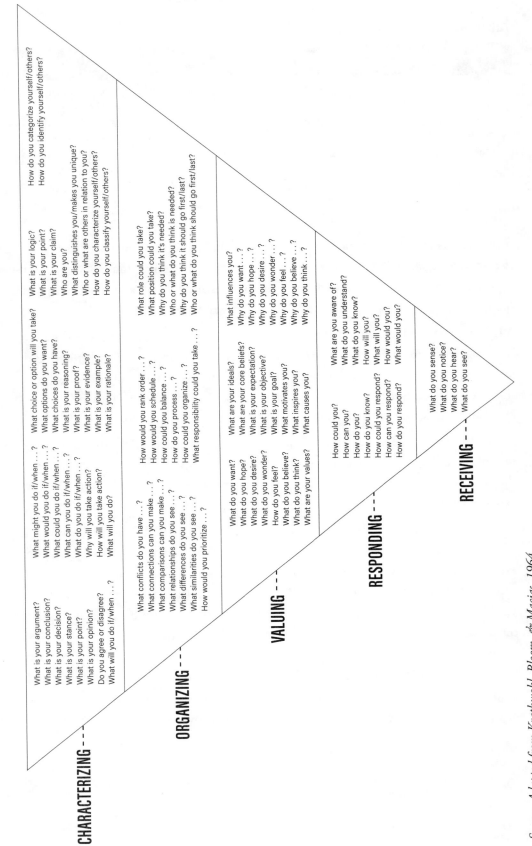

FIGURE 5.2: Affective questioning inverted pyramid

How Could Good Questions Support Social-Emotional Learning?

The Affective Questioning Inverted Pyramid can be used to phrase and pose good questions that support social-emotional learning (SEL). The Collaborative for Academic, Social, and Emotional Learning (CASEL, 2020) defines *SEL* as:

> The process through which all young people and adults acquire and apply the knowledge, skills, and attitudes to develop healthy identities, manage emotions and achieve personal and collective goals, feel and show empathy for others, establish and maintain supportive relationships, and make responsible and caring decisions. (p. 1)

Their framework features five core competencies that focus on the following.

1. **Self-Awareness:** How could you understand your own emotions, thoughts, and values and how they influence behavior across contexts?

2. **Self-Management:** How could you manage your emotions, thoughts, and behaviors effectively in different situations and to achieve goals and aspirations?

3. **Social Awareness:** How could you understand the perspectives of others and empathize with them, including those from diverse backgrounds, cultures, and contexts?

4. **Relationship Skills:** How could you establish and maintain healthy and supportive relationships with diverse individuals and groups and effectively navigate different settings?

5. **Responsible Decision Making:** How could you make caring and constructive choices about personal behavior and social interactions across diverse situations?

The CASEL (2020) framework features examples of affective objectives that expand on and extend how students could address and apply the core competencies. Placing "How could you . . . ?" in front of these objectives transforms them into good questions that will prompt inquiry and personalize social-emotional learning. Table 5.3 (page 128) features the affective objectives rephrased into good questions that could prompt and personalize inquiry-based social-emotional teaching and learning experiences.

Table 5.3: Good Questions That Support Social-Emotional Learning

CASEL Five Core Competencies	Good Questions That Support SEL
Self-Awareness How could you understand your own emotions, thoughts, and values and how they influence behavior across contexts?	• How could you integrate personal and social identities? • How could you identify personal, cultural, and linguistic assets? • How could you identify your emotions? • How could you demonstrate honesty and integrity? • How could you link feelings, values, and thoughts? • How could you examine prejudices and biases? • How could you experience self-efficacy? • How could you develop and demonstrate a growth mindset? • How could you develop interests and a sense of purpose?
Self-Management How could you manage your emotions, thoughts, and behaviors effectively in different situations to achieve goals and aspirations?	• How could you manage your emotions? • How could you identify and use stress-management strategies? • How could you exhibit self-discipline and self-motivation? • How could you set personal and collective goals? • How could you use planning and organizational skills? • How could you show the courage to take initiative? • How could you demonstrate learner or co-agency?
Social Awareness How could you understand the perspectives of others and empathize with them, including those from diverse backgrounds, cultures, and contexts?	• How could you take others' perspectives? • How could you recognize strengths in others? • How could you demonstrate empathy and compassion? • How could you show concern for the feelings of others? • How could you understand and express gratitude? • How could you identify diverse social norms, including unjust ones? • How could you recognize situational demands and opportunities? • How could you understand the influences of organizations/systems on your or others' behavior?
Relationship Skills How could you establish and maintain healthy and supportive relationships with diverse individuals and groups and effectively navigate different settings?	• How could you communicate effectively? • How could you develop positive relationships? • How could you demonstrate cultural competency? • How could you practice teamwork and collaborative problem solving? • How could you resolve conflicts constructively? • How could you resist negative social pressure? • How could you show leadership in groups? • How could you seek or offer support and help when needed? • How could you stand up for the rights of others?

Responsible Decision Making How could you make caring and constructive choices about personal behavior and social interactions across diverse situations?	• How could you demonstrate curiosity and open-mindedness? • How could you identify solutions for personal and social problems? • How could you make a reasoned judgment after analyzing information, data, or facts? • How could you anticipate and evaluate the consequences of one's actions? • How could you recognize how critical thinking skills are useful both inside and outside of school? • How could you reflect on your role to promote personal, family, and community well-being? • How could you evaluate personal, interpersonal, community, and institutional impacts?

Source: Adapted from CASEL, 2020.

These good questions can serve multiple purposes.

- Pose them as overarching essential questions that ask and address the core ideas and enduring understandings of an SEL competency.

- Present them to encourage students to engage in and experience inquiry in authentic learning experiences, such as project-based learning, problem-based learning, or service learning.

- Use them to fortify intellectual character and foster a spirit of inquiry to establish practical and personal connections between academic, social-emotional, and personalized learning.

How Could You Encourage Students to Ask and Address Their Own Good Questions?

Instead of posing good questions that personalize inquiry and promote expertise, encourage students to pose their own good questions that will prompt them to engage in and experience inquiry. Good questions from the students should come with little to no influence or input from the teacher.

One way to encourage students to pose their own questions is to give them the opportunity to pose a personal question they want to address about the subject, skill, or situation they're studying. These good questions embolden students to do the following.

- Consider what more they want to learn about concepts and content
- Contemplate what else they could learn about a particular text or topic
- Communicate what they have learned about the subject with the class
- Choose how they want to share what they have learned with the class (Francis, 2016)

Personal questions are challenging. It's difficult for students to come up with questions they want to ask about their learning. Challenge students to pose a personal question they want to address about the text, topic, or technique being taught. But do so only after providing them with the opportunity to build the foundational knowledge or develop the functional understanding needed to comprehend the subject, skill, or situation of study. You might ask students, "What do you personally want to know, understand, or learn?" or "What else do you personally want to learn?" Then, have them phrase it as a good question that will initiate the inquiry, inspire further questions, identify the instructional focus, and inform the purpose of learning.

Some students may struggle to come up with their own question. The simplest solution is to give students a list of questions they can choose from. However, the intent and purpose of posing a good personal question is to "pique curiosity—specifically, the innate inquisitiveness that leads us to delve deeper into a subject that interests us personally" (Francis, 2016, p. 141). Engage students and encourage them to come up with their own question without any influence or input by doing the following.

- Provide students with copies of the Bloom's Questioning Inverted Pyramid (figure 3.2, page 71) and the Three-Story Inquiry House of Question Stems (figure 3.3, page 72).
- Ask students good affective questions that gauge their attitudes, emotions, and interests, and guide them to come up with their own questions.
- Reassure students that any questions they ask will be good because it's the questions they want to address.

Students could use the QFT or Rapid-Fire Questioning to come up with and choose their own questions. Do not attempt to change or control students' questions. Instead, guide and support students by rephrasing their question so it stimulates deeper thinking or encourages them to delve deeper into the subject. Avoid assigning a question to students or directing them to ask a specific question.

Be careful not to dismiss a question that you believe or feel is not good. For example, it's acceptable and permissible for a student to ask a factual question that only requires them to recall information or how to do something to answer correctly. Remember, this is their personal question. If that's all they want to ask and address, that's okay. To guide students, ask questions to prompt students to explain how they attained their answer or justify why their response is correct.

The goal of asking a good personal question is for students to take ownership and responsibility for their learning. The expectation is that students will address the question either on their own, with a partner, or within a group. Then, they share with the class what they learned. This allows educators to delve deeper or go further into the subject, skill, or situation beyond what the standards demand, or the curriculum offers through a student-centered and student-driven experience. It also enables students to share and showcase the depth and extent of their education, experiences, emotions, and endowments—or expertise.

Summary

Placing the question stems "How do you . . . ?," "How can you . . . ?," or "How could you . . . ?" before the cognitive action verb of a learning objective or target will rephrase the objective or target into a good standards-based, student-centered question. It also makes the complex language and sentence structure of learning objectives and targets clearer and more comprehensible to students. Good questions promote expertise by encouraging students to think critically and creatively about how they could understand and use their learning innovatively, inventively, or in their own unique way.

Using *you* as the pronoun referent personalizes the learning and prompts conversations about the learning between teachers and students. Good questions that personalize inquiry and promote expertise are socially and emotionally supportive in that they ask students to consider and convey their attitudes, beliefs, or feelings.

Finally, students can pose their own good questions to engage in and experience inquiry. The QFT and Rapid-Fire Questioning are effective instructional strategies that encourage students to ask their own questions and activate—or reactivate—their inquiring mind.

Application: How Could You Rephrase Learning Objectives and Targets Into Good Questions That Personalize Inquiry and Promote Expertise?

Either individually or with your team, rephrase learning objectives and targets into good standards-based, student-centered questions. Decide whether the intent and purpose of the good questions posed do one (or more) of the following.

- Personalize inquiry
- Promote expertise
- Prompt students to express their emotions
- Support social-emotional learning

Use the Generating Good Questions for Expertise reproducible (page 134) to create good questions that personalize learning.

1. Copy the Generating Good Questions for Expertise reproducible on page 134.

2. Identify the learning objective or target that will be addressed and assessed as part of the unit or lesson being taught.

3. On the reproducible, write the statement or objective starting with the cognitive action verb in the column labeled *Learning Objective or Instructional Statement*. With learning targets, remove the first-person introductory phrase (for example, "I can" or "We will").

4. Choose one of the following good question stems.

   ⌑ How do you . . . ? (assessment)

   ⌑ How can you . . . ? (instruction)

   ⌑ How could you . . . ? (inquiry)

5. Write the chosen question stem in the column labeled *Good Question Stem ("You")* next to the statement of objective.

6. To pose a good question that promotes expertise, do the following.

   ⌑ Write the learning objective or instructional statement in the column labeled *Learning Objective or Instructional Statement*.

⛛ Choose a good driving question stem from Table 5.1 (page 122) that states the creative action students must perform or the product students must produce.

⛛ Write the chosen question stem in the column labeled *Good Question Stem ("You")* next to the learning objective or instructional statement.

7. To pose a good question that prompts students to express their emotions, do the following:

⛛ Write the subject, skill, or situation students will study in the column labeled *Learning Objective or Instructional Statement*.

⛛ Choose a good affective question stem from Table 5.2 (page 125) or from the levels of the Affective Questioning Inverted Pyramid in Figure 5.2 (page 126) that prompt students to consider and convey their attitude, beliefs, or feelings.

⛛ Write the chosen question stem in the column labeled *Good Question Stem ("You")* next to the learning objective or instructional statement.

8. To pose a good question that promotes social-emotional learning, do the following.

⛛ Share the scenario or situation you want students to examine or explore in the column labeled *Learning Objective or Instructional Statement*.

⛛ Choose one of the SEL question stems that addresses one of the CASEL five core competencies.

⛛ Write the chosen question stem in the column labeled *Good Question Stem ("You")* next to the imperative statement of objective.

9. Review and rewrite the good question you created.

10. Pose the good question to the class. Be sure to use the pronoun referent *you* to initiate the inquiry and inspire further questioning and conversation.

Generating Good Questions for Expertise

Good Question Stem ("You")	Learning Objective or Instructional Statement

Chapter 6

HOW CAN GOOD QUESTIONS AND INQUIRY ADDRESS AND ASSESS UNDERSTANDING?

Without questions, there is no learning.

—W. Edwards Deming

Reflect and Respond

What does the Deming quote infer or suggest about the impact of questions on teaching and learning? How can good questions set the instructional focus and serve as assessments for student learning? What do you feel is the meaning and measure of true learning—the ability to answer correctly, explain how the answer was obtained, or justify whether the answer is accurate, acceptable, or appropriate?

THE PREVIOUS CHAPTER explored how to create good questions that personalize learning and promote expertise by using question stems that feature the pronoun referent *you*. This chapter discusses how to create good questions that are both subject specific and standards based. It explains how these good questions can set the instructional focus and serve as the assessment for inquiry experiences that prompt students to develop and demonstrate their understanding of concepts and content.

What Distinguishes Good Questions for Understanding?

Good questions for understanding are standards based and subject specific. They address and assess how or why a specific subject or skill can be understood and used to do the following.

- Answer questions correctly
- Address problems successfully
- Accomplish tasks accurately
- Analyze the ideas and information presented in texts or pertaining to topics (Francis, 2016, 2022)

The following criteria for good questions guide students down the Inquiry Pathway to Understanding.

- Analytical questions that challenge students to apply knowledge, concepts, or skills, or use information and basic reasoning to establish and explain how answers can be attained.
- Evaluative questions that engage students to think strategically or use complex reasoning supported by evidence to examine and explain causes, connections, consequences, reasoning, relationships, or results.

Table 6.1 features the different types of question stems teachers and students can use to phrase and pose analytical and evaluative questions for understanding. Notice that they ask and address both *how* and *why*. Most good questions for understanding feature these question stems because that's what they require students to do—establish or examine and explain *how* or *why*. However, what distinguishes both questions is the depth and extent to which they require students to reflect and respond *how* or *why*.

Analytical questions prompt students to apply knowledge, concepts, and skills or use information and basic reasoning to establish and explain answers with examples, which designates them as DOK 2. Evaluative questions are DOK 3 because they engage students to think strategically or use complex reasoning to examine and explain answers with evidence.

Analytical Question Stems

- How can ... ?
- How could ... ?
- How is/are ... ?
- How does/do ... ?
- How has/have ... ?
- Why is/are ... ?
- Why does/do ... ?
- Why can ... ?
- Why could ... ?
- Why has/have ... ?
- What is an example ... ?
- What categorizes ... ?
- What characterizes ... ?
- What classifies ... ?
- What determines ... ?
- What distinguishes ... ?
- What establishes ... ?
- What indicates ... ?

- What are the similarities ... ?
- What are the differences ... ?
- What are the similarities and differences ... ?
- How are ... similar?
- How are ... different?
- How can ... be determined?
- What is the diagnosis ... ?
- What are the circumstances ... ?
- What is the issue ... ?
- What is the problem ... ?
- What is the process ... ?
- What is the function ... ?
- What is the way ... ?

- What role ... ?
- What responsibility ... ?
- What is the basis ... ?
- What is the intent ... ?
- What is the purpose ... ?
- What causes ... ?
- What is the idea ... ?
- What is the lesson ... ?
- What is the meaning ... ?
- What is the message ... ?
- What is the reason ... ?
- What does ... imply?
- What does ... infer?
- What does ... involve?
- What does ... suggest?
- What does ... signify?
- What does ... symbolize?

Evaluative Question Stems

- How was/were ... ?
- How did ... ?
- How had ... ?
- Why could ... ?
- Why was/were ... ?
- Why did ... ?
- Why had ... ?
- What is the evidence ... ?
- What proof ... ?
- What is the reasoning ... ?
- What is the cause and effect ... ?
- What is the connection ... ?
- What is the consequence ... ?

- What is the importance ... ?
- What is the relevance ... ?
- What is the significance ... ?
- What is the value ... ?
- What is the worth ... ?
- What is the outcome ... ?
- What is the result ... ?
- What is the solution ... ?
- What is the pattern ... ?
- What is the relationship?
- What is the tendency ... ?
- What is the trend ... ?
- How accurate ... ?
- How acceptable ... ?
- How appropriate ... ?
- How authentic ... ?
- How credible ... ?
- How convincing ... ?

- How dependable is ... ?
- How effective is ... ?
- How rational is ... ?
- How reliable is ... ?
- How sound is ... ?
- How valid is ... ?
- How viable is ... ?
- What are the advantages or disadvantages ... ?
- What are the benefits ... ?
- What are the drawbacks ... ?
- What are the chances ... ?
- What is the likelihood ... ?
- What are the odds ... ?
- What is the possibility ... ?
- What is the potential ... ?
- What is the probability ... ?
- What is the prospect ... ?
- What is the risk ... ?

What Forms of Inquiry Address and Assess Understanding?

Inquiry for understanding is both instructional and inquisitive. The focus and purpose of the inquiry is to:

- Teach students to learn how to engage in inquiry
- Engage students to learn about a subject through inquiry

To address and assess student understanding, students could be engaged in the following forms of inquiry.

- *Confirmation or controlled inquiry*, in which the teacher dictates expectations and the extent of the experience from start to finish.
- *Structured inquiry*, in which students seek answers; defend, disprove, or draw conclusions; and use data and examples or evidence to support their responses, results, or reasoning.
- *Guided inquiry*, in which the teacher initiates the inquiry and provides guidance and support throughout the experience.
- *Open or free inquiry*, in which the teacher initiates the inquiry experience and students complete it individually and independently.
- *Coupled inquiry*, which combines aspects of guided and open or free inquiry to tier the experience based on students' successes and struggles.

Inquiry for understanding teaches students how to approach learning with an inquiring mind. They learn the essential skills needed to engage in inquiry competently and how to demonstrate proficiency in a specific subject through inquiry and questioning. Teaching and learning with an inquiring mind are student centered, standards based, and subject specific.

How Are Good Questions for Understanding Standards Based?

Good questions for understanding are derived directly from the learning intentions of academic standards and curricular units. However, unlike the good questions that personalize inquiry, these prompt students to establish or examine and explain how subject-specific concepts or procedures could be understood or used. That's why they don't feature the pronoun referent *you*. The subject of the question is the specific text, topic, theory, or technique being taught, not the student.

Table 6.2 (page 140) shows the difference between good questions for expertise that are posed for instruction and good questions for understanding that set the instructional focus and serve as the assessments for standards-based inquiry.

The key difference between good questions for expertise and good questions for understanding is the *purpose* of the question. Good questions for expertise prompt students to consider or demonstrate how and why they personally could understand and use concepts and procedures in depth, insightfully, or in their own unique way.

The pronoun *you* emphasizes personal thinking, individual talent, self-knowledge, and self-awareness. Good questions for understanding target the specific text, topic, technique, or theory being taught. This makes the inquiry experienced instructional rather than personal. The teacher asks these questions to address and assess conceptual and procedural understanding.

Which Academic Standards Should Inquiry for Understanding Address and Assess?

Inquiry for understanding should address and assess academic standards that feature the essential knowledge and skills students need to know to demonstrate proficiency in a certain course or develop competency in a specific subject. Douglas Reeves call these the "power standards" or "priority standards" that "give a student the ability to use the reasoning and thinking skills to learn and understand other curriculum objectives" (as cited in Ainsworth, 2003, pp. 5–6).

To determine whether to address and assess a specific standard as a priority through inquiry and questioning, educators need to check whether it meets the R.E.A.L. criteria developed by Ainsworth (2013) and translated by Thomas W. Many and Ted Horrell (2014):

- **Readiness:** Does the standard provide students with knowledge and skills that will be necessary for success in the next class, course, or grade level?

Table 6.2: Distinguishing Good Questions for Expertise and Understanding

Subject	Learning Intention	Good Questions for Expertise	Good Questions for Understanding
Mathematics	*Solve* with fluency one- and two-step problems involving multiplication and division, including interpreting remainders. (TEKS.MATH.4.2[G])	How could you *solve* with fluency one- and two-step problems involving multiplication and division, including interpreting remainders?	How could one- and two-step problems involving multiplication and division *be solved?* How could remainders *be interpreted?*
English Language Arts	*Determine* the meaning of words and phrases as they are used in a text, including figurative and connotative meanings. (CCRS. ELA-LIT.RI.8.4)	How can you *determine* the meaning of words and phrases as they are used in a text, including figurative and connotative meanings?	How can the figurative meaning of words and phrases as they are used in a text *be determined?* How can the connotative meanings of words and phrases as they are used in a text *be determined?*
Science	*Analyze* and *interpret* data on natural hazards to forecast future catastrophic events and inform the development of technologies to mitigate their effects. (NGSS-MS-ESS3–2)	How could you *analyze* and *interpret* data on natural hazards to forecast future catastrophic events and inform the development of technologies to mitigate their effects?	How could data on natural hazards *be analyzed* and *interpreted* to forecast future catastrophic events and inform the development of technologies to mitigate their effects?
Civics	*Apply* civic virtues and democratic principles in school and community settings. (C4.D2.Civ.7–6–8)	How could you *apply* civic virtues and democratic principles in school and community settings?	How could civic virtues and democratic principles *be applied* in school and community settings?
Economics	*Use* benefits and costs to evaluate the effectiveness of government policies to improve market outcomes. (C4.D2.Eco.8.9–12)	How can you *use* benefits and costs to evaluate the effectiveness of government policies to improve market outcomes?	How can benefits and costs *be used* to evaluate the effectiveness of government policies to improve market outcomes?

	Standard		
Geography	Construct maps and other graphic representations of both familiar and unfamiliar places. (C4.D2.Geo.1.3–5)	How could you construct maps and other graphic representations of both familiar and unfamiliar places?	How could maps and other graphic representations of both familiar and unfamiliar places be constructed?
History	Use other historical sources to infer a plausible maker, date, place of origin, and intended audience for historical sources where this information is not easily identified. (C4.D2.His.11.6–8)	How can you use other historical sources to infer a plausible maker, date, place of origin, and intended audience for historical sources where this information is not easily identified?	How can other historical sources be used to infer a plausible maker, date, place of origin, and intended audience for historical sources where this information is not easily identified?
World Languages	Use the target language to acquire goods, services or information orally and in writing. (AERO.COMM.1.1.G6.)	How can you use the target language to acquire goods, services, or information orally and in writing?	How can the target language be used orally and in writing to acquire goods, services, or information?
Art	Combine ideas to generate an innovative idea for artmaking. (NCAS.VA.CR1.1.6a)	How can you combine ideas to generate an innovative idea for artmaking?	How can ideas be combined to generate an innovative idea for artmaking?
Music	Improvise rhythmic and melodic patterns and musical ideas for a specific purpose. (NCAS.MU:Cr1.1.2a)	How can you improvise rhythmic and melodic patterns and musical ideas for a specific purpose?	How can rhythmic and melodic patterns and musical ideas be improvised for a specific purpose?
Physical Education and Health	Dribble with dominant hand using a change of speed and direction in a variety of practice tasks. (S1.M8.6)	How can you dribble with your dominant hand using a change of speed and direction in a variety of practice tasks?	How can a ball be dribbled with the dominant hand using a change of speed and direction in a variety of practice tasks?

Source for standards: *American Education Reaches Out, 2018; National Center for History in the Schools, 1996; National Core Arts Standards State Education Agency Directors of Arts Education, 2014; National Council for the Social Studies, 2013; NGA & CCSSO, 2010b; NGSS Lead States, 2013; SHAPE America, 2013; Texas Education Agency, 2014.*

- **Endurance:** Does the standard provide students with knowledge and skills that will be applicable and useful beyond a single assignment, lesson, or unit of study?
- **Assessment:** Will the knowledge and skills addressed in the standard be assessed on a standardized or end-of-course summative assessment?
- **Leverage:** Does the standard provide students with knowledge and skills that will be of value in multiple disciplines?

If the standard meets these criteria, rephrase its learning intention and individual objectives into good questions that will set the instructional focus and serve as the assessment for inquiry for understanding.

How Can Academic Standards Be Rephrased as Good Questions for Understanding?

As with good questions that promote expertise, the imperative statements of a standard's learning intention and individual objectives should be rephrased as good questions that prompt inquiry for understanding. However, these good questions should not feature the pronoun referent *you*. The focus of good questions for understanding is the subject being studied, not the student. The subject of the interrogative statement is the noun or noun phrase that names the specific text, topic, technique, or theory being taught. The following is the simplest way to rephrase a standard's learning intention and objectives into good questions for understanding.

1. **Rephrase the standard's learning intention or individual objective into a good question that personalizes learning:** Decide whether to place the question stems "How do you . . . ?," "How can you . . . ?," or "How could you . . . ?" before the statement of objective. If it's a learning target, replace the introductory first-person phrase (for example, "I can" or "We will") with one of the personalized question stems.

2. **Remove the pronoun *you* from the question stem:** This transforms the question stem into an analytical one that asks, "How do . . . ?,"

"How can . . . ?," or "How could . . . ?" It also shifts the subject of the question from the student to the specific text, topic, theory, or technique being taught. The instructional focus of the good question is for students to examine and explain how the subject or skill studied could be understood and used, not how they personally understand or use it.

3. **Move the cognitive action verb after the question stem, rephrase it in the past tense, and pair it with the verb *be*:** The intent and purpose of the cognitive action verb shifts from indicating the type and level of thinking students must demonstrate to informing the specific cognitive action or process students must perform.

Look at the good questions in table 6.2 (page 140). These questions are still standards based because they're derived from the learning intention of the standard being addressed and assessed. However, removing *you* as the pronoun referent shifts the instructional focus of the question from the student to the subject, skill, or situation. The cognitive action verb is expressed or written in past tense and placed after the question stem.

How Can the Cognitive Action Verb Indicate Which Good Question Stem to Use?

Some question stems have a direct correlation with certain cognitive action verbs. These question stems prompt students to demonstrate a specific type of thinking. For example, the question stems "What are the similarities and differences . . . ?" and "What distinguishes . . . ?" prompt students to compare, contrast, or both. Table 6.3 (page 144) features the correlating question stems that will prompt students to demonstrate a specific type or level of thinking. Another way to determine which question stem will prompt students to demonstrate a specific type and level of thinking is to use Bloom's Questioning Inverted Pyramid (see figure 3.2, page 71) or the Three-Story Inquiry House of Question Stems (see figure 3.3, page 72).

Check the level where the cognitive action verb is categorized in either of these visuals first. Then, choose the question stem that will prompt students to demonstrate that specific type and level of thinking.

Table 6.3: Cognitive Action Verbs With Correlating Good Question Stems

Cognitive Action Verb	Correlating Good Question Stem
Appraise Assess Consider Gauge Judge Measure Review	How many? How much? What effect? What extent? What impact? What influence? What is the importance? What is the relevance? What is the significance? What is the value? What is the worth? To what extent? How accurate? How acceptable? How appropriate? How authentic? How effective? How important? How relevant? How significant? How valuable? How worthy?
Associate Connect Relate	What is the affiliation? What is the association? What is the connection? What is the context? What is the correlation? What is the link? What is the relation? What is the relationship?
Calculate Estimate	How many? How much? What is the amount? What is the estimate? What is the cost? What is the price?
Categorize Characterize Classify	What categorizes? What characterizes? What classifies? What designates? What differentiates? What distinguishes? What discriminates? What indicates? What marks? What separates? What signifies? What specifies?
Compare Contrast Compare and contrast Differentiate Distinguish	What are the similarities? What are the differences? What are the similarities and differences? What differentiates? What are the discrepancies? What discriminates? What dissimilarities? What distinctions? What distinguishes? What indicates? What marks? What separates?
Decide Determine Establish Reveal	What causes? What is the cause and effect? What decides? Who decides? What determines? Who determines? What effect? What establishes? What impact? What impression? What influence? What is an example? What is the reason?
Define Describe	Who? What? Where? When? How? Why?
Clarify Convey Explain Illuminate Illustrate Inform Interpret Translate	Who? What? Where? When? How? Why? What is the aim? What is the goal? What are the circumstances? What are the conditions? What indicates? What is the intent? What is the intention? What does it insinuate? What does it mean? What is the meaning? What is the motive? What is the objective? What is the point? What is the purpose? What is the relevance? What is the significance? What suggests? What does it suggest? What are the ways?
Identify Label Mark	Who? What? Where? When? How? Why? What categorizes? What characterizes? What classifies? What discriminates? What distinguishes? What marks? What separates?
Conclude Imply Indicate Infer Insinuate Speculate Suggest	What determines? What implies? What indicates? What does it imply? What does it infer? What does it insinuate? What is the intention? What is the meaning? What is the purpose? What is the reason? What is the reasoning? What signifies? What suggests? What is the conclusion? What is the assumption? What is the presumption? What is the opinion? What is the perception? What is the speculation?
Justify Prove Validate Verify	What confirms? What is the evidence? What indicates? What is the proof? What is the reasoning? What supports? What suggests? What validates? What verifies? How does it reinforce? How does it strengthen? How does it substantiate? How does it support?
Estimate Forecast Predict	What if? What could happen? What would happen? What will happen? How could? How would? How may? How might? How will?

How Does the Auxiliary Verb Determine the Complexity and Demand of a Good Question?

Traditionally, the complexity and quality of a good question have been characterized and critiqued based on the question stem. For example, the question stems *who*, *what*, *where*, and *when* prompt students to demonstrate lower levels of thinking associated with remembering and understanding. They also generally demand students to recall information to answer correctly. Questions that ask students *how* or *why* are both preferable and promoted in teaching and learning because they prompt students to think deeply and provide in-depth responses.

However, it's not the stem alone that measures the cognitive rigor of a good question. It's the words and phrases that follow the question stem that specify how deeply students must address the question by establishing the extent of the response students must provide.

Consider the question stem *what*. Questions that ask *what* typically demand students recall information to answer correctly, designating them a DOK 1. However, question stems, such as "What categorizes?," "What distinguishes?," or "What indicates?" are DOK 2 because they demand students apply knowledge, concepts, and skills or use information and basic reasoning to explain answers with examples.

The question stems "What could?" or "What would?" prompt students to use complex reasoning to explain with evidence, making them DOK 3. The question stem "What else?" could require students to think strategically or extensively, making these questions DOK 3 or DOK 4, depending on the depth and extent to which student must address the question. Conversely, the question stems *how* and *why*—which are often regarded as the most thought-provoking questions—can only be designated as DOK 1 if the context of the question asks, "How did . . . ?" or "Why did . . . ?" or includes the stipulation "according to the source."

The auxiliary verb paired with a question stem also determines the cognitive demand—or DOK level—of the question. The following list explores the verbs *be*, *do*, *have*, *can*, *could*, *must*, *should*, and *will*.

- **The verb *be*:** The verb *be* states presence or provisions. Forms of these verbs include *am*, *is*, *are*, *was*, *were*, *being*, or *been*. These forms follow the question stem. In fact, many analytical and reflective question stems include these verb forms (for example, "What are the similarities or differences?," "What is the meaning?," "What is the effect?,"

"What is the purpose?"). The verb *be* itself is placed before the past tense of a cognitive action verb to specify the conditions or stipulations of the mental processing required (for example, *be understood*, *be used*, *be analyzed*, or *be evaluated*). The level of DOK demanded by good questions featuring these verb forms will vary depending on the tense of the verb and the context in which the question prompts students to understand and use their learning.

- **The verb *do*:** The verb *do* specifies performance or proceedings. The DOK level of the question featuring this auxiliary verb depends on verb tense. For example, questions that ask "How did . . . ?" or "Why did . . . ?" are DOK 1 because they require students to recall information or recall how something was done to answer correctly. Questions that ask "How do . . . ?" or "How does . . . ?" are DOK 2 because they challenge students to apply knowledge, concepts, and skills, or use information and basic reasoning, to establish and explain with examples. Questions that ask "Why do . . . ?" or "Why does . . . ?" could be DOK 2 or DOK 3 depending on the conditions and criteria of the inquiry the question requires students to engage in and experience. That's detailed by the words and phrases that complete the question.

- **The verb *have*:** The verb *have* shows possession or progress. The DOK level of a question featuring this auxiliary verb also depends on verb tense. For example, a good question that asks "How had . . . ?" or "Why had . . . ?" is DOK 1 because it requires students to answer correctly. A good question that asks "How has . . . ?" or "Why has . . . ?" is DOK 2 because it requires students to establish and explain with examples.

- **The verb *can*:** The verb *can* stipulates process, prowess, or possibility. A good question that asks "How can . . . ?" or "Why can . . . ?" is DOK 2 because it requires students to establish and explain answers with examples. The examples used to strengthen and support explanations are the items students must complete. They also can be the information presented in the text or pertaining to the topic being taught.

- **The verb *could*:** The verb *could* suggests prospect, potential, or probability. A good question that asks "How could . . . ?" or "Why could . . . ?" is DOK 3 because it engages students to examine and explain with evidence. It also implies or infers to students that there could be more than one idea or way to justify how an answer could be attained and explained. Other auxiliary verbs that suggest possibility are *shall, may,* and *might.*

- **The verb *must*:** The verb *must* stresses prerequisites. A good question that asks "How must . . . ?" or "Why must . . . ?" could be DOK 2 or DOK 3 depending on whether it requires students to respond with examples or evidence. Examples are the reasons that *explain* how or why. Evidence is the reasoning that *justifies* how or why. When pairing a question stem with the auxiliary verb *must,* consider whether students need to support their responses with examples and reasons or evidence and reasoning.

- **The verb *should*:** The verb *should* submits position or proposition. Like the verb *must,* the level of DOK required by a good question that asks "How should . . . ?" or "Why should . . . ?" depends on the response. If students are challenged to give their opinion supported with information and reasons, then it's DOK 2. If students construct an argument with specific claims and relevant evidence, then the question is DOK 4.

- **The verb *will*:** The verb *will* signifies prediction. A good question that asks "How will . . . ?" or "Why will . . . ?" could be DOK 3 or DOK 4 depending on whether it requires students to examine or explore and explain with examples and evidence. With these questions, the depth and extent of the response students provide depends on the conditions and criteria of the inquiry the question requires students to engage in and experience.

When deciding which auxiliary verb to choose and use with a question stem, determine the purpose of the question. Both the verb and the question stem determine the depth and extent to which the question requires students to perform a particular mental process or provide a precise response.

How Can a Good Question Be Embedded in a Learning Intention or Objective?

Some academic standards may feature the question stem that introduces the good question for understanding. Look at the learning intentions for the academic standards listed in table 6.4. Notice that they feature the question stem *how* or *why* within the standard's statement of objective. That's the question stem that introduces the good question for understanding derived from the standard. Once you identify the question stem, choose the auxiliary verb that defines and delineates the cognitive demand of the inquiry. Both the question stem and the auxiliary verb confirm the depth of the mental processing to be performed and the extent of the response to be provided.

Learning intentions and individual objectives of academic standards may feature keywords that are part of a question stem. Look at the learning intentions and individual objectives in table 6.5 (page 151). Notice how the boldfaced keyword is featured in the good question stem. The keyword also expects students to demonstrate the type and level of thinking indicated by the learning intention or objection from which it is derived. Again, the auxiliary verb paired with the question stem determines the level of DOK required.

How Can an Academic Standard Be "Flipped" to Find the Question?

Chapter 1 (page 13) established how an inquiring mind flips the question to fathom the answer. You can flip the learning intention and individual objectives of an academic standard to find the question to address and assess. To do this, follow these steps.

1. Rewrite the imperative statement of an objective into a declarative one that states the basic facts, core idea, or enduring understanding students must learn.

2. Choose an analytical or reflective question stem that prompts students to perform the cognitive action expected in the standard.

3. Rephrase the declarative statement into an analytical or reflective question that requires students to establish or examine and explain with examples or evidence.

Table 6.4: Using the Question Stem Within the Standard to Create Good Questions

Subject	Learning Intention	Good Questions for Understanding	DOK Skill (DOK Level)	DOK Response (DOK Level)
Mathematics	Explain why the sum or product of two rational numbers is rational; that the sum of a rational number and an irrational number is irrational; and that the product of a non-zero rational number and an irrational number is irrational. (MATH.CONTENT.N.RN.3)	Why *is* the sum or product of two rational numbers rational? Why *is* the sum of a rational number and an irrational number irrational? Why *is* the product of a non-zero rational number and an irrational number irrational?	Use complex reasoning supported by evidence. (DOK 3)	Examine and explain with evidence. (DOK 3)
English Language Arts	Describe how the author's use of figurative language, such as metaphor and personification, achieves specific purposes. (TEKS.ELAR.7.9[D])	How *does* the author's use of figurative language, such as metaphor and personification, achieve specific purposes?	Use information and basic reasoning. (DOK 2)	Establish and explain with examples. (DOK 2)
Science	Use argument supported by evidence for how the body is a system of interacting subsystems composed of groups of cells. (NGSS-MS-LS1-3)	How *is* the body a system of interacting subsystems composed of groups of cells?	Use complex reasoning supported by evidence. (DOK 3)	Examine and explain with evidence. (DOK 3)
Civics	Explain how rules and laws change society and how people change rules and laws. (C4. D2.Civ.12.3-5)	How *do* rules and laws change society? How *can* people change rules and laws?	Use complex reasoning supported by evidence. (DOK 3)	Establish and explain with examples. (DOK 2)
Economics	Explain how economic decisions affect the well-being of individuals, businesses, and society. (C4.D2.Eco.1.6-8)	How *could* economic decisions affect the well-being of the following? · Individuals · Businesses · Society	Use complex reasoning supported by evidence. (DOK 3)	Examine and explain with evidence. (DOK 3)
Geography	Explain why environmental characteristics vary among different world regions. (C4.D2.Geo10.3-5)	Why *do* environmental characteristics vary among different world regions?	Use complex reasoning supported by evidence. (DOK 3)	Examine and explain with evidence. (DOK 3)

continued →

Subject	Learning Intention	Good Questions for Understanding	DOK Skill (DOK Level)	DOK Response (DOK Level)
History	Explain how the French Revolution developed from constitutional monarchy to democratic despotism to the Napoleonic empire. (UCLA.WHE.7.Std1-A.7-12)	How *did* the French Revolution develop from constitutional monarchy to democratic despotism to the Napoleonic empire?	Recall information. (DOK 1)	Answer correctly. (DOK 1)
World Languages	Identify and describe *how* products reflect the lifestyle of people in various communities. (AERO.CULTURE.2.2.G6)	How *do* products reflect the lifestyle of people in various communities?	Apply knowledge, concepts, and skills. (DOK 2)	Establish and explain with examples. (DOK 2)
Art	Explain why some objects, artifacts, and artwork are valued over others. (NCAS.VA:Pr4.1.1a)	Why *are* some objects, artifacts, and artwork valued over others?	Use complex reasoning supported by evidence. (DOK 2)	Examine and explain with evidence. (DOK 3)
Music	Explain how context (such as social, cultural, and historical) informs performances. (NCAS.MU:Pr4.2.5c)	How *do* the following contexts inform performances? • Social • Cultural • Historical	Use information and basic reasoning. (DOK 2)	Establish and explain with examples. (DOK 2)
Physical Education and Health	Define how the RPE scale can be used to determine the perception of the work effort or intensity of exercise. (S4.M14.7)	How *can* the RPE scale be used to determine the following? • The perception of the work effort • The intensity of exercise	Use information and basic reasoning. (DOK 2)	Establish and explain with examples. (DOK 2)

Source for standards: American Education Reaches Out, 2018; National Center for History in the Schools, 1996; National Core Arts Standards State Education Agency Directors of Arts Education, 2014; National Council for the Social Studies, 2013; NGA & CCSSO, 2010c; NGSS Lead States, 2013; SHAPE America, 2013; Texas Education Agency, 2019.

Table 6.5: Finding Good Question Stem Keywords Featured in Academic Standards

Subject	Learning Intention	Good Questions for Understanding	DOK Skill (DOK Level)	DOK Response (DOK Level)
Mathematics	Understand **the relationship** between numbers and quantities. (CCRS.MATH.K.CC.4)	**What is the relationship** between numbers and quantities?	Apply knowledge, concepts, and skills. (DOK 2)	Establish and explain with examples. (DOK 2)
English Language Arts	Analyze **the impact** of a specific word choice on meaning and tone. (CCRS.ELA-LITERACY.RI.7.4)	**What impact** does a specific word choice have on meaning and tone?	Use complex reasoning supported by evidence. (DOK 3)	Examine and explain with evidence. (DOK 3)
Science	Construct a scientific explanation based on evidence for **the role of** photosynthesis in the cycling of matter and flow of energy into and out of organisms. (NGSS-MS-LS1-6)	**What is the role** of photosynthesis in the cycling of matter and flow of energy into and out of organisms?	Use information and basic reasoning. (DOK 2)	Establish and explain with examples. (DOK 2)
Civics	**Distinguish** the powers and responsibilities of citizens, political parties, interest groups, and the media in a variety of governmental and nongovernmental contexts. (C4.D2.Civ.1.6–8)	**What distinguishes** the powers and responsibilities of the following in a variety of governmental and nongovernmental contexts? · Citizens · Political parties · Interest groups · Media	Use information and basic reasoning. (DOK 2)	Establish and explain with examples. (DOK 2)
Economics	Describe **the consequences** of competition in specific markets. (C4.D2.Eco.5.9–12)	**What are the consequences** of competition in specific markets?	Use complex reasoning supported by evidence. (DOK 3)	Examine and explain with evidence. (DOK 3)

continued →

Subject	Learning Intention	Good Questions for Understanding	DOK Skill (DOK Level)	DOK Response (DOK Level)
Geography	Analyze the effects of catastrophic environmental and technological events on human settlements and migration. (C4. D2.Geo.9.3–5)	What are the effects of catastrophic environmental and technological events on human settlements and migration?	Use complex reasoning supported by evidence. (DOK 3)	Examine and explain with evidence. (DOK 3)
History	Assess ways in which the exchange of plants and animals around the world in the late 15th and the 16th centuries affected European, Asian, African, and American Indian societies and commerce. (UCLA:WHE61C.5–12)	What were the ways the exchange of plants and animals around the world in the late 15th and the 16th centuries affected the following societies and commerce? • European • Asian • African • American Indian	Use information and basic reasoning. (DOK 2)	Establish and explain with examples. (DOK 2)
Art	Compare and explain the difference between an evaluation of an artwork based on personal criteria and an evaluation of an artwork based on a set of established criteria. (NCAS. VA:Re9.1.7a)	What is the difference between an evaluation of an artwork based on personal criteria and an evaluation of an artwork based on a set of established criteria?	Apply knowledge, concepts, and skills. (DOK 2)	Establish and explain with examples. (DOK 2)
Music	Describe the rationale for making revisions to the music based on evaluation criteria and feedback from others. (NCAS.MU:Cr4.1.7b)	What is the rationale for revising the music based on evaluation criteria and feedback from others?	Use complex reasoning supported by evidence. (DOK 3)	Examine and explain with evidence. (DOK 3)
Physical Education and Health	Recognize the importance of warm-up and cool-down relative to vigorous physical activity. (S4.E4.3)	What is the importance of warm-up and cool-down relative to vigorous physical activity?	Use information and basic reasoning. (DOK 2)	Establish and explain with examples. (DOK 2)

Source for standards: American Education Reaches Out, 2018; National Center for History in the Schools, 1996; National Core Arts Standards State Education Agency Directors of Arts Education, 2014; National Council for the Social Studies, 2013; NGA & CCSSO, 2010b, 2010c; NGSS Lead States, 2013; SHAPE America, 2013.

Table 6.6 (page 154) shows how to flip the standard into a good analytical or evaluative question that addresses and assesses understanding. Notice how the imperative statement of objective becomes a declarative one that states the basic facts, core idea, or enduring understanding about the specific subject, skill, or situation.

The good question stem not only addresses the type and level of thinking the standard requires students to demonstrate, but it also prompts students to comprehend, consider, or convey the depth and extent of their learning. With some standards, the question stem can deepen the level of DOK by requiring students to provide a more extensive or in-depth response.

Summary

Good questions for understanding are standards based and subject specific. Unlike good questions for expertise that personalize learning and promote expertise, these good questions address and assess the specific text, topic, theory, or technique being taught. Examples are analytical and evaluative questions that prompt students to explain their understanding with examples or evidence.

The question stem prompts students to demonstrate the type and level of thinking the standard's learning intention and individual objectives expect students to demonstrate. However, the depth and extent of students' responses depends on the auxiliary verb paired with the question stem and the context in which the question must be addressed and assessed. There are numerous ways to rephrase the learning intention and individual objectives of academic standards into good questions that address and assess understanding:

- Remove the pronoun referent *you* from the good question for expertise.

- Look for the question stem or keywords embedded within the standard's learning intention and individual objectives.

- Replace the cognitive action verb with a question stem categorized at the correlating level of thinking from Bloom's Questioning Inverted Pyramid (see figure 3.2, page 71) or the Three-Story Inquiry House of Question Stems (see figure 3.3, page 72).

- Rephrase the imperative statement of objective into a declarative one that states the basic facts, core ideas, and enduring understanding students must learn and then rephrase that statement into a good question.

Table 6.6: Flipping the Standard to Find the Question

Subject	Learning Intention	Basic Facts, Core Ideas, Enduring Understanding	Good Question Stem	Good Questions for Understanding
Mathematics	Generate equivalent numerical expressions using order of operations, including whole number exponents, and prime factorization. (TEKS.6.MATH.6.7[A])	Equivalent numerical expressions can be generated using order of operations, including whole number exponents, and prime factorization.	How?	How can numerical expressions be generated using the following? • Order of operations • Whole number exponents • Prime factorization
English Language Arts	Analyze the structure an author uses to organize a text, including how the major sections contribute to the whole and to the development of the ideas. (CCRS.ELA-LIT.RI.7.5)	An author uses structure to organize a text. The major sections of a text contribute to the whole and to the development of ideas.	How?	How does an author use structure to organize a text? How do the major sections of a text contribute to the whole and to the development of ideas?
Science	Analyze and interpret data to determine scale properties of objects in the solar system. (NGSS-MS-ESS1–3)	Data could be analyzed and interpreted to determine scale properties of objects in the solar system.	How?	How could data be analyzed and interpreted to determine scale properties of objects in the solar system?
Civics	Analyze the impact of constitutions, laws, treaties, and international agreements on the maintenance of national and international order. (C4.D2.Civ.4.9–12)	Constitutions, laws, treaties, and international agreements have an impact on national and international order.	What impact?	What impact do constitutions, laws, treaties, and international agreements on the maintenance of national and international order?
Economics	Explain the roles of buyers and sellers in product, labor, and financial markets. (C4.D2.Eco.4.6–8)	Buyers and sellers have roles in product, labor, and financial markets.	What roles?	What roles do buyers and sellers have in product, labor, and financial markets?
Geography	Evaluate the influences of long-term, human-induced environmental change on spatial patterns of conflict and cooperation. (C3 D2.Geo.9.6–8)	Long-term, human-induced environmental change has influenced spatial patterns of conflict and cooperation.	What influence?	What influence has long-term, human-induced environmental change had on spatial patterns of conflict and cooperation?

	Standard	Understanding Statement	Question Type	Question
History	Analyze how the Seven Years' War, Enlightenment thought, the American Revolution, and growing internal economic crisis affected social and political conditions in Old Regime France. (UCLA.WHE7.1A.7–12)	The Seven Years' War, Enlightenment thought, the American Revolution, and growing internal economic crisis affected social and political conditions in Old Regime France.	What effect?	What effect did the following have on the social and political conditions in Old Regime France? • The Seven Years' War • Enlightenment thought • American Revolution • Growing internal economic crisis
Art	Interpret art by analyzing artmaking approaches, the characteristics of form and structure, relevant contextual information, subject matter, and use of media to identify ideas and mood conveyed. (NCAS.VA:Re8.1.7a)	Art could be interpreted by analyzing artmaking approaches, the characteristics of form and structure, relevant contextual information, subject matter, and use of media to identify ideas and mood conveyed.	How could?	How could art be interpreted by analyzing the following to identify ideas and mood conveyed? • Artmaking approaches • Characteristics of form and structure • Relevant contextual information • Subject matter • Use of media
Music	Identify how cultural and historical context inform performances and result in different music interpretations. (NCAS.MU:Pr4.2.7c)	Cultural and historical context inform performances and result in different music interpretations.	How?	How do cultural and historical context inform performances and result in different music interpretations?
Physical Education and Health	Uses a variety of shots (for example, line drive, high arc) to hit the ball into open space. (S2.M10.7)	The ball can be hit into open space using a variety of shots, including the following: • Line drive • High arc • Fly ball • Grand slam	How could?	How could the ball be hit into open space using the following shots? • Line drive • High arc • Fly ball • Grand slam

Source for standards: American Education Reaches Out, 2018; National Center for History in the Schools, 1996; National Core Arts Standards State Education Agency Directors of Arts Education, 2014; National Council for the Social Studies, 2013; NGA & CCSSO, 2010b; NGSS Lead States, 2013; SHAPE America, 2013; Texas Education Agency, 2019.

Application: How Can Standards Be Rephrased Into Good Questions for Understanding?

Either individually or with your team, rephrase the learning intention and individual objectives of academic standards into good questions that address and assess understanding.

1. Copy the Rephrasing Academic Standards Into Good Questions for Understanding reproducible on page 158.

2. Choose one of the following processes to rephrase the learning intention of an academic standard into a good question for understanding that focuses on the subject studied.

    ¤ Rephrase the standard's learning intention or individual objective into a good question that personalizes learning. Remove the pronoun *you* from the question stem. Move the cognitive action verb after the question stem, rephrase it in the past tense, and pair it with the verb *be*. Choose the auxiliary verb that will determine the depth and extent of the response students must provide. Place a question mark at the end of the interrogative statement.

    ¤ Identify the question stem featured within the academic standard's learning intention or individual objective (for example, *who, what, where, when, how,* or *why*). Choose the auxiliary verb to pair with it that will demand students to provide a particular DOK response. Determine whether you need to remove or rephrase the cognitive action verb in the past tense and relocate it after the question stem.

    ¤ Identify the question stem keyword featured in the academic standard's learning intention or individual objective. Replace the cognitive action verb that introduces the academic standard with the question stem featuring the keyword. Choose the auxiliary verb to pair with it that requires students to provide a particular DOK response. Place a question mark at the end of the interrogative statement.

    ¤ Check table 6.3 (page 144) to determine whether the cognitive action verb in the academic standard correlates to a specific question stem. Replace the cognitive action verb with the correlating good question stem. Place a question mark at the end of the interrogative statement.

◻ Check where the cognitive action verb is listed in Bloom's Revised Taxonomy or Costa's Levels of Questioning. Choose a question stem from Bloom's Questioning Inverted Pyramid (see figure 3.2, page 71) or the Three-Story Inquiry House of Question Stems (see figure 3.3, page 72) that addresses the type and level of thinking required by the standard's learning intention or objective. Rephrase the imperative statement of objective into an analytical or reflective question with the chosen question stem. Decide which auxiliary verb to pair with the question stem.

◻ "Flip the standard" by rephrasing the imperative statement of objective into a declarative one that states the basic facts, core idea, or enduring understanding about the subject, skill, or situation. Choose the question stem that will prompt students to demonstrate the type and level of thinking required by the standard's learning intention or target. Choose the auxiliary verb to pair with the question that will prompt students to provide a particular DOK response.

Rephrasing Academic Standards Into Good Questions for Understanding

Learning Intention/Good Question for Understanding	Basic Facts Core Ideas Enduring Understanding	Good Question Stem	Good Question to Address and Assess Understanding

Chapter 7

HOW DO STUDENTS' GOOD QUESTIONS FOSTER AND FURTHER FOUNDATIONAL INQUIRY?

If you don't understand, ask questions.
If you're uncomfortable about asking
questions, say you are uncomfortable about
asking questions and then ask anyway.

—Chimamanda Ngozi Adichie

Reflect and Respond

Do students ask questions to acquire or assess knowledge? What if teachers encouraged students to ask questions to help them acquire the foundational knowledge and functional understanding they need to succeed? How could educators assess the depth of students' knowledge and understanding based on their questions instead of their answers? How could educators use those questions to engage students in foundational inquiry?

PREVIOUS CHAPTERS EXPLORED how to rephrase the learning intentions and individual objectives of academic standards into good questions that address or assess understanding and expand or extend expertise. This chapter discusses how students can use their own questions to build their foundational knowledge and functional understanding of subjects, skills, and stipulations addressed in academic standards.

What Is the Focus of Foundational Inquiry?

Foundational inquiry focuses on students acquiring the fundamental knowledge and functional understanding they need not only to achieve a standard but also succeed in a specific academic area, discipline, or subject. The expectation is for students to do the following:

- Recognize and summarize "just the facts" about the text or topic being read or reviewed.

- Reproduce or apply knowledge, concepts, and procedures by showing and sharing how to "just do it."

Table 7.1 lists the *kinds of academic knowledge* students must develop and demonstrate, including vocabulary, factual, conceptual, procedural, strategic, and conditional or contextual. These kinds of knowledge are categorized in the Knowledge Dimension of Bloom's Revised Taxonomy (Anderson & Krathwohl, 2001). Table 7.1 features good question stems that address and assess different *types of knowledge* categorized within each kind of academic knowledge. Anderson and Krathwohl (2001) describe these *types of knowledge* as "domain specific and contextualized" (p. 41), meaning these categories and subcategories focus on the specifics of a subject area and how one can understand and use them in different contexts.

Table 7.1: The Knowledge Dimension of Bloom's Revised Taxonomy

Kinds of Academic Knowledge	Types of Knowledge	Good Question Stems
Vocabulary Knowledge	Basic or common words, general academic words, literary words, labels, names, symbols, and terminology	What? What does it mean? What is the definition? What is the meaning? What is it called?
Factual Knowledge	Data, specific details, essentials, facts, and information	Who? What? Where? When? How? Why? (according to the source or text)
Conceptual Knowledge	Categories and classifications; principles and generalizations; models, structures, and theories	What? How? Why?
Procedural Knowledge	Subject-specific skills and algorithms; subject-specific methods, strategies, and techniques; criteria for determining when to use appropriate procedures	How can? How does? How do? What is the method? What is the process? What is the strategy? What is the technique? When can? When does? When must?

Strategic Knowledge	Learning processes, methods, strategies, and techniques	What? How? How do? How does? How can? How could? How would? How may? How might?
Conditional or Contextual Knowledge	When and which learning processes, methods, strategies, or techniques to use	What? Where? When? Which? Which one(s)? How? How could? How would? How should? When can? When could? When would? When should? Where can? Where could? Where would? Where should?

Source: Adapted from Anderson & Krathwohl, 2001.

How Is Foundational Inquiry Teacher Led and Student Driven?

Foundational inquiry is traditionally teacher led and instructional. The forms of inquiry students engage in are either controlled or structured. The teacher decides and dictates the expectations and extent of the inquiry. The success of the inquiry is based on:

- The accuracy of students' answers
- The acceptability of students' examples or evidence
- The authenticity of students' claims or conclusions
- The appropriateness of students' responses, results, or reasoning

Foundational teaching and learning with an inquiring mind are a coupled inquiry experience. The teacher selects the subject students will study and shares the following as the QFocus for inquiry.

- A learning intention, objective, or target that addresses and assesses the academic standard students must achieve to demonstrate proficiency or perform successfully
- A stimulus that exemplifies and expands on the core ideas and enduring understandings addressed in the academic standard and associated with the subject

The teacher presents the prompt by asking the following questions.

- What are the words, terms, or details you don't know or understand in the standard and stimulus?

- How could you express and share what you don't know or understand as a question?

The goal is for students to learn—or *relearn*—how to develop and demonstrate their knowledge and understanding through questioning. The expectation is that students will communicate exactly what they don't know or understand about the standard, stimulus, or subject in the form of a question. Students *will* be expected to develop and demonstrate foundational knowledge and functional understanding by addressing their own questions. This makes foundational inquiry not only standards based and subject specific, but also student driven. The time and thinking needed for students to develop their foundational knowledge and functional understanding depends on the amount and complexity of the questions students ask.

How Does Foundational Inquiry Stimulate Students to Acquire Subject Knowledge?

Academic standards and accompanying stimuli provide the data and details—or subject knowledge—students must learn about a text, topic, or technique. This is the background knowledge and basic understanding students must learn to become familiar with a subject. Consider the details featured in this academic standard and accompanying stimulus on World War II: "Assess how the political and diplomatic leadership of such individuals as Churchill, Roosevelt, Hitler, Mussolini, and Stalin affected the outcome of the war" (UCLA.WHE.4B.5–12; National Center for History in the Schools, 1996).

This academic standard features the names of the individuals whose leadership the students will assess. To achieve this standard successfully, students must answer the following questions.

- Who were these leaders?
- When did they lead?
- Which nation did they lead?
- How did they become the leaders of their nation?
- What was their political leadership style?
- What was their diplomatic leadership style?

These are the general good questions that students must ask and address so they can acquire the data and details they need to achieve the demands and expectations of the standard. They use the knowledge and understanding they acquire as examples and evidence to strengthen and support their response to this standard.

How Does Foundational Inquiry Strengthen and Support Language Development?

Foundational inquiry builds foundational knowledge and functional understanding as well as strengthens and supports language development. Students learn to comprehend the specifics of subject matter as well as communicate fluently, maturely, and properly when discussing texts, topics, or techniques.

Look back at the history standard for World War II. It features the facts students must know and understand. Students must know the definition of the general vocabulary words (for example, *assess, individuals, affect, outcome*) and comprehend the meaning of subject-specific terms (for example, *political leadership, diplomatic leadership, war*) stated in the standard. Foundational inquiry engages students to ask and address questions about words and terms they may not recognize or understand.

You can categorize the complexity of the vocabulary in foundational inquiry into the three different tiers, identified by Isabel Beck, Margaret McKeown, and Linda Kucan (2013):

- **Tier 1:** These are high-frequency words used in casual or everyday conversations in a target language. Examples of tier 1 words are basic or sight words, such as *book, chair, dog, girl, happy, look, run, swimming, warm,* and *yellow.* These words do not have multiple meanings. They are defined through identification (for example, "That's a picture of a chair") or as a description (for example, "They are running" or "I feel warm"). That's why these words rarely require direct instruction for meaning. However, these words are taught explicitly to develop basic literacy or language fluency in a target language, such as in second-language courses in which the tier 1 word is accompanied by a visual for identification and pronunciation.

- **Tier 2:** These are high-utility words featured and used in different academic disciplines, literary fiction and nonfiction texts, formal communications, or professional conversations. Examples of tier 2 words are the cognitive action or Bloom's verbs featured in learning objectives (for example, *analyze, evaluate, clarify, exemplify, interpret,* *assess*) and abstract descriptors featured in literary texts and works of fiction and nonfiction (for example, *obvious, situational, auspicious, frequently, industrious, benevolent*). These words and phrases "are characteristic of written text and are found only infrequently in conversation" (Beck, McKeown, and Kucan, 2013, p. 9). They also have abstract, broad, or multiple meanings. However, high-utility words are essential to learn to develop and demonstrate literacy and language comprehension and competency. These words should be taught in context so students can use context clues to determine meaning (DOK 2) or analyze the impact of specific word choice (DOK 3).

- **Tier 3:** These are low-frequency words that are specific to an academic or vocational area, domain, field, or subject. Examples of tier 3 words include *algorithm, democracy, filibuster, metaphor, octave, photosynthesis, ratio, shading,* and *theme.* These words and terms are essential to know and understand the content, concepts, and procedures of a specific subject. They should be integrated and used in teacher instruction and student communication about the specific subject being taught and learned.

The words and terms featured in academic standards are tier 2 and tier 3 words. Examples of tier 2 words in academic standards are the cognitive action (or Bloom's) verbs that introduce statements of objectives. Tier 3 words are the subject-specific terminology that names the specific kind of knowledge being studied.

Consider the following mathematics standard: "Fluently multiply multi-digit numbers using a standard algorithm" (MATH.NYS.5.NBT.1; New York State Department of Education, 2019). Note that the learning intention of the academic standard features both tier 2 words (*fluently, multi, digit, standard*) and tier 3 terms (*multiply, multidigit whole numbers, standard algorithm*) students must know and understand.

The image in figure 7.1 serves as the stimulus that supplements and supports the standard. It showcases the tier 3 subject-specific terms students should learn to develop and deepen their understanding of the concept (*multiplicand, multiplier, factors, product*). These are the words and terms students must understand and use when demonstrating and discussing their learning.

Good questions that assess and build vocabulary knowledge are primarily factual ones that ask *"What . . . ?"* However, the form of the *what* question depends on the vocabulary word's part of speech.

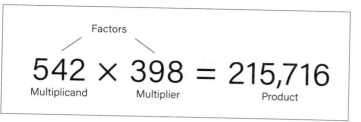

FIGURE 7.1: Parts of a multiplication problem with multidigit numbers.

Table 7.2 features the question stems and starters for words, phrases, and terms based on their part of speech (for example, nouns, verbs, adjectives, adverbs). Give this list to students to help them come up with and create questions about the words, phrases, and terms featured in the academic standard and accompanying QFocus.

Table 7.2: Good Question Starters for Vocabulary Knowledge Based on Parts of Speech

Noun	Verb
• Who is or are . . . ?	• What does it mean to . . . ?
• Who was or were . . . ?	• What does . . . mean?
• What is or are . . . ?	• What does it mean to . . . in mathematics?
• What was or were . . . ?	• What does it mean to . . . in literature?
• What is or are . . . ?	• What does it mean to . . . in science?
• When is or are . . . ?	• What does it mean to . . . in civics?
• When was or were . . . ?	• What does it mean to . . . in economics?
• Where is or are . . . ?	• What does it mean to . . . in geography?
• Where are or were . . . ?	• What does it mean to . . . in art?
• Who is an example of a . . . or an . . . ?	• What does it mean to . . . in music?
• What is an example of a . . . or an . . . ?	• What does it mean to . . . in (subject)?
Adjective	**Adverb**
• What does . . . mean?	• What does . . . mean?
• What does it mean to be . . . ?	• What does it mean to do something . . . ?
• What does it mean to look . . . ?	• What does it mean to be . . . ?
• What does it mean to act/behave . . . ?	• What does it mean to look . . . ?
• What does it mean to appear . . . ?	• What does it mean to act/behave . . . ?
• What does it mean to seem . . . ?	• What does it mean to appear . . . ?
• What does it mean to sound . . . ?	• What does it mean to sound . . . ?
• What does it mean to feel . . . ?	• What does it mean to feel . . . ?
• What does it mean if someone is . . . ?	• What does it mean if someone is . . . ?
• What does it mean if something is . . . ?	• What does it mean if something is . . . ?
• What does it mean when someone is . . . ?	• What does it mean when someone is . . . ?
• What does it mean when something is . . . ?	• What does it mean when something is . . . ?
• What time is it if someone is . . . ?	• What time is it if someone is . . . ?
• What time is it when something is . . . ?	• What time is it when something is . . . ?

continued →

Preposition	
• What does it mean to go . . . ? • What does it mean to be . . . ? • What does mean to be something . . . ? • What does mean to be somewhere . . . ? • Which direction or way is . . . ? • What does it mean when someone or something is (prepositional phrase)?	

Learning these tiered words in context and through inquiry and questioning will not only build students' foundational knowledge and functional understanding about the subject. It also strengthens and supports students' literacy and language skills as these words and terms become part of their vocabulary and personal speech.

How Does Foundational Inquiry Strengthen Reading Retention and Comprehension?

Foundational inquiry stimulates students to read closely to retain and comprehend the essential information and ideas presented in texts. It promotes active reading by prompting students to ask questions about the content and craft of the text. Educators can elicit and encourage questions from students by prompting them to consider and convey the following as they read and review the text.

- What are the literary words you don't know or recognize?
- What are the details or phrases you don't understand?

You can teach students how to employ research-based reading comprehension methods or study skills that utilize questioning for retention and comprehension. For example:

- **Scan-Question-Read-Recite-Review (SQ3R):** This process, developed by Francis P. Robinson (1946), is a reading comprehension method that stimulates students to comprehend, consider, and convey the key details and ideas presented in a text. In this method, students pose questions about an assigned text after they scan or survey it with a quick read-through. After they generate their questions, students read the text actively and closely to respond to both their questions and the standards-based question that addresses and assesses their understanding.

- **Preview-Question-Read-Summary-Test (PQRST):** This method was researched and developed by Ellen Lamar Thomas and H. Alan Robinson (1972) and George D. Spache and Paul Berg (1978). It is both a reading methodology and a study skills strategy. It follows the same sequence as the SQ3R method. However, students use their questions to check and confirm their understanding continuously in preparation for an assessment.

- **Preview-Question-Read-Reflect-Recite-Review (PQ4R):** This method, developed by Ellen Lamar Thomas and H. Alan Robinson (1972), extends both the SQ3R and PQRST methods by prompting students to reflect on both their questions about the text as well as their responses.

- **KWL Charts:** KWL Charts, designed by Donna Ogle (1986), organize foundational learning into three columns: What I Know (K), What I Want to Know (W), and What I Learned (L). Students can pose questions about the text or topic under the W column of the chart. Students can express what they know and learned as questions to help them organize their thoughts or quiz themselves later. Author and literacy specialist Katherine McKnight (2019) recommends adding a fourth column—What Does It Mean?—that prompts students to pose analytical and reflections questions that synthesize their comprehension of the key details and ideas in the text and the meanings of words, phrases, and terms used in the text.

- **T-Charts:** The T-Chart, developed by McKnight (2019), organizes knowledge and understanding into two columns: What Did I Learn? and What Am I Thinking? By answering these questions, students express their knowledge and understanding while also expressing themselves in the form of good questions that guide their reading and help them retain and review the key details and ideas in the text.

- **Cornell Note-Taking System:** This note-taking system, developed by Walter Pauk (with Ross J. Q. Owens, 2011), strengthens comprehension and retention by engaging students to write questions in the margins of a text or their notebook next to the details and information presented on a particular page or the notes they have summarized and transcribed in their notebook. McKnight (2019) emphasizes that students pose good questions they can draw on and use to develop and demonstrate both literal and abstract comprehension. These good questions challenge students to summarize key details and ideas, which would designate these and their responses DOK 2.

- **Annotation:** Annotation engages students to pose their own questions about the text or topic being read or reviewed. Students highlight the key details, ideas, words, or phrases they do not know or understand and write their questions in the margin next to the highlighted segment. Students can use these questions to develop comprehension or as references for retaining and reviewing details or ideas presented in the text.

Each of these methods utilizes questioning as part of the process for retaining and comprehending textual information. The expectation is that students will use their questions to develop their knowledge and understanding of content and craft of the text as well as to guide their reading.

What Does Planning for Foundational Inquiry Involve?

Foundational inquiry should be student centered and student driven. The questions fostering and furthering inquiry should come from the students and reflect what they need to know and understand to achieve the standard or succeed in the subject. Planning for foundational inquiry involves:

- Selecting a standard that students must achieve
- Sharing a stimulus that will stimulate students' thinking
- Singling out the words, terms, and details students must know and understand

Both the academic standard and accompanying stimulus serve as the QFocus for the foundational inquiry. The academic standard features:

- The general academic vocabulary or literary words students must define
- The subject-specific terminology students must describe
- The data and details students must explain

The stimulus should be an audio, print, or visual text that exemplifies and expands on the core ideas and enduring understandings addressed in the standard. Consider the following stimulus that exemplifies and expands on the standard on cells:

Develop and use a model to describe the function of a cell as a whole and ways the parts of cells contribute to the function. [Emphasis is on the cell functioning as a whole system and the primary role of identified parts of the cell, specifically the nucleus, chloroplasts, mitochondria, cell membrane, and cell wall.] (NGSS-MS-LS1–1; NGSS Lead States, 2013)

Notice that the learning intention of the academic standard and its emphasis statement features general academic words (for example, *to develop, to use, function, to contribute, system, primary, identified*) as well as subject-specific terms (for example, *model, cell, nucleus, chloroplasts, mitochondria, cell membrane, cell wall*) students must define and describe. It also includes specific details (for example, *the function of a cell as a whole, how parts of cells contribute to the function, the primary role of identified parts of the cell*) students must explain. These words, terms, and phrases should serve as the subject for the good questions that will foster and further foundational inquiry.

Figure 7.2 (page 170) shows two cells, one animal and one plant, that serve as the stimulus. It labels and locates the key parts of each cell that are essential to learn, according to the standard. This is the background knowledge and basic understanding students must acquire to achieve the standard and become familiar with the subject. Other parts of the cell that are important to understand and "nice to know" are not essential to learn; however, they expand students' knowledge about other parts of a cell. They also extend students' understanding or awareness of how they contribute to the cell's function. All the names of these parts should serve as the subject for foundational inquiry questions focusing on subject-specific terminology. The data and detail questions could ask students to explain the function of these parts.

Once you have selected the standard and stimulus, identify and isolate the words, terms, and details featured in both. Check the curricular text for any keywords, terms, or details that are not stated in the standard but are essential to know or understand. These words, terms, and details will serve as the subject for the questions that assess and build foundational knowledge and functional understanding of the subject.

When composing foundational questions and choosing the subject, presume students know and understand absolutely nothing presented in the standard and stimulus or pertaining to the subject. Take the approach and attitude that this may be the first time students have seen the academic words, subject-specific terms, and data and details shared, shown, or stated.

Don't be concerned if you find yourself coming up with numerous questions. Of all the pathways to inquiry in the Inquiring Minds Framework, students are asked to address the most questions along the Foundational Pathway to Inquiry.

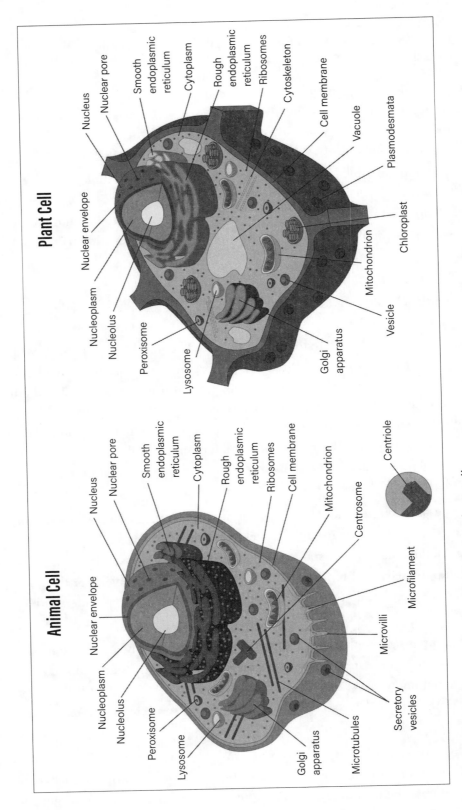

FIGURE 7.2: Parts of an animal cell and a plant cell.

Keep in mind the purpose of foundational inquiry—to assess and build foundational knowledge and functional understanding. Some subjects may involve knowing and understanding a lot of concepts, content, procedures, and vocabulary.

What Is the Process for Foundational Inquiry?

Initiate foundational inquiry by posting the academic standard and presenting the accompanying stimulus to students. Do not make the standard or stimulus text student friendly by replacing the advanced or complex vocabulary or verbiage with synonymous, yet simpler words. Ask questions about those complex words, phrases, and terms so students can develop and deepen their literacy and language skills. Also, read the complex words, phrases, and terms aloud to students so they can hear and learn how to pronounce them accurately.

Do not share the foundational questions students need to address—at least, not yet. Instead, prompt students to reflect, "What are the words, terms, and details you don't know or understand? How could you express this as a question?" Use the QFT or Rapid-Fire Questioning to engage students in this experience. Either technique will help students create their own questions for foundational inquiry.

How you elicit and encourage questions from students depends on their grade level, reading ability, and language competency. For example, consider the following.

- *With students who know how to comprehend text and communicate in the target language*, present the academic standard and accompanying stimulus and ask, "What are the words, terms, and details you do not understand? How could you express this as a question?" Students go through the QFT or Rapid-Fire Questioning process of writing down their questions, which should feature the words, terms, or details they do not know or understand. Some students may pose questions that delve deeper into the subject or go beyond the standard. Do not dissuade students from posing these questions. In fact, encourage them by saying their question is good enough for the whole class to address, or it could serve as a good personal question they want to address.

- *With students who are learning to read in the target language*, present a printed form of the statement of objective and pull out the keywords, terms, and details students must know and understand. For example, isolate the cognitive action verbs in a statement of objective and provide a definition that students can understand. That's when the communication should be student friendly. Provide students with the opportunity to define, describe, or explain in their own words; offer examples; or use the words in their own communication.

- *With second language learners who are learning to comprehend and communicate in the target language,* present the words, terms, and details both in context, in printed form, and in isolation in their base form (for example, *to use* instead of *use* or *using*). Ask students to identify and pronounce the words, terms, and details they do not understand, and guide them to use those words, terms, or details in an interrogative statement. This extends the foundational inquiry to focus on both knowledge and language acquisition. Use a combination of direct instruction and guided practice to support students in pronouncing and using the words, terms, or details accurately and fluently in a question and a response.

After students come up with their questions, ask them to share with the class. Inform them that their questions will set the instructional focus for the foundational inquiry to help them feel invested in learning about the subject. This lets them know they have a voice in the instructional planning and learning process and learn how to advocate for themselves and their learning through inquiry and questioning.

It may feel awkward for students to share their questions initially—especially older students in the upper grade levels for whom questioning might have become uncomfortable and even embarrassing. That's why you should build a culture of respect and trust in the classroom and among students. Instill in students that questioning reflects a need or want to learn, not a lack of knowledge or understanding. Assure and ensure that all questions are regarded and responded to respectfully by everyone in the class.

One way to ease students into this experience is by pairing or organizing them into small groups in which they share their questions with each other. The goal is for students to recognize that they may have the same questions. Also challenge and encourage students to answer any of their classmates' questions. For example, if one student asks, "What is multiplication?" or "Who is Winston Churchill?," another student may be able to answer the question. Having students learn from each other promotes collaborative inquiry and learning. After students meet and confer about their questions, bring them together to share their questions and answers. This allows students to realize they may have the same questions. Their responses provide them with the opportunity to learn from each other while allowing you the opportunity to check for understanding and inform future instruction.

Once you have students' questions, plan the foundational inquiry. Combine your questions with students' questions to create a bank of questions to address. Make sure to eliminate any questions students were able to answer.

How Does the Inquiry Grid Organize Good Questions for Foundational Inquiry?

Inquiry Grids as a concept are introduced in figure 2.4 (page 53) and featured at the end of chapter 4 (page 91). Here, you can use them to organize foundational questions into the following three categories.

1. **Academic vocabulary:** This column lists the foundational questions featuring the tier 2 general academic and literary words students must define.

2. **Subject-specific terminology:** This column lists the foundational questions featuring the tier 3 terminology students must describe.

3. **Data and details:** This column lists the questions that ask and address the facts, figures, ideas, and information students must explain.

Figure 7.3 (page 174) shows a completed Inquiry Grid for multiplying multidigit whole numbers. The questions in these columns come from both the teacher and students. Completing this grid allows the foundational inquiry to be a collaborative process. The bottom row of the grid informs how students must respond to each categorized foundational question:

- Define academic vocabulary.
- Describe subject-specific terminology.
- Explain data and details.

The Inquiry Grid also can include questions that require students to delve deeper into the subject or go beyond the standard. For example, in figure 7.4 (page 175), note how some questions in the Explain Data and Details column ask about Emperor Hirohito, who was not one of the leaders listed in the standard. However, he did play an important role in World War II, and his impact and influence should be assessed. The questions also analyze the political and diplomatic leadership style of each leader, which is essential for students to know and understand so they can address the standard proficiently and its good question successfully.

Subject	Perform Operations With Multidigit Whole Numbers
Standard (QFocus)	Fluently multiply multi-digit numbers using a standard algorithm. (MATH.NYS.5.NBT.1)
Prompt (Good Questions)	• How can multidigit whole numbers be multiplied fluently using a standard algorithm? (DOK 2) • How could you multiply multidigit numbers fluently using a standard algorithm? (DOK 3)
Socratic (Discussion)	Is there only one way to "do the mathematics," or could arithmetic problems be solved using multiple methods? Has the way to do mathematics changed, or has how the ways we teach and learn mathematics changed? How many ways could multidigit numbers be multiplied? Which algorithm do you prefer using, and why?
Stimulus (QFocus)	Factors $542 \times 398 = 215{,}716$ Multiplicand Multiplier Product

Define Academic Vocabulary	Describe Subject-Specific Terminology	Explain Data and Details
• What does it mean to perform? • What is an operation? • What does fluently mean? • What does multi mean? • What is a digit? • What is a standard?	• What is an operation in mathematics? • What is multiplication? • What does it mean to multiply? • What is grouping? • What is repeated addition? • What is a factor? • What is the multiplicand? • What is the multiplier? • What is the product? • What is a digit in mathematics? • What is a multidigit whole number? • What is an algorithm?	• What is an example of a multidigit number? • What are the standard algorithms for multiplying multidigit numbers? • What are the values of the digits in the multidigit whole numbers in the stimulus problem? • Which factor is the number that will be multiplied? • Which factor informs how many times the number will be multiplied? • What does the featured multiplication problem mean? • What would happen if the positions of the numbers were flipped or reversed?

Source for standard: New York State Department of Education, 2019.

FIGURE 7.3: Inquiry Grid for multiplying multidigit whole numbers.

Subject	World War II
Standard (QFocus)	Assess how the political and diplomatic leadership of such individuals as Churchill, Roosevelt, Hitler, Mussolini, and Stalin affected the outcome of the war. (UCLA.WHE.4B.5–12)
Prompt (Good Questions)	How did the political and diplomatic leadership of the following individuals affect the outcome of the war? (DOK 3) • Winston Churchill • Franklin D. Roosevelt • Adolf Hitler • Benito Mussolini • Josef Stalin • Emperor Hirohito
Socratic (Discussion)	What makes a leader "great"? What are the measures of great leadership? What are the skills a "great" leader should possess? What are the lasting impact and influences a leader could have or make? How could a leader have a positive or negative impact or influence? What makes a leader "bad"? What distinguishes a "bad" leader from "poor" leadership? How could a leader be "bad" but have a "great" impact or influence? Is the mark and measure of a "great" leader based on what they do while they serve in the position, or what happens after they leave or step down? How could a leader possess strong skills but still be a "bad" leader?
Stimulus (QFocus)	(Show photos of Winston Churchill, Franklin D. Roosevelt, Adolph Hitler, Benito Mussolini, Josef Stalin, and Emperor Hirohito.)

Define Academic Vocabulary	Describe Subject-Specific Terminology	Explain Data and Details
• What does it mean to assess? • What is leadership? • What is an individual? • What does it mean to affect? • What is an outcome? • What is an ally? • What is appeasement?	• What does political mean? • What is political leadership? • What does diplomatic mean? • What is diplomacy? • What is diplomatic leadership? • What is a war? • What is a total war?	• When was World War II? • What caused World War II? • What was the outcome of World War II? • How was World War II a total war? • Who were the Axis Powers? • Who were the Allied Powers? • Who were the "big three" of the Allied Powers? • Who was Winston Churchill?

FIGURE 7.4: Inquiry Grid for World War II.

continued →

Define Academic Vocabulary	Describe Subject-Specific Terminology	Explain Data and Details
		• Who was Franklin D. Roosevelt?
		• Who was Adolf Hitler?
		• Who was Benito Mussolini?
		• Who was Josef Stalin?
		• Who was Emperor Hirohito?
		• What was Winston Churchill's leadership style?
		• What was Franklin D. Roosevelt's leadership style?
		• What was Adolf Hitler's leadership style?
		• What was Benito Mussolini's leadership style?
		• What was Josef Stalin's leadership style?
		• What was Emperor Hirohito's leadership style?

Source for standard: National Center for History in the Schools, 1996.

You can also use the Inquiry Grid to expand on the questions asked in each column. Look at the subject-specific terminology and data and detail questions in the Inquiry Grid in figure 7.5. Note how the data and details questions expand on the subject-specific terminology questions by asking for examples of specific organisms and cells, the function of a particular part of a cell, the similarities and differences between cells and its parts, and the *how* and *why* about the function and structure of cells.

Students can use the Inquiry Grid to record their questions as they read fiction and nonfiction texts. Figure 7.6 (page 179) shows an Inquiry Grid a student may complete as they read, reflect, and respond to Emily Dickinson's poem "I Like to See It Lap the Miles (a.k.a. The Railway Train)."

Subject	From Molecules to Organisms: Structures and Processes
Standard (QFocus)	Develop and use a model to describe the function of a cell as a whole and ways the parts of cells contribute to the function. [Clarification Statement: Emphasis is on the cell functioning as a whole system and the primary role of identified parts of the cell, specifically the nucleus, chloroplasts, mitochondria, cell membrane, and cell wall.] (NGSS-MS1-LS-1)
Prompt (Good Questions)	• How does a cell function? (DOK 2) • What are the ways the parts of the cell contribute to its function? (DOK 2) • How could you develop and use a model to describe the function of a cell as a whole and ways the parts of cells contribute to the function? (DOK 3)
Socratic (Discussion)	What is life? What do all living things have in common? What are the basic functions of living things? What is the difference between a scientific law and a scientific theory? How can a scientific theory become a scientific law? Why is the concept of cells a theory? What would it take for cell theory to become a scientific law?
Stimulus (QFocus)	

Define Academic Vocabulary	Describe Subject-Specific Terminology	Explain Data and Details
• What does it mean *to develop*? • What does it mean *to use*? • What does *function* mean? • What is an *apparatus*? • What does *uni* mean? • What does *multi* mean?	• What is an *organism*? • What is a *cell*? • What is a *eukaryotic cell*? • What is a *eukaryote*? • What is a *prokaryotic cell*? • What is a *prokaryote*? • What does *unicellular* mean? • What does *multicellular* mean? • What is a *unicellular organism*? • What is a *multicellular organism*? • What is the *nucleus*? • What is the *cytoplasm*? • What are the *chloroplasts*?	• What is an example of an organism? • What is an example of a cell? • What is an example of a eukaryotic cellular organism? • What is an example of a prokaryotic cellular organism? • What distinguishes eukaryotic cells from prokaryotic cells? • What is an example of a unicellular organism? • How does a unicellular organism function? • What is an example of a multicellular organism?

FIGURE 7.5: Inquiry Grid for animal and plant cells.

continued →

Define Academic Vocabulary	Describe Subject-Specific Terminology	Explain Data and Details

	• What are *mitochondria*?
	• What is the *cell membrane*?
	• What is *plasma*?
	• What is the *cell wall*?
	• What is an *organelle*?
	• What are *vacuoles*?
	• What are *vesicles*?
	• What are *centrioles*?
	• What are *centrosomes*?
	• What are *lysosomes*?
	• What are *ribosomes*?
	• What is the *nucleolus*?
	• What is the *nuclear membrane*?
	• What is the *cell membrane*?
	• What is the *cytoskeleton*?
	• What is the *endoplasmic reticulum*?
	• What is the *Golgi apparatus*?
	• What is the *druse crystal*?
	• What is the *raphide crystal*?
	• What is the *amyloplast*?
		• How could eukaryotes be unicellular or multicellular?
		• Why are prokaryotes only unicellular?
		• What are the differences between unicellular and multicellular organisms?
		• What are the similarities and differences between plant and animal cells?
		• How do the following contribute to the function of a cell?
		  ¤ The nucleus
		  ¤ Chloroplasts (in plant cells)
		  ¤ Mitochondria
		  ¤ Cell membrane
		  ¤ Cell wall
		• What distinguishes the cell membrane in animal and plant cells?
		• What is the difference between the druse and raphide crystals in plant cells?
		• Why don't animal cells have chloroplasts but plant cells do?
		• Why don't plant cells have centrosomes and lysosomes but animal cells do?
		• How are the function of lysosomes in animal cells and vacuoles in plants similar?

Source for standard: NGSS Lead States, 2013.

In the first column, students list the tier 2 literary words from the poem that they may not recognize or know. In the middle column, the teacher lists tier 3 terms students must know to address the standard proficiently and its good question successfully. In the third column, both the teacher and students list questions they have about the data and details in the poem.

Subject	Figurative Language in Poetry: Emily Dickinson
Standards (QFocus)	• Describe how the author's use of figurative language such as metaphor and personification achieves specific purposes. (TEKS.ELA.6.9[E]) • Compose literary texts such as personal narratives, fiction, and poetry using genre characteristics and craft. (TEKS.ELA.6.11[A])
Prompt (Good Questions)	• How does an author's use of figurative language achieve specific purposes? (DOK 3) • How does Emily Dickinson use figurative language to depict the train as a giant, powerful, living, horse-like creature? (DOK 2) • How does Emily Dickinson's use of figurative language support the poem's central idea or theme of the advancement, power, and wonder of technology? (DOK 3) • How could you compose a narrative poem that attributes humanlike or animallike qualities, characteristics, or behaviors to inanimate objects (for example, a car, home, or toy), intangible concepts (for example, love, fear, anger, or progress), or natural events or phenomena (for example, thunderstorms, earthquakes, or waves in the ocean)? (DOK 4)
Socratic (Discussion)	How can technology be amazing and unsettling? What are the benefits and costs of technological progress? How can technology have animallike or humanlike behaviors, characteristics, qualities, or traits? Do you prefer stories, songs, poems, or dramas that state the meaning concretely and explicitly or infer ideas abstractly and subtly?
Stimulus (QFocus)	"I Like to See It Lap the Miles" (a.k.a. "The Railway Train") by Emily Dickinson I like to see it lap the miles, And lick the valleys up. And stop to feed itself at tanks; And then—prodigious, step Around a pile of mountains, And, supercilious, peer In shanties by the sides of roads And then a quarry pare To fit its sides, and crawl between, Complaining all the while In horrid, hooting stanza; Then chase itself down hill And neigh like Boanerges; Then, punctual as a star, Stop—docile and omnipotent— At its own stable door.

Define Academic Vocabulary	Describe Subject-Specific Terminology	Explain Data and Details
(Students write the tier 2 words they do not know or recognize in the poem here.)	(The teacher writes the tier 3 terminology students must understand to address the standard and answer the question successfully.)	(The teacher writes the questions that ask students about the key details and ideas and craft and structure. The students write their questions about the details they do not understand in the poem.)

Source for standards: Texas Education Agency, 2019.

FIGURE 7.6: Inquiry Grid for figurative language in Emily Dickinson's poem.

The Inquiry Grid serves as a tool for planning instruction and as a resource students can use to categorize their foundational inquiry questions. After presenting the prompt or sharing the stimulus, students write their questions in the appropriate columns. This personalizes the Inquiry Grid for individual students because it features the questions they have about the prompt or stimulus. Educators can use it as another curricular tool to teach and learn through inquiry and questioning.

Summary

In the Foundational Pathway to Inquiry, students will ask and address the most questions. The number of questions, however, depends on both the demand of the standards and the needs of students. Some standards require students to acquire or possess a significant amount of knowledge and understanding. Plus, some students may lack the background knowledge and basic understanding they need to achieve the standard or succeed in the subject at a certain grade level or at the specific DOK level required. That's why both teachers and students should never be concerned about the number of foundational questions asked—be it too little or too many.

These questions not only represent the foundational knowledge and functional understanding they need to achieve the standard. They also reflect the depth and extent of the background knowledge and basic understanding students either already possess or need to succeed in the subject.

Application: How Can You Plan and Provide Foundational Inquiry Using Students' Questions?

Either individually or with your team, plan a foundational, inquiry-based experience that addresses both your and your students' questions.

1. Copy the Foundational Inquiry Grid on page 182.

2. Write the name of the subject or skill being studied in the row labeled *Subject*.

3. Choose the learning intention or individual objective from an academic standard that will be addressed and assessed. Write the statement of objective in the row labeled *Standard*.

4. Rephrase the learning intention of the standard into a good question that prompts inquiry for understanding or a good question that promotes inquiry for expertise.

5. Choose or create an audio, print, or visual stimulus that exemplifies, elaborates, or expands on the subject addressed in the standard.

6. Come up with good questions that prompt and promote Socratic inquiry.

7. Read and review the standard and stimulus to identify and isolate the following.

   ¤ What are the general academic words students must be able to define?

   ¤ What subject-specific terms must students be able to describe?

   ¤ What are the key data and details students must be able to explain?

8. Create good questions that feature these identified and isolated words, terms, and details as the subject.

9. Write the foundational questions you composed in the appropriate column of the Foundational Inquiry Grid. However, don't share the questions with students—yet!

10. Initiate the inquiry by sharing the standard and showing the stimulus. Ask students, "What are the words, terms, and details you do not understand? How could you express this as a question?"

11. Give students time to reflect on and respond to the standard and stimulus with their questions.

12. Pair or group students to share their questions with each other. Encourage them to share their responses to any of the questions shared.

13. Bring the class together to share the questions posed and any answers provided.

14. Write students' questions on the board, or have students write their questions on paper to display around the room.

15. Add students' questions in their designated columns on the Foundational Inquiry Grid.

16. Distribute a copy of the Foundational Inquiry Grid to students. Have them address the foundational questions that they and their classmates asked.

Foundational Inquiry Grid

Subject	
Standard (QFocus)	
Prompt (Good Question)	
Socratic (Discussion)	
Stimulus (QFocus)	

Define Academic Vocabulary	Describe Subject-Specific Terminology	Explain Data and Details

Chapter 8

HOW COULD INQUIRY AND QUESTIONING DEEPEN TEACHING AND LEARNING?

Questions are creative acts of intelligence.
—Francis (Frank) Kingdon-Ward

Reflect and Respond

How is questioning a creative act of intelligence for both students and educators? What does it mean to engage in deep inquiry and questioning? What determines the depth of inquiry—the cognitive complexity and demand of the question, or the depth and extent to which students must address and answer the question? How could educators share their proficiency in and passion for the subject they teach through deep inquiry? How could technology enhance deep inquiry for students and educators?

N THE PREVIOUS chapters, you learned how to develop and pose good questions that ask about the subjects and skills addressed by academic standards. This chapter explores how to create good questions to engage students in deep inquiry experiences that expand on the subjects studied and extend beyond the standards.

What Distinguishes Deep Inquiry and Questioning?

Deep inquiry enables and encourages students to do the following.

- Expand their knowledge and extend their thinking about a text, topic, or process.

- Delve deeper into the subject or skills addressed by the standards.

- Go beyond the expectations and stipulations set by the standards and curriculum.

- Investigate what's important or interesting about the subject studied.

These are the inquiry expectations that expand students' knowledge and thinking. The goal of deep inquiry and questioning is for students to develop the following.

- Deeper awareness (knowledge) of the subject studied

- Deeper aptitude (skills) in a certain content area

- Deeper appreciation (feelings) of the text, topic, or technique being taught

- Deeper acumen (expertise) in a discipline or field of study

Figure 8.1 is the Deep Inquiry Grid, which features examples of good questions that encourage students to engage in a deep inquiry about fractions.

Standard	Apply and extend previous understandings of multiplication and division to multiply and divide fractions. (CCRS.MATH.CONTENT.5.NF.3–7)
Deep Inquiry	Why is it important to understand how to multiply and divide fractions?

How could understanding how to multiply and divide fractions be helpful in the following real-world situations?
- Telling time
- Splitting the bill or check at a restaurant
- Following a recipe to prepare a meal or a drink
- Cutting a pizza into slices so everyone can have at least one slice
- Shopping for groceries with coupons
- Determining the cost of an item that's on sale
- Measuring the distance a track athlete jumps or throws an object
- Analyzing the performance of a sports team or player
- Counting and exchanging money
- Filling the gas tank of a car and determining the total cost
- Calculating a grade on an assignment or test
- Evaluating progress
- Planning a party

Source for standard: NGA & CCSSO, 2010c.

FIGURE 8.1: Deep inquiry into fractions.

The first row specifies the standard—or in this case, cluster of standards—to be addressed and assessed. It enables teachers to address and assess multiple standards within a single deep inquiry experience. The second row features a good question that will hook 'em into deep inquiry. This question sets the focus and purpose for deep inquiry. However, it does not serve as an assessment. The subsequent questions are what students will inquire about and investigate through deep inquiry.

Educators could share a stimulus to start a deep inquiry experience and spark in-depth conversations about the subject. Figure 8.2 features a popular quote—shared widely on the internet—showing deep inquiry: "Another day has passed, and I still haven't used Pythagoras's theorem." This figure also outlines examples for students to understand and apply how the Pythagorean theorem fits into real-world contexts.

Standard	Understand and apply the Pythagorean theorem. (CCRS.MATH.CONTENT.8.G.6–8)
Deep Inquiry	"Another day has passed and I still haven't used Pythagoras's theorem." —Author Unknown

How could the Pythagorean theorem be applied in the following real-world contexts?
- Finding the distance between two locations on a map or global positioning system (GPS)
- Finding or surveying the steepness of the slopes of mountains or hills
- Calculating the length of staircase required to reach a window
- Painting a wall or side of a building or house
- Confirming the size of a TV or monitor
- Determining the length of the longest item that can be fit in a room
- Plotting a garden or landscaping a yard
- Determining the height of a fully grown or broken tree
- Calculating the steepness of mountains or hills
- Positioning a ladder on a fire truck to fight a fire
- Hitting a baseball
- Hitting and returning serves, shots, and strokes in tennis
- Kicking a soccer ball into a goal

How could the Pythagorean theorem be applied in the following vocations?

• Architecture	• Painting
• Construction	• Sports
• Interior and exterior design	• Firefighting
• Art	• Archeology
• Landscaping and land surveying	• Cartography and mapping
• Geography	• Navigation

Source for standard: NGA & CCSSO, 2010c.

FIGURE 8.2: Deep inquiry into understanding and applying the Pythagorean theorem.

To initiate deep inquiry, a mathematics teacher could hook 'em with the quote and encourage students to express their feelings and thoughts about what the quote infers and suggests. These discussions and questions would lead to a deep inquiry experience that enables students to do the following.

- Examine and explain with evidence how the Pythagorean theorem could be applied in real-world contexts.

- Explore and explain with examples and/or evidence how different disciplines and professions utilize the Pythagorean theorem.

Any good question could enhance and encourage deep inquiry for students. What distinguishes these questions are both the complexity of the content and context they address. They refer to the subject studied; however, they go beyond what the standard requires and the curriculum covers to stimulate deep inquiry.

What Does Planning a Deep Inquiry Experience Involve?

In planning a deep inquiry experience, draw on your intellectual character to determine the following questions.

- What does and doesn't the standard stipulate and the curricular program cover about the subject studied? (*Think critically.*)
- What do I know or understand about the subject studied, and why do I feel it is important or interesting for students to learn? (*Think reflectively.*)
- How could students discover what's important and interesting about the subject studied through deep inquiry and deeper questioning? (*Think creatively.*)

Figure 8.3 features the guiding questions that enable and encourage teachers to plan the deep inquiry students will engage in and experience. Each question addresses a specific dimension of thinking and augments a teacher's level of thinking and DOK of the text, topic, or technique.

Considering these questions will help you choose the appropriate pathway to inquiry for teaching and learning. For example, you could address and assess the power or priority standards deemed essential to learn as part of the Inquiry Pathway to Understanding or Expertise, depending on whether the focus of and purpose are for students to demonstrate proficiency or develop their expertise. The standards that address and assess ideas and information that are important to understand or nice to know could be inquired and investigated through deep inquiry.

Thinking Dimension	Thinking Dispositions and Intellectual Characteristics
Critical Thinking	• What do the standards specify and stipulate about the subject studied? (Attentiveness) • What is the content the curricular program provided to me, and what does it cover or offer? (Carefulness) • What is essential to learn, important to understand, and "nice to know" about the text, topic, or technique I am teaching? (Thoroughness)
Reflective Thinking	• What do I personally want students to learn about the subject or skill I am teaching? (Autonomy) • What is the depth and extent of my learning about the text, topic, or technique I am teaching? (Humility) • What don't I know or understand about the subject or can't I do with the skill? (Courage) • How deeply or extensively am I willing to expand my knowledge and extend my thinking about the subject or skill? (Tenacity) • Do I believe my students could learn what I need to teach them and should learn what I want to teach them? (Honesty)
Creative Thinking	• What else could or should be taught and learned about the text, topic, or technique? (Curiosity) • How else could the subject or skill be taught and learned? (Open-mindedness or fair-mindedness)

FIGURE 8.3: Tapping into educators' intellectual character to plan deep inquiry.

Which Forms of Inquiry Enable and Encourage Deep Inquiry and Questioning?

Deep inquiry and questioning enable and encourage students to engage in and experience the following forms of inquiry.

- Guided inquiry facilitated by the teacher and furthered by students
- Open or free inquiry that starts with the teacher and shifts to the students

- Coupled inquiry that fluctuates between being teacher led and student driven
- Authentic inquiry that addresses and appeals to students' interests
- Synergistic inquiry engaged in by both students and the teacher

The form of deep inquiry students engage in depends on the following.

- Who poses the question or shares the stimulus that initiates the inquiry experience
- Who provides the information, items, resources, or tools needed to engage in the inquiry experience
- Who asks the questions that determine and drive the depth and direction of the inquiry experience
- Who sets the procedures performed or decides the design produced through the inquiry experience

These guiding questions also determine the difficulty of the deep inquiry students could engage in and experience. For example, deep forms of inquiry that are more teacher led may be easier for students due to the amount of information and instructions provided to them. Deep forms of inquiry that are more student driven may be harder or more difficult for students who struggle to ask and address questions, acquire data and details, or apply resources and tools they need to succeed. The demands of the form of inquiry students engage in depends on the depth of reflection and extent of the response students must provide to address the prompt or analyze the stimulus that initiates the inquiry.

Which Good Questions Enable and Encourage Deep Inquiry and Questioning?

Any good question could initiate a deep inquiry experience—even factual questions that only require students to acquire or apply the knowledge to answer correctly. However, good questions should neither be easy nor simple to answer through basic recall or rote memorization. The questions that enable and encourage deep inquiry should require students to do the following.

- Reflect insightfully or introspectively before responding.

- Research a response, result, or reasoning in detail or in-depth.

Look at the good question in figure 8.4, which initiates the deep inquiry into the presidents appointed under the Articles of Confederation. It's a good factual question that only requires students to answer correctly. However, the answer is not obvious or even common knowledge. Students would have to research the response. Plus, the intent and purpose of the question is not to obtain an answer—at least, not immediately or initially. It's meant to initiate deep inquiry and inspire further questions.

Standard	Identify the issues that led to the creation of the U.S. Constitution, including the weaknesses of the Articles of Confederation. (TEKS.HIS. 5.3[A])
Deep Inquiry	Who were the Presidents of the United States before George Washington?

- Who were the eight Presidents of the United States in Congress Assembled appointed under the Articles of Confederation?
- When did these eight Presidents of the United States in Congress Assembled serve in this position?
- What distinguished the position and power of the presidency under the Articles of Confederation from the presidency under the U.S. Constitution?
- Why are these appointed presidents are not credited as Presidents of the United States?
- What impact or influence did these eight Presidents who were appointed under the Articles of Confederation have on United States' history and society?
- How did the U.S. Constitution address the weakness of the position of the presidency under the Articles of Confederation?
- What if the power and position of presidency remained or reverted to what it was under the Articles of Confederation?
- Should George Washington continue to be credited as the first President of the United States, or should the eight Presidents of the United States in Congress Assembled also be acknowledged?

Source for standard: Texas Education Agency, 2022.

FIGURE 8.4: Deep inquiry into the weaknesses of the Articles of Confederation.

What distinguishes good questions that enable and encourage deep inquiry is that they are interesting and introspective. Students should find the questions so captivating or sensational that they want to inquire and investigate them. Look at the good questions in figure 8.5 (page 190), which prompt and provoke a deep inquiry into analyzing and interpreting data on natural hazards.

Standard	Analyze and interpret data on natural hazards to forecast future catastrophic events and inform the development of technologies to mitigate their effects. (NGSS-MS-ESS2–2)
Deep Inquiry	Will "The Big One" earthquake destroy California?

- What is a "big" earthquake?
- What is "The Big One" earthquake?
- When was California struck by "big" earthquakes, and where were they?
- Why does California have earthquakes?
- What are the major fault lines in California that cause earthquakes?
- What could happen to California when "The Big One" occurs?
- Is "The Big One" a theory, fact, or myth?
- Could earthquakes be forecasted, or are they too unpredictable?
- How could past and present data on earthquakes in California be analyzed and interpreted to predict where and when "The Big One" might occur?
- Will "The Big One" be triggered by the San Andreas fault or one of the major fault lines that connect to it?
- What causes buildings and architectural structures to collapse due to an earthquake?
- Which types of buildings or houses generally pose exceptionally high risks of collapse due to an earthquake?
- How could the collapse of an architectural structure due to an earthquake be prevented?

Source for standard: NGSS Lead States, 2013.

FIGURE 8.5: Deep inquiry into natural hazards.

This deep inquiry experience enables and encourages students to analyze and interpret data to forecast earthquakes—specifically, "The Big One" earthquake that will strike California and allegedly sink the entire state into the Pacific Ocean. Notice how the good question that initiates the deep inquiry hooks 'em right from the start by piquing students' curiosity, interest, imagination, or wonder about the possibility and practicality of a giant earthquake that could destroy the entire state of California. The subsequent questions enable and encourage students to delve deeper into the topic and draw their own conclusions about the potential of this natural hazard, whether it could be predicted or prevented, and how people could be protected.

There are specific good questions, however, that will enable and encourage students to engage in deep inquiry experiences. These good questions are highly abstract, demanding that students reason and respond with relevant examples and evidence rather than reply with basic facts or information. These questions also prompt deeper reflection and provoke in-depth discussions. Table 8.1 features abstract good questions that stimulate and support deep inquiry.

Table 8.1: Abstract Good Questions That Stimulate and Support Deep Inquiry

Hypothetical Questions	Argumentative Questions
• What if?	• Is . . . or . . . ?
• What could?	• Was . . . or . . . ?
• What would?	• Does . . . or . . .?
• What could happen?	• Could . . . or . . . ?
• What would happen?	• Would . . . or . . . ?
• What may?	• Should . . . or . . .?
• What might?	• Will . . . or . . .?
• How may?	• Which one or ones?
• How might?	• Which is the best?
• How would?	• Which is the most accurate?
• What will?	• Which is the most appropriate?
• How will?	• Which is the most effective?

None of the good questions posed in a deep inquiry experience should be used to evaluate student learning. Their primary purpose is to expand students' knowledge and extend their thinking about the text, topic, or technique being taught. They also serve more as a stimulus that sparks curiosity and interest to learn than a prompt that sets the instructional focus and purpose for learning.

What Are the Levels of DOK Required by Deep Inquiry?

Deep inquiry experiences do not automatically engage students to comprehend and convey their learning at deeper levels of thinking or DOK. The cognitive rigor of a deep inquiry experience depends on:

- The instructional focus and purpose for learning
- The demand of the task students must complete

Table 8.2 (page 192) shows how deep inquiry enables and encourages students to develop and demonstrate their learning at different DOK levels. It also specifies the goals and expectations for teaching and learning through deep inquiry at each DOK level. Note that deep inquiry experiences can enable and encourage students to attain (DOK 1) or explain (DOK 2) answers through in-depth research, experimentation, and analyses.

Table 8.2: DOK Levels of Deep Inquiry and Questioning

DOK Level	Overarching Essential Question for Deep Inquiry	Instructional Focus and Purpose	Goal and Expectations	Deep Inquiry Experience
DOK 1	What is the knowledge?	Knowledge acquisition	Students develop and demonstrate deeper awareness.	Students read and respond to a text or research a topic that's connected to the curriculum.
DOK 2	How or why can the knowledge be understood or used?	Knowledge application	Students develop and demonstrate deeper aptitude.	Students conduct experiments or complete tasks that are rigorous and relevant.
DOK 3	How or why could the knowledge be understood or used?	Knowledge analysis	Students develop and demonstrate deeper appreciation.	Students conduct in-depth investigations, engage in debates or discussions, or use their imagination.
DOK 4	What else could be done with the knowledge?	Knowledge augmentation	Students develop and demonstrate deeper acumen.	Students extend their learning beyond the classroom and curriculum.

Which Academic Standards Could Deep Inquiry Address?

Deep inquiry addresses and assesses supporting standards—academic standards "that do not receive the same degree of instructional and assessment emphasis" (p. 17). Luis Cruz (2023) clarifies supporting standards further by describing them as:

- Important standards educators believe should be taught
- "Nice-to-know" standards educators want to teach

The subjects and skills addressed in supporting standards are neither essential nor evaluated for competency or proficiency in a certain content area or grade level. However, they expand students' knowledge and extend their thinking about the text, topic, or technique being taught. Consider the following ELA standards addressed in a novel study of *The Outsiders* by S. E. Hinton: "Compare and contrast a written story, drama, or poem to its audio, filmed, staged, or multimedia version, analyzing the effects of techniques unique to each medium (e.g., lighting, sound, color, or camera focus and angles in a film)" (CCRS.ELA-LIT.RL.7.7; NGA & CCSSO, 2010b).

According to the R.E.A.L. criteria for prioritization (p. 139), this standard does not address or assess the essential knowledge or skills students need to demonstrate content-area competency or grade-level proficiency. It's also not an important standard that students must achieve to understand the key ideas or craft and structure of *The Outsiders*. However, it does focus on a subject-related concept that's nice to know—specifically, how literary fiction and nonfiction texts can be presented and produced in different formats and media. It enables students to consider a broader question that goes beyond the standard and text—specifically, the question, "Which is better, the book or the movie?"

Figure 8.6 features the good questions that enable and encourage students to engage in a deep inquiry into the novel and film adaptation of *The Outsiders*. This inquiry experience is standards based and allows students to expand their knowledge about the impact and influence of both the novel and film. It encourages students to extend their thinking about bigger ideas and broader issues regarding adapting and presenting stories in different formats and mediums.

Standard	Compare and contrast a written story, drama, or poem to its audio, filmed, staged, or multimedia version, analyzing the effects of techniques unique to each medium (e.g., lighting, sound, color, or camera focus and angles in a film). (CCRS.ELA-LIT.RL.7.6)
Deep Inquiry	Which is better—the book or the film adaptation of *The Outsiders*?

- Who is Francis Ford Coppola, the director of *The Outsiders*? What other novels did he adapt into films?
- What is the story behind the film adaptation and production of *The Outsiders*?
- Who were the actors in *The Outsiders*? How and why were they cast in their respective roles? How did *The Outsiders* start or strengthen the careers of these actors?
- What are the key differences between the novel and the film adaptation of *The Outsiders*?
- How faithful is the film adaptation of *The Outsiders* to the novel? What changes and cuts were made to the film adaptation? Were those changes and cuts important, inappropriate, or insignificant?
- How does the film adaptation of *The Outsiders* maintain the first-person point of view of the novel?
- Which is better—the book or the film adaptation of *The Outsiders*?
- Which version of the film adaptation of *The Outsiders* should have been released—the one that was released in theaters in 1983 or the complete novel adaptation that was later released?

Source for standard: NGA & CCSSO, 2010b.

FIGURE 8.6: Deep inquiry into *The Outsiders* by S. E. Hinton.

Enabling and encouraging students to inquire and investigate supporting standards through deep inquiry and questioning ensures teaching and learning with an inquiring mind is a well-rounded experience that's rigorous and relevant. It provides teachers with the ability to prioritize and pick which academic standards could and should be inquired and investigated along a particular pathway of the Inquiring Minds Framework.

Which Academic Standards Are Better Suited for Deep Inquiry?

Some academic standards are better suited for deep inquiry and questioning. The context of these standards requires students to delve deeper into a subject or go beyond the curriculum and classroom. For example, consider the following.

- Mathematics standards that reference real-world problems in their learning intentions or objectives or encourage students to deepen their learning by applying the processes and proficiencies identified in the Standards for Mathematical Practice (NGA & CCSSO, 2010c)

- ELA standards that focus on how texts integrate knowledge and ideas—specifically, the standards that state students must read and review multiple texts, or specify that students must evaluate how content is integrated and presented in diverse formats or media visually, quantitatively, and in words

- Science standards that enable students to examine or explore the effects of natural events or phenomena, or encourage students to deepen their learning through a STEM experience that promotes scientific experimentation and investigation or engineering design

- History standards that enable and encourage students to establish, examine, or explore and explain an idea, incident, idea, individual, or issue in broader contexts

- Arts standards that reference how choices and contexts (for example, social, cultural, historical) influence and inform the creation and performance of art, music, theater, or dance

- World language standards that enable and encourage students to establish or examine the comparisons and connections between a target language or exploring cultures and communities that speak and use a target language

- Health and physical education standards that address and assess physical activity knowledge, fitness knowledge, health, or nutrition

Keep in mind, however, that academic standards that feature these keywords or focus on these topics do not automatically make them more suitable for deep inquiry and questioning. Educators still need to use the R.E.A.L. criteria to check and confirm whether the subjects and skills they address make them power or priority standards. You also should consider whether you could rephrase these standards into good driving questions that personalize learning or promote expertise.

Another set of standards suited for deep inquiry includes those that focus on social-emotional learning. You can draw on and use these standards to phrase and pose abstract good questions that students can examine and explore through inquiry experiences such as Socratic seminars, problem-based learning, or social stories. These questions differ from the social-emotional learning students experience through inquiry for expertise in that they focus on the idea or issue, not the individual student and how they would react or respond. The questions that define and drive deep inquiry are more abstract than affective, prompting students to think critically instead of reflectively about the idea, issue, theme, or topic.

Figure 8.7 features an example of a deep inquiry that enables and encourages students to inquire and investigate one of the competencies of social awareness from the CASEL (2020) frameworks.

Standard	Demonstrate empathy and compassion. (CCRS.ELA-LIT.RL.7.6)
Deep Inquiry	What is empathy?

- What is the definition of *empathy*?
- What does it mean to be empathetic?
- What is the difference between empathy, pity, sympathy, and compassion?
- How does empathy contribute to individual well-being and mental health?
- How could empathy support building positive relationships?
- How could empathy strengthen understanding between individuals?
- Is empathy a natural trait or a learned behavior?
- How could empathy be developed, nurtured, or strengthened?
- What role does empathy play in communicating effectively?
- What role does empathy play in resolving conflict or problems?
- How could empathy promote a more inclusive and diverse society?
- How could empathy impact or influence decision making?
- What are the consequences for lacking empathy?

Source for standard: NGA & CCSSO, 2010b.

FIGURE 8.7: Deep inquiry into social awareness and empathy.

How Could Deep Inquiry Enable and Encourage Educators to Share Their Expertise?

Deep inquiry experiences not only expand students' knowledge and extend their thinking about a specific area or aspect of the subject studied, but they also enable and encourage us, as educators, to share our expertise on the text, topic, or technique we are teaching.

However, don't copy from or rely on technology for the good questions that promote and prompt deep inquiry. You should consider and critique the complexity or quality of the good questions an e-resource or tech tool provides. You also should use questions suggested by technology as a stimulus or starting point to craft or create your own good questions that promote and prompt deep inquiry.

Educators are highly proficient in a specific subject area. They also have a strong passion for the content they teach and enthusiasm for why the content is important or interesting for students to learn. Traditionally, teachers share their DOK or show skills through demonstrations or presentations in the hope that students will find the subject as fascinating or fun as they do. However, these teaching and learning experiences can become more of a showcase for teacher knowledge and understanding, rather than a shared experience with students.

Deep inquiry enables us, as educators, to show our proficiency and share our passion for what we are teaching. However, instead of discussing what we know and understand or demonstrating what we can do, we pose good questions that will prompt students to discover what's important and what's interesting about the text, topic, or technique. These questions should encourage students to delve deeper into the subject. The delivery of the teaching and learning experience should be more conversational and exploratory than informational and instructional.

For example, I am a tremendous fan of Edgar Allan Poe. I am deeply aware of Poe's influence not only on literature but other disciplines such as art, music, theater, and criminology. I have a deep appreciation for the impact of Poe's works on society, historically and presently. One of the fun facts I know about Poe is that he established the genre of detective fiction with his three short stories featuring a sleuth named C. Auguste Dupin (National Park Service, 2017). Poe called these short stories "tales of ratiocination" because the main character used deductive logic and reasoning to solve crimes that were perplexing and seemingly unsolvable. Sir Arthur Conan Doyle, who created Sherlock Holmes, credited Poe as a major influence on his writing, stating, "Where was the detective story until Poe breathed the breath of life into it?" (as cited in Eschner, 2017).

I could have created a captivating presentation in which I shared this information through a lecture with a PowerPoint. However, instead, I initiated the inquiry by asking students, "How did Edgar Allan Poe create an entire genre of literary fiction?" My students kept silent either because they did not know or were unsure of the answer. However, I neither expected nor required them to respond. I posed the question as a prompt to hook 'em into inquiry.

After a moment of silence, I asked students, "What if I told you that Edgar Allan Poe wrote the first story that featured an investigator or sleuth who was smarter than the police and used logical reasoning to solve a crime?" Students responded that this sounded like Sherlock Holmes.

Then I asked, "What if I told you that Sir Arthur Conan Doyle, who created Sherlock Holmes, acknowledged he was highly influenced by Poe and based his Holmes on a character Edgar Allan Poe created over forty years earlier?"

Now they were hooked! At that point, I had students use their cell phones or classroom computers to inquire about and investigate how Edgar Allan Poe created the subgenre of detective fiction mystery with his short story "The Murders in the Rue Morgue" and the character C. Auguste Dupin (Poe, 1841). This short story was not included in the unit on Edgar Allan Poe in my textbook. However, I provided students with a link so they could download the story and printed copies for those students who did not have access to a device or preferred to read a hard copy.

I asked students to conduct a literary analysis in which they examined and explained how Edgar Allan Poe established the common elements, motifs, style, and themes of detective mystery fiction with his short story "The Murders in the Rue Morgue." That was the topical essential question they had to address as they read the story. I also encouraged students to choose a Sherlock Holmes short story to read on their own and compare the key details and craft of their chosen mystery to Poe's tale.

After students completed the assignment, I asked them, "What if I told you Poe wrote two more tales featuring C. Auguste Dupin?" One of my students always asked, "So he wrote this as a trilogy?" They knew what a trilogy was because of their familiarity with film series. After I said *yes*, someone in the class would ask, "Did Edgar Allan Poe create the trilogy?"

That would lead into an even deeper inquiry in which students discovered the trilogy format dates to ancient civilizations and was used by the playwrights of Greek drama. That led to another deep inquiry experience that enabled students to examine the influence of the legends and literature of ancient civilizations on Edgar Allan Poe and his works.

Notice that I did not share this information through a presentation. Instead, I asked good questions that enabled and encouraged students to discover the knowledge and deepen their awareness through inquiry. They learned about the subject. However, I did not inform them about the subject through direct instruction or discourse. I invited them to engage in a conversation and consider what I was asking them. This was a memorable experience for students, which they took away and made their own. In fact, to this day, when I engage with former students either in person or through social media, they often tell me how this was one of their favorite lessons but also one of their cherished memories from school.

Figure 8.8 features the good questions students inquired and investigated in the Deep Inquiry Passion Project on Edgar Allan Poe. These questions encouraged students to expand their knowledge and extend their thinking about Edgar Allan Poe. They also enabled me to share my expertise on and enjoyment of Edgar Allan Poe, which is what made this inquiry experience a passion project.

Standard	Demonstrate knowledge of eighteenth-, nineteenth-, and early-twentieth-century foundational works of American literature, including how two or more texts from the same period treat similar themes or topics. (CCRS.ELA-LIT.RL.11–12.9)
Deep Inquiry	How did Edgar Allan Poe create an entire genre of literary fiction?

- What is detective fiction?
- How did Edgar Allan Poe establish the common elements, motifs, style, and themes of detective mystery fiction with "The Murders in the Rue Morgue"?
- What influence did Edgar Allan Poe have on Sir Arthur Conan Doyle and his stories featuring Sherlock Holmes?
- What are the similarities and differences between Edgar Allan Poe's "Murders in the Rue Morgue" and a Sherlock Holmes short story written by Sir Arthur Conan Doyle?

Source for standard: NGA & CCSSO, 2010b.

FIGURE 8.8: Deep inquiry into the impact and influence of Edgar Allan Poe.

Teaching and learning through deep inquiry is more challenging for teachers than students. The challenge for teachers is to instruct students through inquiry and interact with them by questioning—even when they want to share or show something. The teacher also must be comfortable with the silence that could follow questions. They must be quick to respond by posing another question or prompting students to turn and talk.

How Could Technology Enhance and Encourage Deep Inquiry and Questioning?

While deep inquiry enables and encourages educators to share their expertise in a subject, it does not expect them to be experts in every single text, topic, or technique they teach. Teachers are not expected to teach everything possible about the subject studied; there's just not enough time to address all the content. However, technology provides the option and opportunity for both students and teachers to delve deeper into subjects and go beyond what the standards stipulate and the curriculum covers through deep inquiry.

Chapter 3 (page 65) established that questions that can be googled are good questions, and that googling is an essential skill that benefits students in learning and life. Deep inquiry involves googling—and students should be empowered and encouraged to do so. The questions inquired and investigated through deep inquiry necessitate students use Google and other electronic platforms or technical tools. The rigor of deep inquiry also could depend on the extent students must use these e-resources to engage in and experience deep inquiry.

Technology could provide suggestions for good questions that will prompt and promote deep inquiry. For example, you might enter the question, "What are good questions to ask about cells?" into Google, Bing, or Yahoo. Each search engine will provide a link to a webpage hosted by the United States Department of Health and Human Services titled "Cell Day Frequently Asked Questions," which feature a list of good questions students could investigate through deep inquiry. Students don't have to use the questions. However, they can feel confident these questions are coming from a credible source.

Advances in technology continue to revolutionize how teachers and students engage in and experience deep inquiry and questioning. Voice assistants such as Alexa, Bixby, Google Assistant, Microsoft Cortana, and Siri not only retrieve but also respond to requests for answers and cite the source. Generative AI, such as ChatGPT, shares and summarizes ideas and information in a language and tone that is both comprehendible and conversational (from a DOK perspective, generative AI responds at DOK 2 because it explains the answer). Deep machine learning establishes connections and makes suggestions based on the data it retrieves and requests it receives. It can also make logical decisions and predictions by valuing, organizing, and characterizing data and details. Think about how Netflix suggests shows to watch and how social media platforms such as Facebook and Instagram feature posts on feeds based on a person's viewing history. These advances in technology make deep inquiry an easier, yet enriching experience for students.

Educators could also use generative AI to come up with good questions that students could investigate through a deep inquiry into a specific subject. For example, you might go into ChatGPT (https://chat.openai.com) and type, "What are good questions students could inquire and investigate through a deep inquiry into . . . ?," and name the text, topic, or technique being taught. ChatGPT will generate questions (at least ten, in my experience) that differ in their cognitive complexity and demand. In fact, some of the questions featured in this book were suggested and influenced by ChatGPT. Again, as with Google, you don't have to use these questions. However, they could provide a frame of reference or inspiration for planning and providing a deep inquiry experience for students.

To plan and provide effective and engaging deep inquiry experiences, become familiar with how technology could enhance and encourage deep inquiry for both you and your students. Technology is a tool both you and your students can use to engage in and experience deep inquiry. Technology has transformed deep inquiry from an activity that requires researching and investigating answers to an experience that involves searching for examples or seeking evidence that expands knowledge and extends thinking. However, don't copy from or rely on technology for the good questions that prompt deep inquiry. You should consider and critique the complexity or quality of the good questions an e-resource or a tech tool provides and use these resources to help craft your inquiry experiences.

Summary

Deep inquiry requires critical and creative thinking from both educators and students. As teachers craft good questions, students are encouraged to delve deeper into subjects and go beyond what the standards require or the curriculum covers.

Through deep inquiry, students expand their knowledge and extend their thinking about the subject studied. It gives teachers the opportunity to show their proficiency and share their passion for the texts, topics, or techniques they teach. That's what makes these inquiry experiences both educational and enjoyable.

The experience of deep inquiry has been transformed by technological advancements such as voice assistants and generative AI. These e-resources and tech tools not only make it easier to conduct in-depth investigations; they also could provide the good questions that drive deep inquiry. However, teachers and students should always consider the questions provided by technology with a critical lens. They should think creatively about how they could come up with their own good (or better) questions that will promote deep inquiry.

Application: How Can You Plan and Provide Deep Inquiry Experiences?

Either individually or with your team, plan a deep inquiry experience that enables students to delve deeper into the subject and allows you to share your expertise through inquiry and questioning.

1. Copy the Deep Inquiry Grid reproducible on page 204.

2. Write the learning intention and individual objectives of the standard to be addressed in the first row labeled *Standard*. This standard could be the following:

   ¤ A priority standard that addresses and assesses a subject or skill students must learn

   ¤ An important standard that addresses a subject or skill that's important to understand

   ¤ A supporting standard that addresses ideas or issues that are "nice to know"

3. Check the teacher edition of your curricular program or text for good questions students could investigate through deep inquiry.

4. Create the good questions students must investigate through deep inquiry. These questions should range in the level of DOK they require students to understand and use their learning. However, they should not rephrase the learning intention of the priority standard or feature the pronoun referent *you*. These questions should expand students' knowledge and extend their thinking about the subject.

5. Use an e-resource or technical tool to come up with good questions students could investigate through deep inquiry. For example:

   ¤ Conduct an online search for ideas, information, or issues about the subject that aren't specified in the standards or covered by the curriculum. You could enter the name of the subject, skill, or situation in the search window or specify the content, conditions, and criteria (for example, *different ways to add numbers*; *using logarithms in the real world*; *the connections between poetry and music*; *Edgar Allen Poe's influence on art, literature, and society*; *engineering problems involving energy*; *causes and consequences of World War I*). Your search will either provide sample questions or inspire ideas about the deep inquiry students could engage in and experience.

   ¤ Conduct an online search for details, facts, ideas, and information that would expand students' knowledge and extend their thinking about the subject. Your search will provide sample questions or inspire ideas about the deep inquiry students could engage in and experience. For example:

     · What are interesting facts about fractions?
     · How could linear equations be used in a real-world context?
     · What influence has Roald Dahl had on society historically and in the present?
     · What could rock formation inform about the history of Earth?
     · What are interesting facts or little-known information about the Renaissance?
     · What are the origins of a form or style of art or music?
     · Which words in English came from Spanish?

   ¤ Conduct an online search for examples of good questions that address and ask about the text, topic, or technique being taught. Your search will provide sample questions or inspire you to come up with your own good questions that enable and encourage deep inquiry. For example:

     · What are good questions students that would deepen students understanding of place value?

- What are good questions students should research on Greek mythology?
- What are good questions to ask about cells?
- What are good questions students could inquire and investigate about World War II?
- What are good questions to ask students about a specific form of art of music?

⌐ Ask generative AI, such as ChatGPT, to come up with good questions students could investigate through a deep inquiry of the subject they are studying. Use the sentence frame, "What are good questions students could inquire and investigate through a deep inquiry into [subject, skill, situation, text, topic, technique]?"

6. List the good questions students will investigate through deep inquiry in the section labeled *Deep Inquiry* on the Deep Inquiry Grid.

Deep Inquiry Grid

Standard	
Deep Inquiry	

Epilogue

CONSIDERATIONS FOR TEACHING AND LEARNING WITH AN INQUIRING MIND

An intelligent mind is an inquiring mind. It is not satisfied with explanation, with conclusions. Nor is it a mind that believes, because belief is again another form of conclusion. An intelligent mind is one which is constantly learning, never concluding.

—Bruce Lee

Reflect and Respond

Is teaching and learning through inquiry and questioning an intellectual or emotional experience? How is inquiry and questioning complex intellectually, yet difficult emotionally? How could teaching and learning with an inquiring mind be rigorous intellectually? How could teaching and learning with an inquiring mind be respectful socially and emotionally? What are some precautions you should consider when teaching and learning with an inquiring mind? How could teaching and learning with an inquiring mind be a rigorous, respectful, and rewarding experience for educators and students?

• • •

TEACHING AND LEARNING with an inquiring mind can be challenging and complex intellectually and emotionally. It encourages creative thinking by piquing curiosity, imagination, and wonder. It expands knowledge and extends thinking with an open mind. Critical thinking requires one to be attentive, careful, and thorough in how they address or answer questions as well as how they ask them. It prompts and stimulates reflective thinking and enables you to "activate, regulate, evaluate, and direct [your] thinking" when you ask, address, and answer questions—be those questions your own or someone else's (Ritchhart, 2002, p. 28).

It does not matter whether the level of thinking expected is higher or lower, or the DOK level demanded is deeper or reduced. Inquiry and questioning challenges you to think about what you are learning and requires you to understand and use your learning in detail, in depth, and in your own unique way. That's what makes the experience complex.

Teaching and learning with an inquiring mind can be difficult socially and emotionally for both respondents and questioners. People generally don't like being asked questions or asking them. They may feel questions challenge them personally instead of intellectually. They might feel pressured to provide an answer and put off if their response is questioned. They might fear being judged as foolish, ignorant, or unintelligent if they ask questions or cannot answer them accurately, acceptably, or appropriately. They also may feel embarrassed or self-conscious about asking or answering, possibly suspecting that questions are meant to "test" their intellect instead of triggering them to think.

However, a person with an inquiring mind loves to ask questions. They need answers, seek explanations, and want justifications. Their yearning to learn can make them relentless with their questions and come off as ruthless with their questioning. This can make teaching and learning through inquiry and questioning uncomfortable and upsetting both for the respondent and the questioner.

Cautionary Tips for Effective Inquiry

To teach and learn effectively with an inquiring mind, ensure the experience of teaching and learning through inquiry and questioning is rigorous intellectually and respectful socially and emotionally. Encourage students to be curious to learn through inquiry and questioning; however, be cognizant of how to properly engage students in this process. To accomplish this, the following sections provide some "fair warnings" for teaching and learning with an inquiring mind.

Don't Emphasize Answering Questions Correctly

Teaching and learning with an inquiring mind are not about answering questions correctly. It's about asking and addressing questions to attain, explain, justify, or extend responses, results, and reasoning through inquiry and questioning. That's how you can engage students to acquire, apply, and analyze academic and social-emotional knowledge, skills, and dispositions—or learning. Students need to understand that true learning is not about whether questions can be answered but rather, the depth and extent to which they can address and ask them.

Don't Put Students "on the Spot" to Answer Questions

Teaching and learning with an inquiring mind engage *all students* to ask and address questions. However, do not pick students or put them on the spot to provide a response. Instead, enable and encourage students to address and ask questions through whole-class, small-group, or one-on-one discussions. The good questions posed can serve as checks for understanding. However, they can also act as conversation starters that initiate the inquiry and inspire further questioning. Invite students to share their responses, results, or reasoning openly and willingly; do not insist on an answer or instruct them to respond.

Don't Push Students to Answer Questions

We should be careful and cognizant not to pump or push students with questions. Teaching and learning with an inquiring mind neither expect nor require students to provide an answer—at least, not immediately or initially. If they can, great! However, remember a good question prompts students to reflect before responding. Also, the intent and purpose of a good question is to initiate the inquiry and commence conversations. That's what effective teaching and learning with an inquiring mind enables and encourages—reflections and conversations about responses. Keep reminding students that teaching and learning with an inquiring mind is about asking and addressing questions—be it their own or those posed by others—about a prompt presented or stimulus shared, not answering them.

Don't Put Down or Put Off Students' Responses to Questions

In teaching and learning with an inquiring mind, there are three ways students can respond—correctly, incorrectly, or expressively as "right" or "wrong." Regardless of the accuracy of the answer or whether you agree with an assertion, respect the response. Responses are both academic and affective. They reflect who someone is and represent what they know, think, or feel.

However, that does not mean you must accept incorrect answers or acquiesce to a wrong assertion. You should challenge those responses, results, or reasoning through inquiry and questioning. For example, ask clarifying questions such as, "What do you mean?" so students can check their reasoning and even correct themselves. Ask probing questions such as, "Why do you believe, feel, or say that?" so students can clarify their contention. Not only do those questions prompt students to comprehend and consider responses, but they also communicate and convey a care and curiosity to learn, which is what teaching and learning with an inquiring mind cultivates.

Don't Prevent Students From Directing an Inquiry Discussion

Teaching and learning with an inquiring mind promote a shared inquiry approach to discussion. According to the Great Books Foundation (2020), a shared inquiry discussion "is about the give-and-take of ideas, a willingness to listen to others, and [a commitment to] talk to them respectfully" (p. 1). However, in some circumstances or classes, there may be students who like to direct or dominate the discussions. Let them. Don't ask, "How about someone else sharing their thoughts?" Don't ask the domineering dialoguer directly, "How about letting someone else answer or talk?" The student might back off for the moment, but they could also "shut down" from saying or sharing anything in the future.

Instead, you could ask, "What else . . . ?" or "How else . . . ?" to encourage other students to speak. You might even ask the domineering dialoguer, "Who would you like to hear from next?," and have them pick classmates to respond and continue the conversation. In fact, that's how you can shift the inquiry and questioning to students—take the role of a facilitator and turn over the discussion to students so they can teach and learn from each other.

Don't Preclude Students From Sharing Responses or Reasoning

Teaching and learning with an inquiring mind provide students not only choice but also voice. Enable and encourage students to share their responses and reasoning freely, yet respectfully, without fear of repercussions or reproach. If students feel they can share their answer, argument, or attitude without the risk of rejection or ridicule—even if their answer is incorrect or "wrong"—they will more readily engage in the inquiry.

However, that does not mean you should permit disrespectful discourse or rude reactions. Everyone needs to respect the response but be aware of the audience and sensitive with students. Just because you know, think, or feel it doesn't mean you should share it; the response will cause more harm than help. Let students learn through inquiry and questioning that leads to discovery and discussion. Give them the opportunity recognize how they are incorrect and realize why they may be "wrong" instead of just teaching or telling them. Enable them to learn from and correct their mistakes. Be sure students understand that they can agree to disagree on arguments or attitudes but remain respectful to each other.

Don't Present or Promote Your Opinions, Perspectives, or Thoughts

Teaching and learning with an inquiring mind involve engaging and encouraging students to discover and discuss through inquiry and questioning. Serve as a facilitator who poses questions to prompt inquiry, not as a participant involved in the discussions. Share what you know through inquiry and questioning, but do not let students know what you think or how you feel about the text, topic, or technique being taught. This holds true for all forms of inquiry—even synergistic inquiry experiences that involve teachers and students working together as colleagues.

With synergistic inquiry, you collaborate to answer a question, address a problem, or accomplish a task through inquiry and questioning. But do not participate by offering your opinions. Be careful about asking leading or loaded questions that present one position or promote a particular perspective or point of view—especially your own. You cannot control what students say or the responses they provide, but you can control how you ask and address the questions you pose.

Don't Prohibit Students From Responding, "I Don't Know"

As with the debate over "googleable" questions, there is some disagreement among educators over whether students should be permitted or prohibited from responding, "I don't know." Many educators view the answer, "I don't know" as a sign of disinterest or disrespect. In fact, education articles and authors offer alternatives students could say instead of "I don't know." Conversely, articles and authors in other professions suggest and even stress responding, "I don't know" to questions that expect an answer at that moment, which is when and why student usually reply, "I don't know."

Some businesspeople and other professionals regard replying "I don't know" not only as responsive but also respectful. It's an honest answer. What's also interesting is that businesspeople and other professionals look at the response from the point of view of the responder, while educators who are against "I don't know" look at the answer from the perspective of the questioner. Personally, I'm of the opinion and thought that it's OK for both students and even teachers to answer or respond, "I don't know." In fact, I encourage and welcome "I don't know" responses from students and participants in professional development seminars and workshops. I don't take the statement as a sign of disinterest or disrespect.

I agree with veterinarian Robert Sedam (2020), who explains in his article, "It's Okay to Say, 'I Don't Know'": "By saying, 'I don't know,' you're opening a discussion with the questioner that can benefit both parties in the end. I see how it could be used to spark cognition and start conversations." That's how I understand and use "I don't know" responses—as a conversation starter and indicator of the pathway the inquiry needs to take. For example, I often follow an "I don't know" response with a probing question such as, "What is it you don't know or understand?" This question is not meant to be challenging or confrontational (although it could be taken that way, so be mindful of tone). It's meant to check, clarify, and confirm understanding.

I pose this question to gather information about what I may need to address, explain, or teach. I also use this question to encourage discussion and engage students to express themselves with a question. Then, I use their question to set the instructional focus for the inquiry. Plus, remember that teaching and learning with an inquiring mind involves respecting the response because it reflects the responder. If a student—or anyone—answers, "I don't know," then accept their answer. Don't challenge them or try to get them to change their response or how they communicate it. That's what they know, and that's who they are. How you react or respond to "I don't know" will impact and influence the nature of the inquiry and need to ask and address further questions.

Don't Pound Students With Questions

While teaching and learning with an inquiring mind is a Socratic process, be conscious and considerate about how you phrase and pose questions. If you pound students with questions, you might risk disengagement or shut down. This is something I had to learn as someone with an inquiring mind who teaches and learns through inquiry and questioning.

Sometimes, I would phrase my questions or pose them in such a way that students in my class or participants in professional development would shut down rather than share their response or reasoning. For example, whenever someone would give an answer, I would ask, "What do you mean?" The purpose of my question is to give them a chance to clarify their response or reasoning. This was a technique I learned from my father. He taught me to ask, "What do you mean?" because it naturally prompts people to elaborate or explain.

This is an effective way to work with adults (especially parents) who make blanket or unfounded statements without examples or evidence to support their response or reasoning. It is also an effective questioning method to prompt students to check and convey their learning. However, it can have an opposite and detrimental effect—especially asking participants in my professional development sessions who felt frustrated because they could not elaborate on or explain their responses or reasoning. It seemed as if I was pressuring for responses rather than prompting for reflection. That's why it's essential to be aware of your audience and how they react and respond to questioning.

It's important to teach students the philosophy and practice of teaching and learning with an inquiring mind through inquiry and questioning. It's not about answering questions. It's about asking questions to acquire, apply, analyze, or augment learning. It's also about attaining, explaining, justifying, or extending responses, results, or reasoning.

Don't Pump or Push Students With Questions

You should be careful and cognizant not to pump or push students with questions. Believe it or not, this concept was popularized as "pimping the questions" by Frederick L. Brancati (1989). This describes a formal practice in the medical field that physicians used to train their attendants, residents, or students. Questions posed through pimping "are administered in rapid succession [and] should be essentially unanswerable" (Brancati, 1989, p. 89). The term *pimping* comes from the German word *pumprage*, which means "pump questions." It refers to the practice of posing a series of quick questions that demand an immediate response. The purpose of these questions is to assess but also abase someone for their knowledge, or lack thereof.

This may seem applicable and appropriate for teaching and learning with an inquiring mind. However, according to numerous medical articles and journals discussing the practice, "pimping the question" is meant primarily to assert authority and instill respect (Brancati, 1989; Cooper, 2017; Ezeok, 2020; Karan, 2017; Kost & Chen, 2015). It also contrasts sharply with the spirit of inquiry medical nurses are educated in and encouraged to practice. In education, this practice would be like posing a hard or trick question that is meant to shame or single out students for what they don't know or understand, or what they can't do. Educators might also pepper students with unanswerable questions to establish their expertise and authority by conveying to students, "I know the answer, and you don't, so you need to listen to and learn from me." That's why it's important to make sure the questions you ask students to address actually develop their learning, not discipline their behavior. Pumping or pushing—or "pimping"—questions is an insensitive, not constructive, way to use inquiry and questioning.

Conclusion

As you finish this book and reflect on what you have read, keep in mind that teaching and learning through inquiry and questioning is complex intellectually and difficult socially and emotionally. It not only takes time and thought but also training and trial and error to transition to this method and mindset of teaching and learning.

To take the first step in this process, shift how you perceive and practice inquiry and questioning. Don't ask questions to answer or assess. Instead, pose questions to stimulate different levels of thinking—to pique curiosity, interest, imagination, and wonder, and to prompt reflection or review. Use these questions to check for, clarify, or confirm knowledge, understanding, or awareness. Ask questions to expand knowledge, extend thinking, and encourage deeper examination or exploration.

Don't forget that good questions help students acquire knowledge, demonstrate understanding, deepen awareness, and develop personal expertise through inquiry. These are all the things a person with an inquiring mind wants from learning and life. It's what teaching and learning with an inquiring mind involves, and it's how teaching and learning with an inquiring mind can be a rigorous, respectful, and rewarding experience for all.

REFERENCES AND RESOURCES

Ainsworth, L. (2003). *Power standards: Identifying the standards that matter the most.* Englewood, CO: Lead + Learn Press.

American Education Reaches Out. (2018). *2018 AERO world language standards and benchmarks.* Washington DC: Office of Overseas Schools U.S. Department of State. Accessed at http://projectaero.org/AEROplus/languages/AERO_world_language _standards.pdf on October 21, 2023.

Anderson, L. W., & Krathwohl, D. R. (Eds.). (2001). *A taxonomy for learning, teaching, and assessing: A revision of Bloom's taxonomy of educational objectives.* Boston: Addison-Wesley.

Baehr, J. (2011). *The inquiring mind: On intellectual virtues and virtue epistemology.* New York: Oxford University Press.

Baehr, J. (2013). *Intellectual Virtues Academy: Master virtues.* Accessed at www.iva longbeach.org/academics/master-virtues on October 22, 2023.

Baehr, J. (2017). *Cultivating good minds: A philosophical and practical guide to educating for intellectual virtues.* Author.

Baehr, J. (2021). *Deep in thought: A practical guide to teaching intellectual virtues.* Cambridge, MA: Harvard Educational Press.

Banchi, H., & Bell, R. (2008, October). The many levels of inquiry. *Science and Children, 9*(2), 26–29. Accessed at www.michiganseagrant.org/lessons/wp-content /uploads/sites/3/2019/04/The-Many-Levels-of-Inquiry-NSTA-article.pdf on October 23, 2023.

Beck, I., McKeown, M., & Kucan, L. (2013). *Bringing words to life: Robust vocabulary instruction* (2nd ed.). New York: The Guilford Press.

Beresford, J. (2021, July 25). *Job applicant who put "googling" under skills on resume lands interview.* Accessed at www.newsweek.com/job-applicant-who-put-googling-under -skills-resume-lands-interview-1612883 on October 21, 2023.

Berger, W. (2014). *A more beautiful question: The power of inquiry to spark breakthrough ideas.* New York: Bloomsbury.

Berger, W. (2018). *The book of beautiful questions: The powerful questions that will help you decide, create, connect, and lead.* New York: Bloomsbury.

Berger, W., & Foster, E. (2020). *Beautiful questions in the classroom: Transforming classrooms into cultures of curiosity and inquiry.* Thousand Oaks, CA: Corwin.

Bird, B. (2018). *Incredibles 2* [Film]. Pixar Animation Studios.

Bloom, B. S. (Ed.). (1956). *Taxonomy of educational objectives: The classification of educational goals. Handbook 1: The cognitive domain.* Philadelphia: David McKay.

Brancati, F. L. (1989). The art of pimping. *JAMA: Journal of the American Medical Association, 262*(1), 89–90.

Bronson, P., & Merryman, A. (2010, July 10). The creativity crisis. *Newsweek.* Accessed at www.newsweek.com/2010/07/10/the-creativity-crisis.html on April 3, 2022.

Buck, L. B., Lowery Bretz, S., & Towns, M. H. (2008, September). Characterizing the level of inquiry in the undergraduate laboratory. *Journal of College Science Teaching, 38*(1), 52–58. Accessed at www.chem.purdue.edu/towns/Towns%20Publications /Bruck%20Bretz%20Towns%202008.pdf on April 17, 2022.

Cazden, C. B. (2001). *Classroom discourse: The language of teaching and learning* (2nd ed.). Portsmouth, NH: Heinemann.

Clapton, E., & Robertson, R. (1986). It's in the way that you use it [Song]. On *August.* Burbank, CA: Warner Bros.

Collaborative for Academic, Social, and Emotional Learning. (2020, November). *CASEL's SEL framework: What are the core competence areas and where are they promoted?* Chicago, IL: CASEL. Accessed at https://casel.org/casel-sel -framework-11-2020 on October 13, 2023.

Cooper, J. (2017, February 10). *Are you asking students questions or "pimping"?* [Blog post]. Accessed at www.kevinmd.com/2017/02/asking-students-questions-pimping .html on May 29, 2023.

Coppola, F. F. (1983). *The Outsiders* [Film]. Burbank, CA: Warner Bros.

Costa, A. L. (2000). Using questions to challenge students' intellect. In A. L. Costa & B. Kallick (Eds.), *Activating and engaging habits of mind: Book 2* (pp. 34–45). Alexandra, VA: Association for Supervision and Curriculum Development.

Cotton, K. (1988). Classroom questioning. *School Improvement Research Series, 5.* Accessed at https://educationnorthwest.org/sites/default/files/Classroom Questioning.pdf on December 23, 2022.

Cruz, L. F. (2023). *Embracing the five vessels: Learning the non-negotiables to becoming a high-functioning PLC.* Presented at the Professional Learning Communities® Institute in Pasadena, California, September 23, 2023. Accessed at https://solutiontree.s3.us -west-2.amazonaws.com/solutiontree.com/media/pdf/event-materials/sacramento -plc-23/Cruz_EmbracingTheFive_(HO).pdf on October 22, 2023.

Curry, J., & Samara, J. (1993). *Curriculum guide for the education of gifted high school students.* Austin: Texas Association for the Gifted and Talented.

Dickinson, E. (1891). *The railway train*. Accessed at https://americanliterature.com /author/emily-dickinson/poem/the-railway-train on February 27, 2023.

Doherty, J. (2017, July 9). *Skilful* [sic] *questioning: The beating heart of good pedagogy*. Accessed at https://impact.chartered.college/article/doherty-skilful-questioning -beating-heartpedagogy on December 23, 2022.

Dow, P. E. (2013). *Virtuous minds: Intellectual character development for students, educators and parents*. Downers Grove, IL: InterVarsity Press.

Dunkhase, J. A. (2003). The coupled-inquiry cycle: A teacher concerns-based model for effective student inquiry. *Science Educator, 12*(1), 10–15.

Engel, S. (2013, February 1). The case for curiosity. *Educational Leadership, 70*(5). Accessed at www.ascd.org/el/articles/the-case-for-curiosity on December 23, 2022.

Eschner, K. (2017 April 20). *Without Edgar Allan Poe, we wouldn't have Sherlock Holmes*. Accessed at www.smithsonianmag.com/smart-news/edgar-allan-poe-invented -detective-story-180962914 on October 29, 2023.

Ezeoke, O. M. (2020, July 23). *A guide to pimping in medical education*. Accessed at www.wolterskluwer.com/en/expert-insights/a-guide-to-pimping-in-medical -education# on May 29, 2023.

Fisher, D., & Frey, N. (2013). *Better learning through structured teaching: A framework for the gradual release of responsibility* (2nd ed.). Alexandria, VA: Association for Supervision and Curriculum Development.

Fisher, D., & Frey, N. (2021). *Better learning through structured teaching: A framework for the gradual release of responsibility* (3rd ed.). Alexandria, VA: Association for Supervision and Curriculum Development.

Floyd, W. D. (1960). *An analysis of the oral questioning activity in selected Colorado primary classrooms* [Unpublished doctoral dissertation]. Fort Collins, CO: Colorado State University.

Francis, E. M. (2016). *Now that's a good question! How to promote cognitive rigor through classroom questioning*. Alexandria, VA: Association for Supervision and Curriculum Development.

Francis, E. M. (2022). *Deconstructing depth of knowledge: A method and model for deeper teaching and learning*. Bloomington, IN: Solution Tree Press.

Francis, F. L. (1971). *Handbook for the disabled students of Brooklyn College C. U. N. Y.* Accessed at https://files.eric.ed.gov/fulltext/ED072576.pdf on November 6, 2023.

Friesen, S., & Scott, D. (2013, June). *Inquiry-based learning: A review of the research literature*. Accessed at https://galileo.org/focus-on-inquiry-lit-review.pdf on August 21, 2023.

Gagné, F. (2009). Building gifts into talents: Brief overview of the DMGT 2.0. *Gifted*, *152*, 5–9. Accessed at www.researchgate.net/publication/287583969_Building _gifts_into_talents_Detailed_overview_of_the_DMGT_20 on October 21, 2023.

Gall, M. D. (1970). The use of questions in teaching. *Review of Educational Research*, *40*(5), 707–721.

Gano-Phillips, S. (2009). *Affective learning in general education*. Accessed at www.oge .cuhk.edu.hk/wp-content/uploads/journal/issuu-6/01_SusanGanoPhilips.pdf on December 27, 2022.

Gardner, H. (1999). *Intelligence reframed: Multiple intelligences for the 21st century*. New York: Basic Books.

Gardner, H. (2022, July 8). *A resurgence of interest in existential intelligence: Why now?* [Blog post]. Accessed at www.howardgardner.com/howards-blog/a-resurgence-of -interest-in-existential-intelligence-why-now on December 31, 2022.

Gholam, A. (2019). Inquiry-based learning: Student teachers' challenges and perceptions. *Journal of Inquiry and Action in Education*, *10*(2), 112–134.

Great Books Foundation. (2020, April). *The five guidelines for shared inquiry discussion*. Accessed at www.greatbooks.org/wp-content/uploads/2020/04/Five-Guidelines-for -Shared-Inquiry-Discussion.pdf on October 21, 2023.

Harris, P. L. (2012). *Trusting what you're told: How children learn from others*. Cambridge, MA: The Belknap Press of Harvard University Press.

Harvey, S., & Goudvis, A. (2007). *Strategies that work: Teaching comprehension for understanding and engagement*. Portland, ME: Stenhouse.

Hattie, J. (2009). *Visible learning: A synthesis of over 800 meta-analyses relating to achievement*. New York: Routledge.

Hattie, J. (2012). *Visible learning for teachers: Maximizing impact on learning*. New York: Routledge.

Hattie. J. (2023). *Visible learning: The sequel: A synthesis of over 2,100 meta-analysis related to achievement*. New York: Routledge.

Herron, M. D. (1971). The nature of scientific enquiry. *The School Review*, *79*(2), 171–212. Accessed at www.journals.uchicago.edu/doi/abs/10.1086/442968 on October 23, 2023.

Hess, K. J. (2006). *Exploring cognitive demand in instruction and assessment* [White paper]. Dover, NH: National Center for Assessment. Accessed at http://quality assessment.pbworks.com/w/file/fetch/45823115/DOK_ApplyingWebb_KH08.pdf on February 19, 2022.

Hess, K. J. (2013). *Linking research with practice: A local assessment toolkit to guide school leaders.* Accessed at www.uen.org/literacyresources/downloads/linking_research _with_practice.pdf on October 20, 2023.

Hess, K. J. (2018). *A local assessment toolkit to promote deeper learning: Transforming research into practice.* Thousand Oaks, CA: Corwin.

Hess, K. J., Carlock, D., Jones, B., & Walkup, J. R. (2009). *What exactly do "fewer, clearer, and higher standards" really look like in the classroom? Using a cognitive rigor matrix to analyze curriculum, plan lessons, and implement assessments* [Paper presentation]. National Conference on Student Assessment, Detroit, MI. Accessed at http://media.wix.com/ugd/5e86bd_2f72d4acd00a4494b0677adecafd119f.pdf on March 28, 2023.

Hess, K. J., Jones, B. S., Carlock, D., & Walkup, J. R. (2009). *Cognitive rigor: Blending the strengths of Bloom's taxonomy and Webb's depth of knowledge to enhance classroom-level processes.* Accessed at https://files.eric.ed.gov/fulltext/ED517804.pdf on March 28, 2023.

Hinton, S. E. (1967). *The Outsiders.* New York: Viking Press.

Hoque, M. E. (2016). Three domains of learning: Cognitive, affective, and psychomotor. *The Journal of EFL Education and Research, 2*(2), 45–52.

Hsee, C. K., & Ruan, B. (2016). The pandora effect: The power and peril of curiosity. *Psychological Science, 27*(5), 659–666. Accessed at https://doi.org/10.1177 /0956797616631733 on October 20, 2023.

Hunter, R. (2004). *Madeline Hunter's mastery teaching: Increasing instructional effectiveness in elementary and secondary schools.* Thousand Oaks, CA: Corwin.

Hurwitz, M., & Knowles, C. (2016). *The complete X-files* (Rev. ed.). San Rafael, CA: Insight Editions.

Jarrett, C. (2016). *Why are humans so curious?* Accessed at www.sciencefocus.com/the -human-body/why-are-humans-so-curious on October 20, 2023.

Jonassen, D. H. (2011). *Learning to solve problems: A handbook for designing problem-solving learning environments.* New York: Routledge.

Karan, A. (2017, February 3). Medical students need to be quizzed, but "pimping" isn't effective. *STAT News.* Accessed at www.statnews.com/2017/02/03/medical-students -pimping-testing-knowledge on May 29, 2023.

Kost, A., & Chen, F. M. (2015). Socrates was not a pimp: Changing the paradigm of questioning in medical education. *Academic Medicine, 90*(1), 20–24. Accessed at https://journals.lww.com/academicmedicine/Fulltext/2015/01000/Socrates_Was _Not_a_Pimp__Changing_the_Paradigm_of.11.aspx on May 29, 2023.

Krathwohl, D. R., Bloom, B. S., & Masia, B. B. (1964). *Taxonomy of educational objectives: The classification of educational goals. Handbook II: Affective domain.* New York: Longman.

Kuntzleman, T. (2019, January 3). *Synergistic inquiry.* Accessed at www.chemedx.org /article/synergistic-inquiry on March 20, 2023.

Lamb, A., & Johnson, L. (2010, April). Beyond googling: Applying Google Tools to inquiry-based learning. *Teacher Librarian, 37*(4), 83–86. Accessed at https:// scholarworks.iupui.edu/items/d4c0483e-e8a1-41df-bff4-dbf2eb9e52a0 on October 20, 2023.

Larmer, J., Mergendoller, J., & Boss, S. (2015). *Setting the standard for project-based learning: A proven approach to rigorous classroom instruction.* Alexandria, VA: Association of Supervision and Curriculum Development.

Larsen-Freeman, D., Driver, P., Gao, X., & Mercer, S. (2021). *Learner agency: Maximizing learner potential.* Accessed at https://elt.oup.com/feature/global/expert /learner-agency?cc=us&selLanguage=en on October 21, 2023.

Leadbeater, C. (2017, December). *Student agency: Learning to make a difference* [Seminar series 269]. Melbourne, Victoria, Australia: Centre for Strategic Education. Accessed at https://fusecontent.education.vic.gov.au/68349a5d -6c79-4662-a395-bceec4293eae/Charles%20Leadbeater-Seminar%20Series %20269-December2017-REV-Secure.pdf on July 29, 2023.

Lemov, D. (2010). *Teach like a champion: 49 techniques that put students on the path to college.* San Francisco, CA: Jossey-Bass.

Levin, T. (1981). *Effective instruction.* Alexandria, VA: Association for Supervision and Curriculum Development.

Many, T. W., & Horrell, T. (2014 January/February). Prioritizing the standards using R.E.A.L. criteria. *TEPSA News, 7*(1), 1–2. Accessed at https://absenterprisedotcom .files.wordpress.com/2016/06/real-standards.pdf on October 23, 2023.

Martin-Hansen, L. (2002, February). Defining inquiry: Exploring the many types of inquiry in the science classroom. *Science Teacher, 69*(2), 34–37. Accessed at http://people.uncw.edu/kubaskod/SEC_406_506/Classes/Class_3_Inquiry /DefiningInquiry.pdf on April 17, 2022.

Marzano, R. J., & Simms, J. A. (2014). *Questioning sequences in the classroom.* Bloomington, IN: Marzano Resources.

McKnight, K. S. (2019). *Literacy and learning centers for the big kids: Building literacy skills and content knowledge for grades 4–12* (2nd ed.). Antioch, IL: Engaging Learners.

McTighe, J., & Wiggins, G. (2013). *Essential questions: Opening doors to student understanding.* Alexandria, VA: Association for Supervision and Curriculum Development.

Mehan, H. (1979). *Learning lessons: Social organization in the classroom.* Cambridge, MA: Harvard University Press.

Miller, M. (2010). Teaching and learning in the affective domain. In M. Orey (Ed.), *Emerging perspectives on learning, teaching, and technology* (pp. 93–103). Zurich, Switzerland: The Global Text Project. Accessed at https://textbookequity.org /Textbooks/Orey_Emergin_Perspectives_Learning.pdf on December 27, 2022.

Mitchell, K. L. (2019). *Experience inquiry: 5 powerful strategies, 50 practical experiences.* Thousand Oaks, CA: Corwin.

Morgan, G., & Wong. J. (1994, February 18). E.B.E. (Season 1, Episode 17) [TV series episode]. In C. Carter, *The X-files.* Los Angeles: 20th Century Fox Studios.

Moss, C. M., & Brookhart, S. M. (2012). *Learning targets: Helping students aim for understanding in today's lesson.* Alexandria, VA: Association for Supervision and Curriculum Development.

Murdoch, K. (2015). *The power of inquiry: Teaching and learning with curiosity, creativity, and purpose in the contemporary classroom.* Melbourne, Australia: Seastar Education.

National Academies of Sciences, Engineering, and Medicine. (2012). *A framework for K–12 science education: Practices, crosscutting concepts, and core ideas.* Washington, DC: National Academies Press. Accessed at https://doi.org/10.17226/13165 on December 16, 2022.

National Center for History in the Schools. (1996). *History standards.* Los Angeles: UCLA Public History Initiative. Accessed at https://phi.history.ucla.edu/nchs /history-standards on August 21, 2023.

National Commission on Excellence in Education. (1983, April). *A nation at risk: The imperative for educational reform.* Washington, DC: U.S. Department of Education.

National Core Arts Standards State Education Agency Directors of Arts Education. (2014). *National core arts standards.* Accessed at www.nationalartsstandards.org on October 23, 2023.

National Council for the Social Studies. (2013). *College, career, & civic life (C3) framework for social studies state standards: Guidance for enhancing the rigor of K–12 civics, economics, geography, and history.* Silver Spring, MD: Author.

National Endowment for the Humanities and National Trust for the Humanities. (2018, August). *Who was really our first president? A lost hero.* Accessed at https://edsitement. neh.gov/curricula/who-was-really-our-first-president-lost-hero on October 22, 2023.

National Governors Association Center for Best Practices & Council of Chief State School Officers. (2010a). *Common core state standards*. Washington, DC: Authors.

National Governors Association Center for Best Practices & Council of Chief State School Officers. (2010b). *Common core state standards for English language arts and literacy in history/social studies, science, and technical subjects*. Washington, DC: Authors.

National Governors Association Center for Best Practices & Council of Chief State School Officers. (2010c). *Common core state standards for mathematics*. Washington, DC: Authors.

National League for Nursing. (2014). *Practical/vocational nursing program outcome: Spirit of inquiry*. Washington, DC: Author. Accessed at www.nln.org/docs/default-source/uploadedfiles/default-document-library/spirit-of-inquiry-final.pdf?sfvrsn=acc6df0d_0# on December 16, 2022.

National Park Service (2017, October). *Edgar Allan Poe invents the modern detective story*. Accessed at www.nps.gov/articles/poe-detectivefiction.htm on November 7, 2023.

New York State Department of Education. (2019). *New York State Next Generation Mathematics Learning Standards*. Accessed at www.nysed.gov/sites/default/files/programs/curriculum-instruction/nys-next-generation-mathematics-p-12-standards.pdf on October 22, 2023.

NGSS Lead States. (2013). *Next generation science standards: For states, by states*. Washington, DC: National Academies Press.

Ogle, D. (1986). K-W-L: A teaching model that develops active reading of expository text. *The Reading Teacher, 39*(6), 564–570. Accessed at www.jstor.org/stable/20199156 on February 28, 2023.

Organisation for Economic Co-operation and Development. (2019). *OECD Future of Education and Skills 2030 Concept Note*. Accessed at www.oecd.org/education/2030-project/teaching-and-learning/learning/student-agency/Student_Agency_for_2030_concept_note.pdf on October 21, 2023.

Patson, N. D. (2020, May 29). *Getting students to discuss by channeling the affective domain*. Accessed at www.facultyfocus.com/articles/teaching-and-learning/getting-students-to-discuss-by-channeling-the-affective-domain on December 28, 2022.

Pauk, W., & Owens, R. J. Q. (2011). *How to study in college* (10th ed.). Boston: Wadsworth.

Pearson, P. D., & Gallagher, M. C. (1983, October). *The instruction of reading comprehension* (Technical Report No. 297). Champaign, IL: Center for the Study of Reading.

Pelka, F. (2012). *What have we done: An oral history of the disability rights movement.* Amherst, MA: University of Massachusetts Press.

Poe, E. A. (1841, March). The murders in the Rue Morgue. *Graham's Lady's and Gentleman's Magazine.* Philadelphia: George R. Graham.

Quigley, C., Marshall, J. C., Deaton, C. C. M., Cook, M. P., & Padilla, M. (2011). Challenges to inquiry teaching and suggestions for how to meet them. *Science Educator, 20*(1), 55–61. Accessed at https://files.eric.ed.gov/fulltext/EJ940939.pdf on December 26, 2022.

Ritchhart, R. (2002). *Intellectual character: What it is, why it matters, and how to get it.* San Francisco: Jossey-Bass.

Rittel, H. W. J., & Webber, M. M. (1973, June). Dilemmas in a general theory of planning. *Policy Science, 4*(2), 155–169. Accessed at www.jstor.org/stable/4531523 on November 2, 2023.

Robinson, F. P. (1946). *Effective study.* New York: Harper & Brothers.

Rothstein, D., & Santana, L. (2011). *Make just one change: Teach students to ask their own questions.* Cambridge, MA: Harvard Education Press.

Ruggeri, A., Walker, C. M., Lombrozo, T., & Gopnik, A. (2021). How to help young children ask better questions. *Frontiers in Psychology, 11,* Article 586819.

Sanders, N. M. (1966). *Classroom questions: What kinds?* New York: Harper and Row.

Schmoker, M. (2018). *Focus: Elevating the essentials to radically improve student learning* (2nd ed.). Alexandria, VA: Association for Supervision and Curriculum Development.

Schwab, J. J. (1962). The teaching of science as inquiry. In J. J. Schwab & P. F. Brandwein (Eds.), *The teaching of science* (pp. 3–103). Cambridge, MA: Harvard University Press.

Sedam, R. (2020, October 11). *It's okay to say, "I don't know."* Accessed at https://medium.com/age-of-awareness/its-okay-to-say-i-don-t-know-326effcb296b on May 29, 2023.

Seels, B., & Glasgow, Z. (1990). *Exercises in instructional design.* Columbus, OH: Merrill.

SHAPE America. (2013). *National standards for K–12 physical education.* Accessed at www.shapeamerica.org/Common/Uploaded%20files/document_manager/standards/pe/Grade-Level-Outcomes-for-K12-Physical-Education.pdf on October 23, 2023.

Sizer, T. R. (1992). *Horace's school: Redesigning the American high school.* New York: Houghton Mifflin Harcourt.

Spache, G. D., & Berg, P. C. (1978). *The art of efficient reading* (3rd ed.). New York: Macmillan.

Stevens, R. (1912). *The question as a measure of efficiency in instruction: A critical study of classroom practice*. New York: Teacher's College Press.

Telegraph Staff and Agencies. (2013, March 28). *Mothers asked nearly 300 questions a day, study finds*. Accessed at www.telegraph.co.uk/news/uknews/9959026/Mothers-asked-nearly-300-questions-a-day-study-finds.html on February 20, 2022.

Texas Education Agency. (2014). *Chapter 111.A. Texas essential knowledge and skills for mathematics: Elementary*. Accessed at https://tea.texas.gov/about-tea/laws-and-rules/sboe-rules-tac/sboe-tac-currently-in-effect/ch111a.pdf on October 20, 2023.

Texas Education Agency. (2019). *Chapter 110.B. Texas essential knowledge and skills for English language arts and reading: Middle*. Accessed at https://tea.texas.gov/academics/subject-areas/english-language-arts-and-reading/vertical-alignmentk-12english06-20190.pdf on October 20, 2023.

Texas Education Agency. (2022). *Chapter 113.A. Texas essential knowledge and skills for social studies: Elementary*. Accessed at https://tea.texas.gov/about-tea/laws-and-rules/texas-administrative-code/19-tac-chapter-113 on October 20, 2023.

Thomas, E. L., & Robinson, H. A. (1972). *Improving reading in every class*. Boston: Allyn & Bacon.

Timmins, A. C. B. (1998). Classroom questions. *Practical Assessment, Research, and Evaluation, 6*, Article 6. Accessed at https://scholarworks.umass.edu/cgi/viewcontent.cgi?article=1075&context=pare on April 3, 2022.

Vegas, E. (2022, March 11). *Education technology post-COVID-19: A missed opportunity?* Brookings. Accessed at www.brookings.edu/blog/education-plus-development/2022/03/11/education-technology-post-covid-19-a-missed-opportunity on July 17, 2022.

Webb, N. L. (1997). *Criteria for alignment of expectations and assessments on mathematics and science education* (Research Monograph No. 6). Madison, WI: National Institute for Science Education. Accessed at https://files.eric.ed.gov/fulltext/ED414305.pdf on March 6, 2021.

Webb, N. L. (1999). *Alignment of science and mathematics standards and assessment in four states* (Research Monograph No. 18). Madison, WI: National Institute for Science Education. Accessed at https://files.eric.ed.gov/fulltext/ED440852.pdf on March 6, 2021.

Wiggins, G. P., & McTighe, J. (2005). *Understanding by design* (expanded 2nd ed.). Alexandria, VA: Association for Supervision and Curriculum Development.

Wilichowski, T., & Cobo, C. (2021, June 2). *Transforming how teachers use technology* [Blog post]. Accessed at https://blogs.worldbank.org/education/transforming-how-teachers-use-technology on July 17, 2022.

INDEX

Deconstructing Depth of Knowledge
Erik M. Francis
If your understanding of depth of knowledge (DOK) is a little cloudy, you're not alone. This resource is your one-stop-shop for learning what it is and how to use it to provide learning experiences that are academically rigorous, socially and emotionally supportive, and student responsive.
BKF960

Raising the Rigor
Eileen Depka
This user-friendly resource shares questioning strategies and techniques proven to enhance students' critical thinking skills, deepen their engagement, and better prepare them for college and careers. The author also provides a range of templates, surveys, and checklists for planning instruction, deconstructing academic standards, and increasing classroom rigor.
BKF722

Inspiring Lifelong Readers
Jennifer McCarty Plucker
Grounded in practices that promote adolescent literacy, inquiry, motivation, inspiration, and engagement, *Inspiring Lifelong Readers* provides secondary teachers with tried-and-true, evidence-based strategies. Discover how you can advance literacy learning so your students become competent, confident, and engaged readers.
BKF947

The Power of Effective Reading Instruction
Karen Gazith
Through research-supported tools and strategies, this book explores how children learn to read and how neuroscience should inform reading practices in schools. K–12 educators will find resources and reproducible tools to effectively implement reading instruction and interventions, no matter the subject taught.
BKG104

Solution Tree | Press
a division of
Solution Tree

Visit SolutionTree.com or call 800.733.6786 to order.

Wait! Your professional development journey doesn't have to end with the last pages of this book.

We realize improving student learning doesn't happen overnight. And your school or district shouldn't be left to puzzle out all the details of this process alone.

No matter where you are on the journey, we're committed to helping you get to the next stage.

Take advantage of everything from **custom workshops** to **keynote presentations** and **interactive web and video conferencing**. We can even help you develop an action plan tailored to fit your specific needs.

Let's get the conversation started.

Call 888.763.9045 today.

SolutionTree.com